SCIENCE.
BAD.

JONATHAN HICKMAN
WRITER

NICK PITARRA
ARTIST

JORDIE BELLAIRE
COLORS

RUS WOOTON
LETTERS

WITH

RYAN BROWNE
ARTIST (CHAPTER 21)

IMAGE COMICS, INC.
Robert Kirkman – Chief Operating Officer
Erik Larsen – Chief Financial Officer
Todd McFarlane – President
Marc Silvestri – Chief Executive Officer
Jim Valentino – Vice-President

Eric Stephenson – Publisher
Ron Richards – Director of Business Development
Jennifer de Guzman – Director of Trade Book Sales
Kat Salazar – Director of PR & Marketing
Corey Murphy – Director of Retail Sales
Jeremy Sullivan – Director of Digital Sales
Emilio Bautista – Sales Assistant
Branwyn Bigglestone – Senior Accounts Manager
Emily Miller – Accounts Manager
Jessica Ambriz – Administrative Assistant
Tyler Shainline – Events Coordinator
David Brothers – Content Manager
Jonathan Chan – Production Manager
Drew Gill – Art Director
Meredith Wallace – Print Manager
Monica Garcia – Senior Production Artist
Addison Duke – Production Artist
Tricia Ramos – Production Assistant
IMAGECOMICS.COM

THE MANHATTAN PROJECTS, VOLUME 5
First Printing / December 2014 / ISBN: 978-1-63215-184-1

MP

THE MANHATTAN PROJECTS

5

BLARG! BLARG! BLARG!
BLARG!

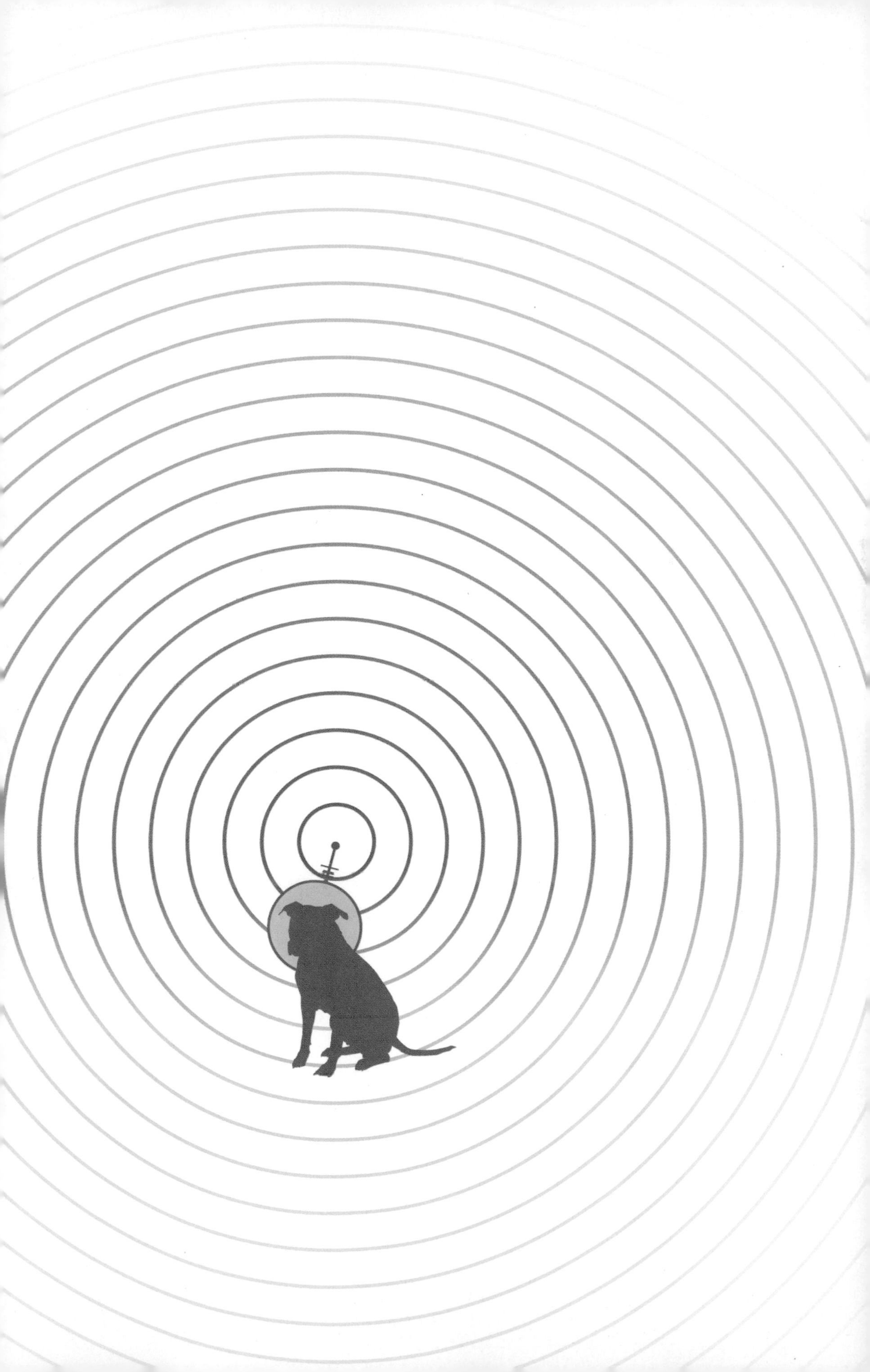

Now.

IMPORTED RUSSIAN VODKA

Polichnaya vodka

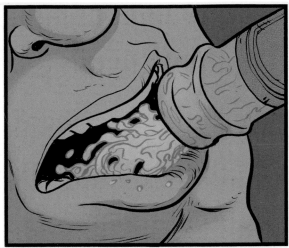

The whole universe is divided into two parts: One is she, and there is all happiness, hope, light...

The other is where she is not, and there is dejection and darkness...

Oh, Laika...

Where are you?

21

SPACE DOG

"IT WAS THE YEAR OF GREAT CHANGE, AND NO ONE WAS SPARED. NO MAN OF THE WORLD. NO WOMAN OF THE EARTH. NO BEAST OF THE FIELD."

CLAVIS AUREA
THE RECORDED FEYNMAN | **VOL. 3**

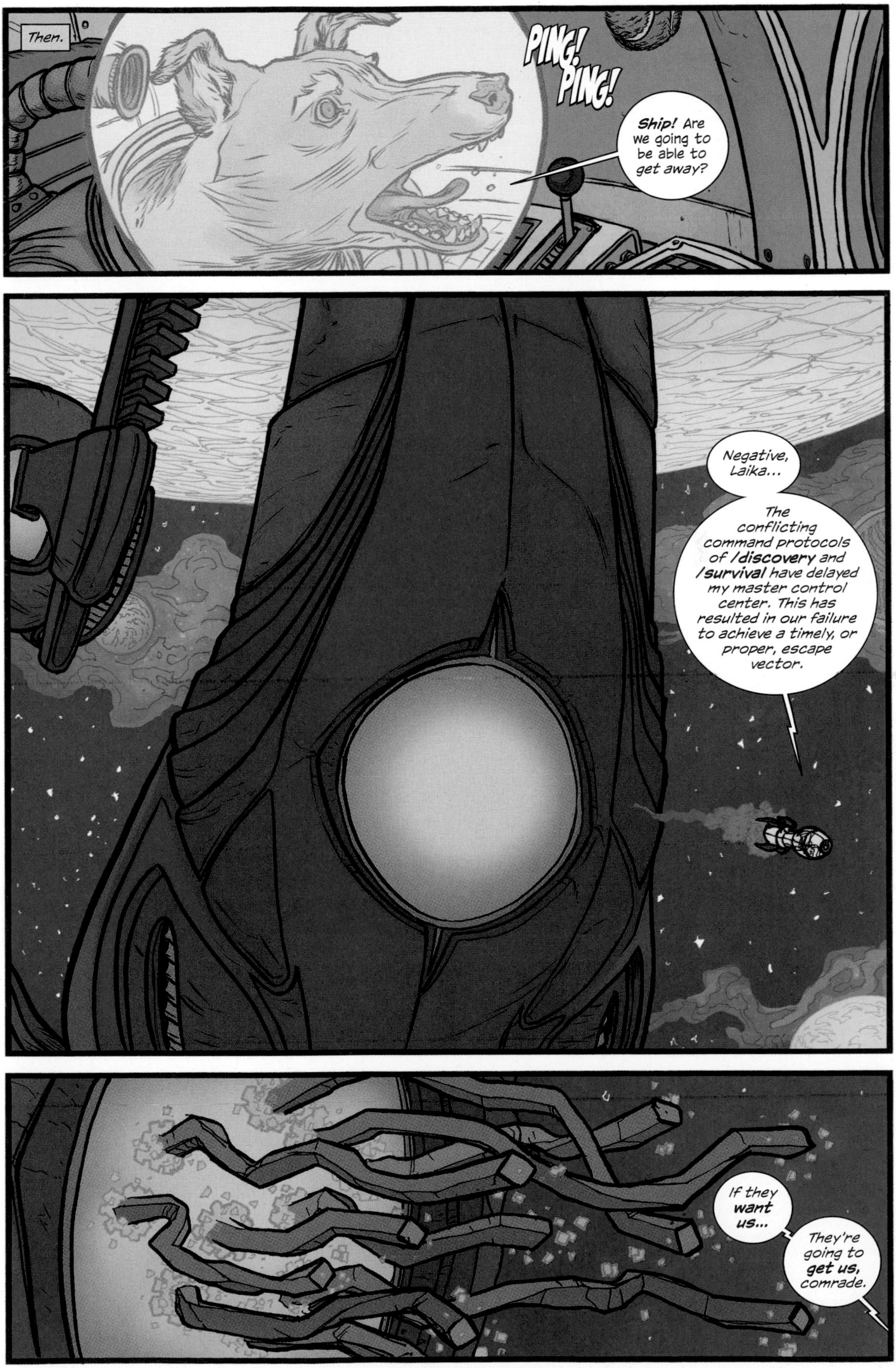

Then.
PING! PING!
Ship! Are we going to be able to get away?
Negative, Laika...
The conflicting command protocols of /discovery and /survival have delayed my master control center. This has resulted in our failure to achieve a timely, or proper, escape vector.
If they want us...
They're going to get us, comrade.

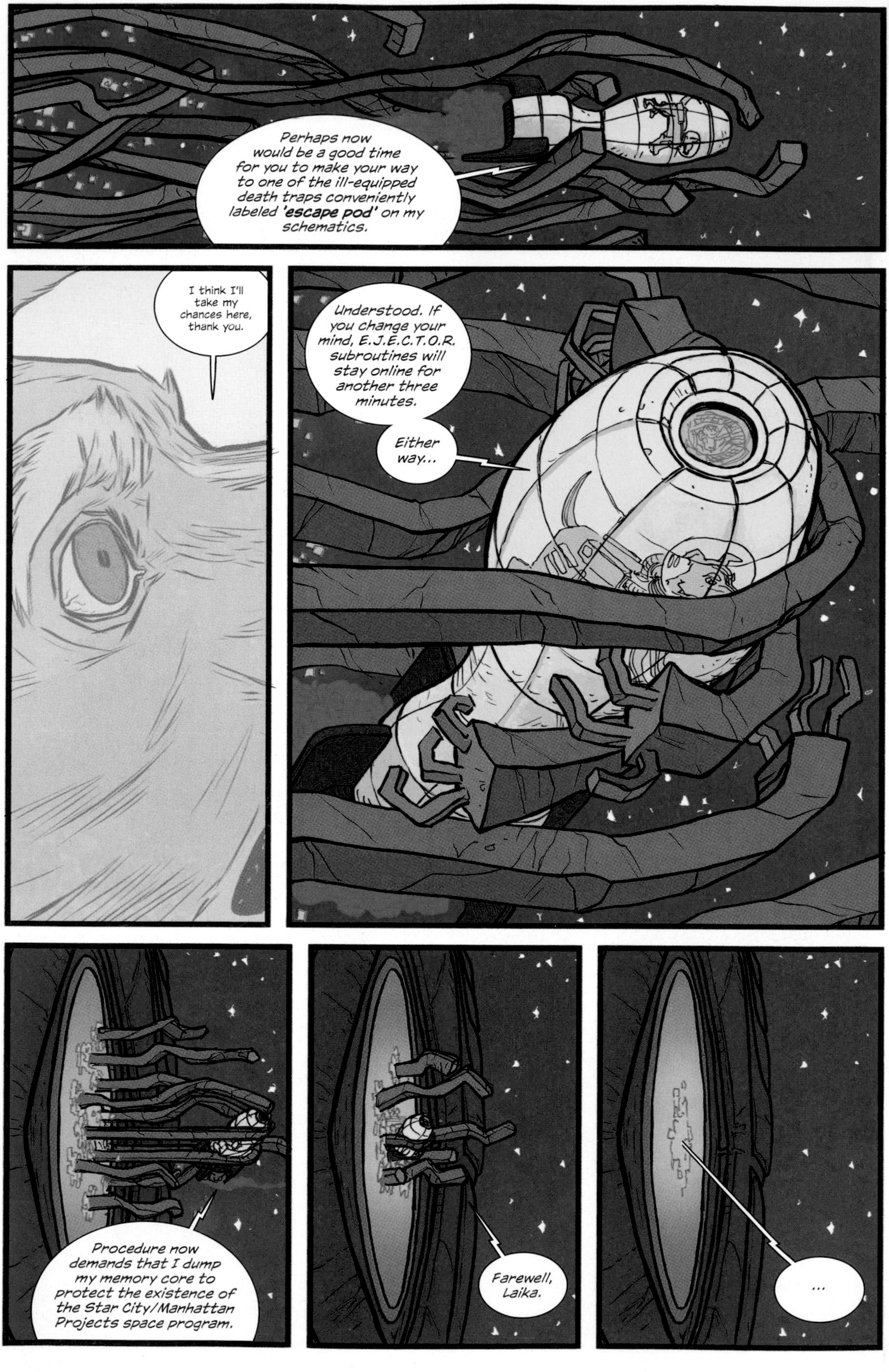
Perhaps now would be a good time for you to make your way to one of the ill-equipped death traps conveniently labeled **'escape pod'** on my schematics.
I think I'll take my chances here, thank you.
Understood. If you change your mind, E.J.E.C.T.O.R. subroutines will stay online for another three minutes.
Either way...
Procedure now demands that I dump my memory core to protect the existence of the Star City/Manhattan Projects space program.
Farewell, Laika.
...

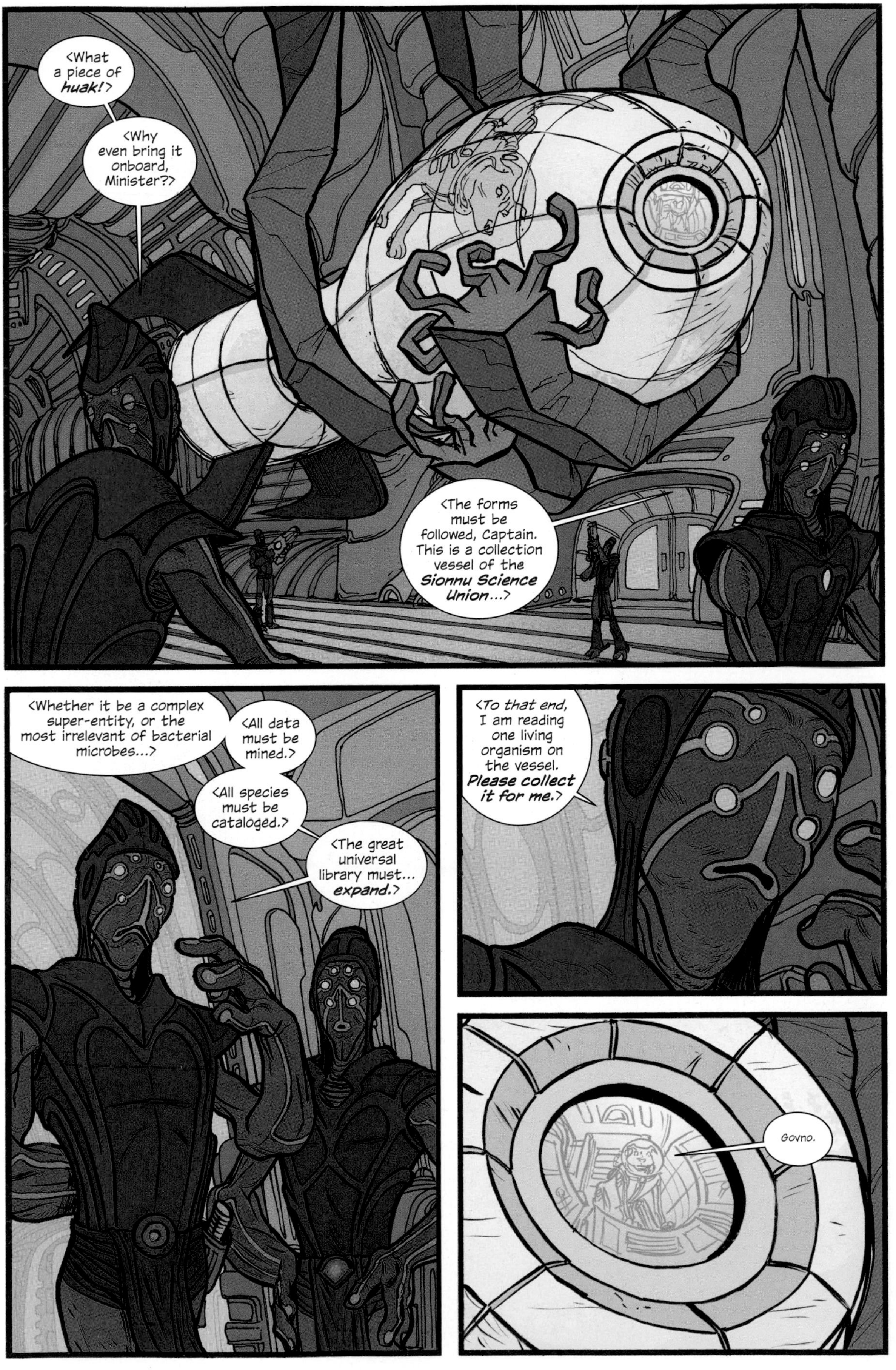
<What a piece of huak!>
<Why even bring it onboard, Minister?>
<The forms must be followed, Captain. This is a collection vessel of the Sionnu Science Union...>
<Whether it be a complex super-entity, or the most irrelevant of bacterial microbes...>
<All data must be mined.>
<All species must be cataloged.>
<The great universal library must... expand.>
<To that end, I am reading one living organism on the vessel. Please collect it for me.>
Govno.

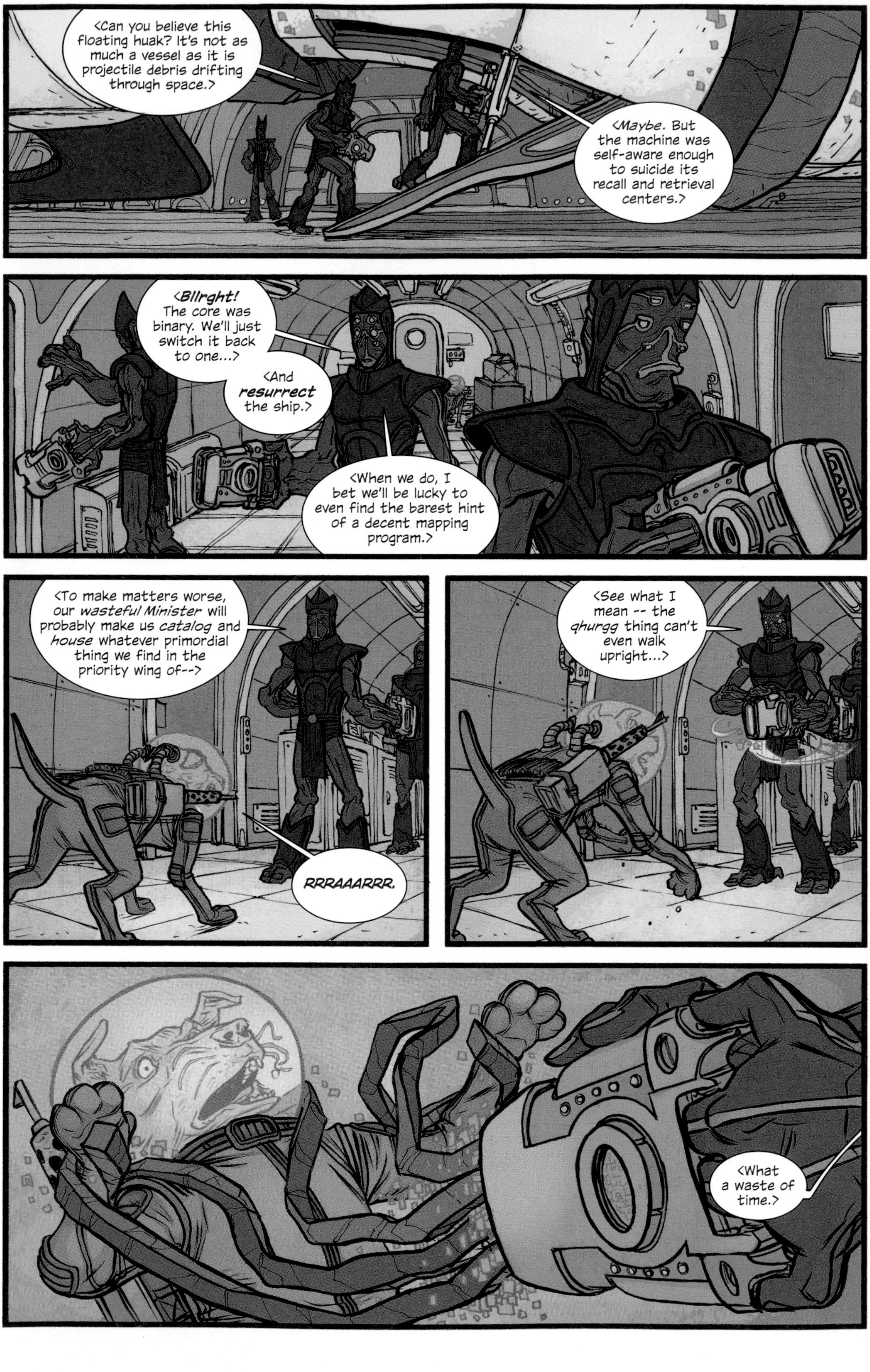
<Can you believe this floating huak? It's not as much a vessel as it is projectile debris drifting through space.>
<*Maybe*. But the machine was self-aware enough to suicide its recall and retrieval centers.>
<***Bllrght!*** The core was binary. We'll just switch it back to one...>
<And ***resurrect*** the ship.>
<When we do, I bet we'll be lucky to even find the barest hint of a decent mapping program.>
<To make matters worse, our *wasteful Minister* will probably make us *catalog* and *house* whatever primordial thing we find in the priority wing of-->
RRRAAARRR.
<See what I mean -- the *qhurgg* thing can't even walk upright...>
<What a waste of time.>

Later.

Hey! You can't just lock me in here. I have rights.

Okay, maybe rights is *a stretch*...but I'd like for you to politely consider my seeing whatever constitutes a lawyer in these parts?

Understand? Lawyer? Please? *Rarrr?*

<Listen to the sounds it makes.>

<Like two Siills mating during a dry season...>

ᚥ ᚥᚷᚥᚤᚾᚷᚾ ᚥᚤ ᚥᚤᚢᚷᚤᚾ ᚥᚤᚥᚷ ᚾᚷᚥᚥᚾᚢᚾᚷᚾ ᚢᚷᚥᚥᚥ ᚥᚥᚷᚥᚥ ᚥᚢᚥᚥᚥᚷᚾᚥᚥᚥᚷᚥᚢ ᚥᚥᚢᚢ

What?

<I'm sorry, I don't understand you...and you clearly don't even understand **standard basic**...>

<But on the odd chance that those awful sounds you're producing **are** a language of **some sort**. Then perhaps this will help.>

<You have to eat it for the translators to bind to your speech centers.>

You want me to eat this?

Sigh...

Chomp. Chomp. Chomp.

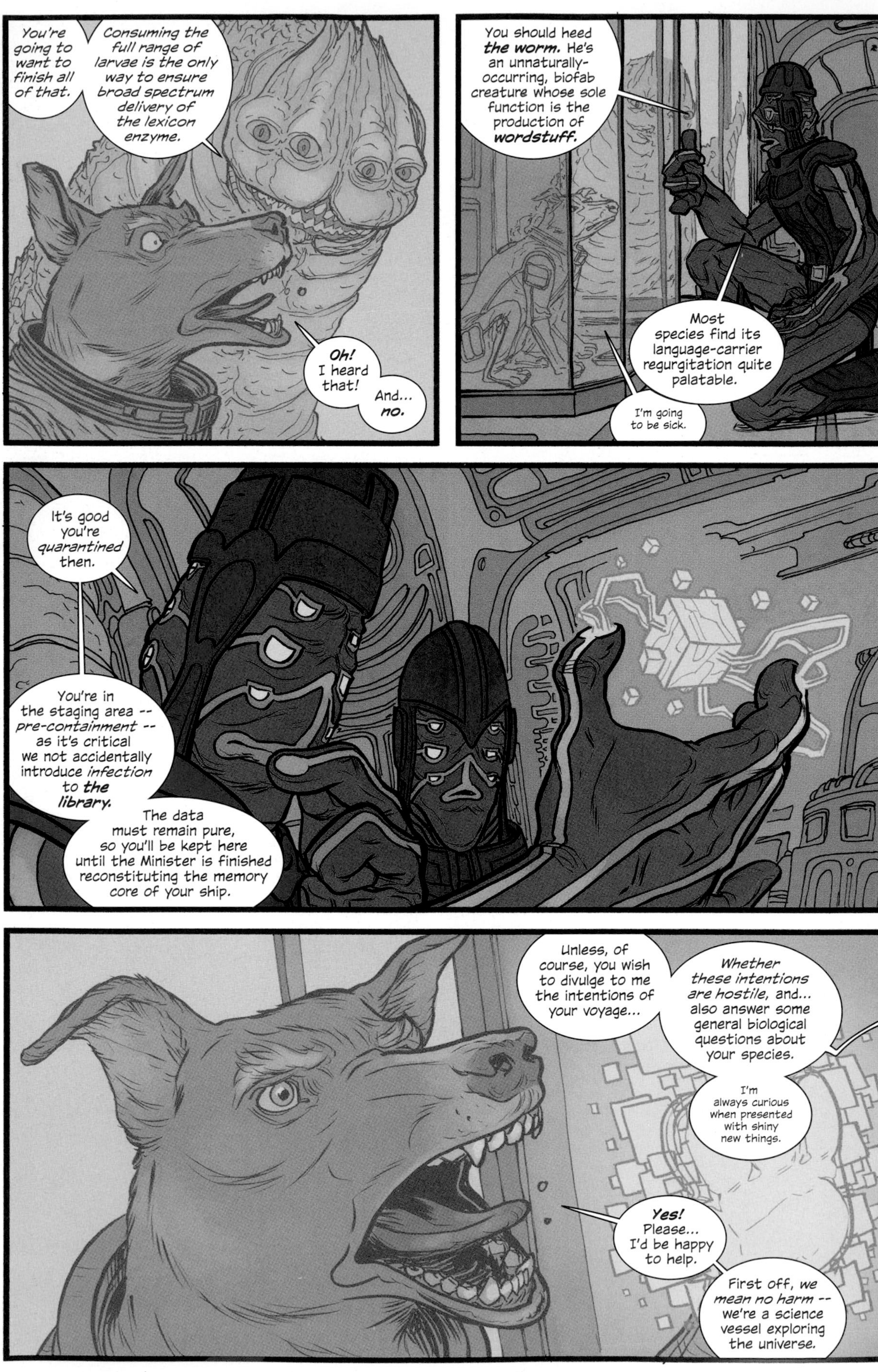
You're going to want to finish all of that.
Consuming the full range of larvae is the only way to ensure broad spectrum delivery of the lexicon enzyme.
Oh! I heard that!
And... ***no.***
You should heed ***the worm.*** He's an unnaturally-occurring, biofab creature whose sole function is the production of ***wordstuff.***
Most species find its language-carrier regurgitation quite palatable.
I'm going to be sick.
It's good you're *quarantined* then.
You're in the staging area -- *pre-containment* -- as it's critical we not accidentally introduce *infection* to ***the library.***
The data must remain pure, so you'll be kept here until the Minister is finished reconstituting the memory core of your ship.
Unless, of course, you wish to divulge to me the intentions of your voyage...
Whether these intentions are hostile, and... also answer some general biological questions about your species.
I'm always curious when presented with shiny new things.
Yes! Please... I'd be happy to help.
First off, we *mean no harm* -- we're a science vessel exploring the universe.

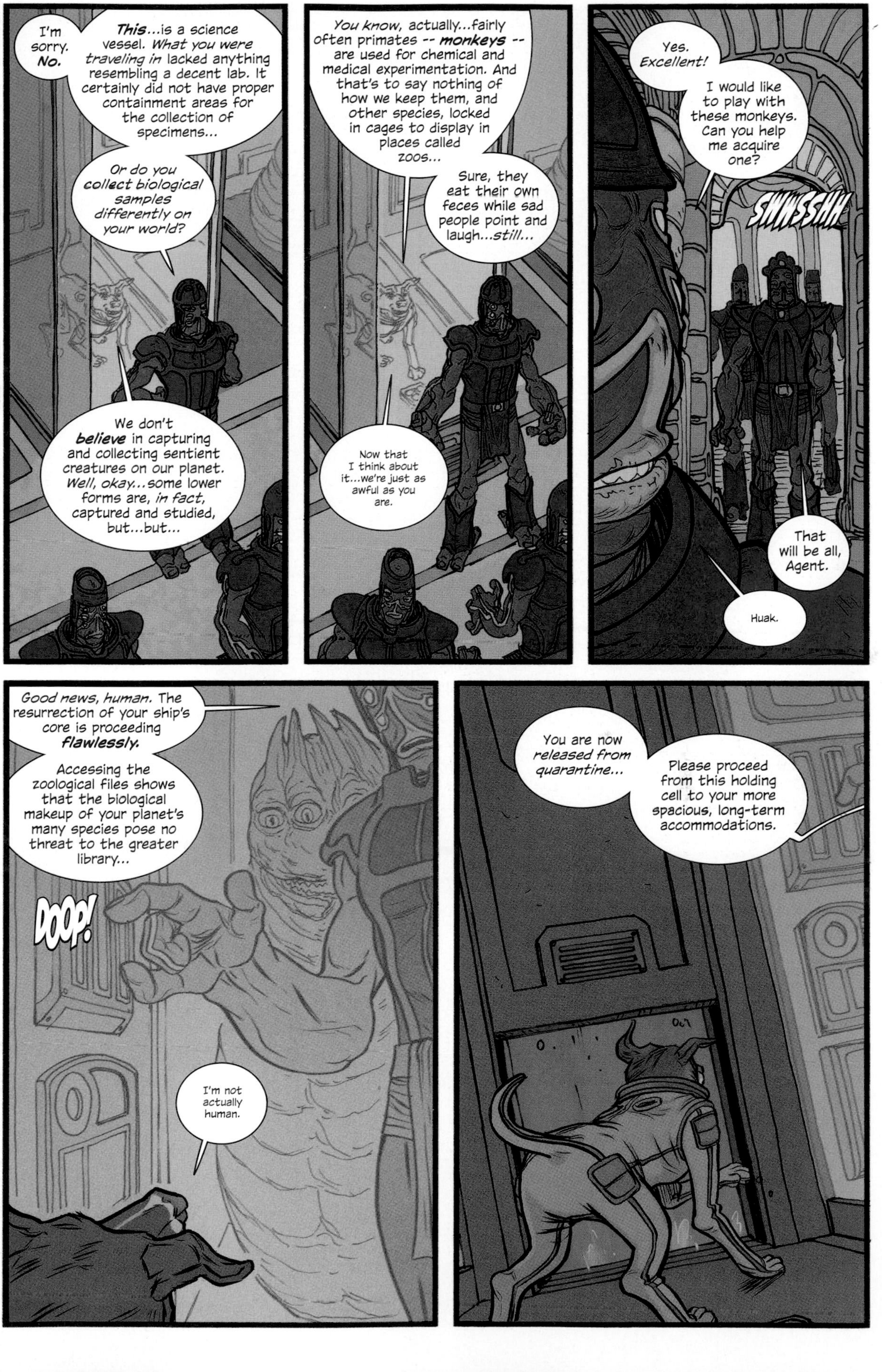
I'm sorry. No.
This...is a science vessel. What you were traveling in lacked anything resembling a decent lab. It certainly did not have proper containment areas for the collection of specimens...
Or do you collect biological samples differently on your world?
We don't believe in capturing and collecting sentient creatures on our planet. Well, okay...some lower forms are, in fact, captured and studied, but...but...
You know, actually...fairly often primates -- monkeys -- are used for chemical and medical experimentation. And that's to say nothing of how we keep them, and other species, locked in cages to display in places called zoos...
Sure, they eat their own feces while sad people point and laugh...still...
Now that I think about it...we're just as awful as you are.
Yes. Excellent!
I would like to play with these monkeys. Can you help me acquire one?
SWWSSHH
That will be all, Agent.
Huak.
Good news, human. The resurrection of your ship's core is proceeding flawlessly.
Accessing the zoological files shows that the biological makeup of your planet's many species pose no threat to the greater library...
DOOP!
I'm not actually human.
You are now released from quarantine...
Please proceed from this holding cell to your more spacious, long-term accommodations.

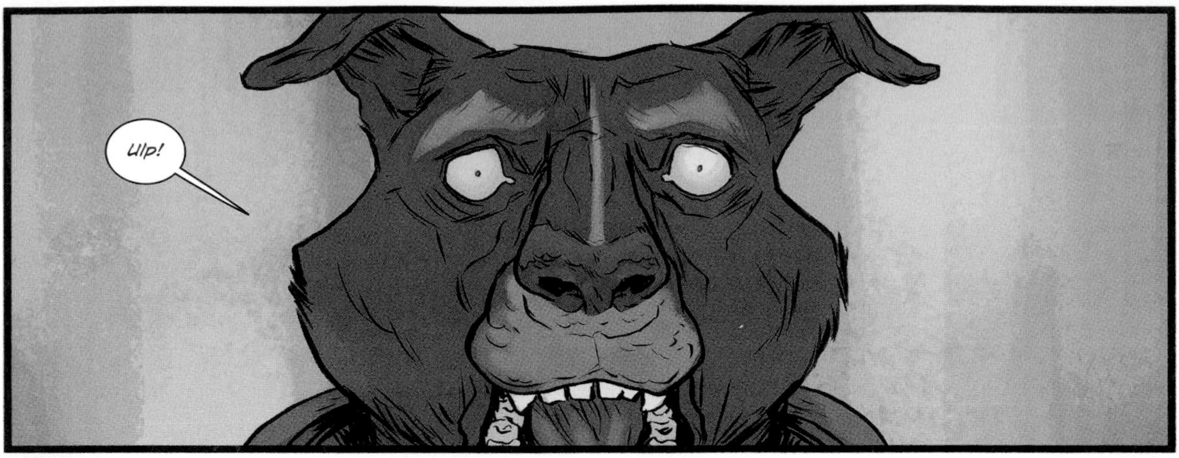
Ulp!

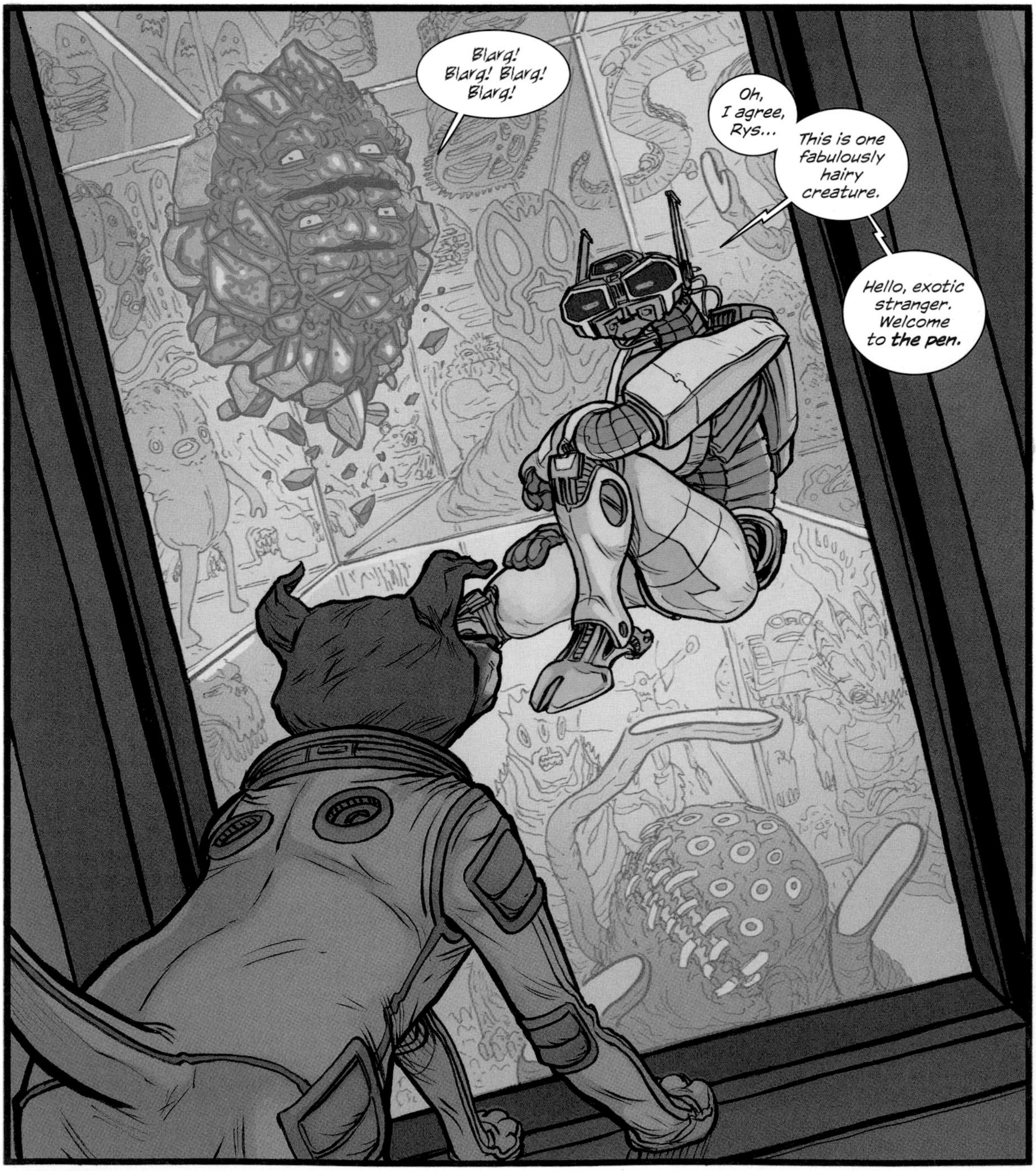
Blarg! Blarg! Blarg! Blarg!
Oh, I agree, Rys...
This is one fabulously hairy creature.
Hello, exotic stranger. Welcome to **the pen.**

My surveillance package is top of the line -- I could hear that you are something called human, and that you ate the wordjunk.
So you can understand me, yes? You have a proper name of some kind?
I'm not a **human**...I'm a **dog** -- my name is Laika.
Well, I am **UNa.** A series nine infiltration and espionage droid -- disinformation a specialty.
And this is **Rys,** the reincarnated space twins from the binary system of Cygnus.
BLARG!
Fine. He's actually a bioconstruct built for interstellar cartography.
Sorry... it's my programming. **I lie a lot.**
It's nice to meet you, Laika.

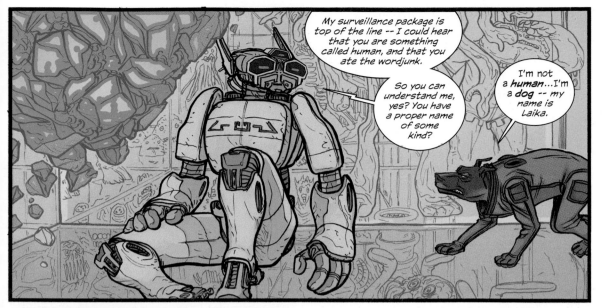

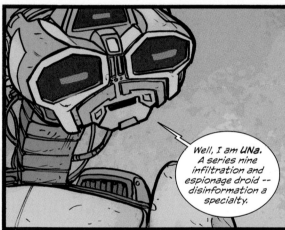

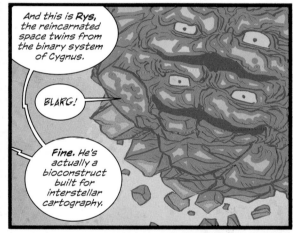

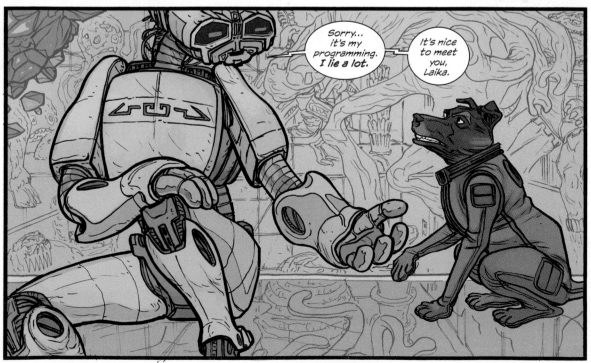

Wait, do you really mean that? *That it's nice to meet me?*
Yes.
Does that really mean no?
No.
This is going to get old very quickly, isn't it?
We have to entertain ourselves somehow.
After all, these Sionnu collection missions have been known to last decades.
What?
Yes. Very thorough, the Sionnu.
Rys, where are we now?
Blarg! Blarg!
Blarg!
Right.
And that's at the edge of Sionnu space. Badlands gone even worse with the fall of the Siill Empire.
Far from the **Sionnu library world.** We'll be here for quite some time.

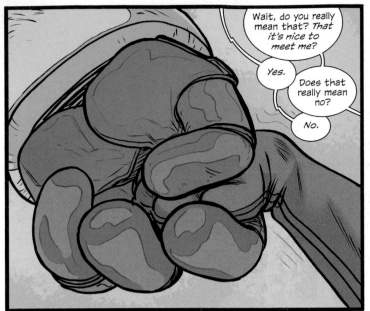

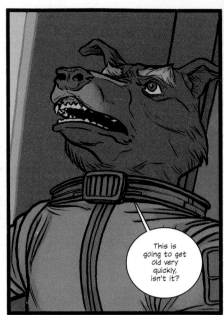

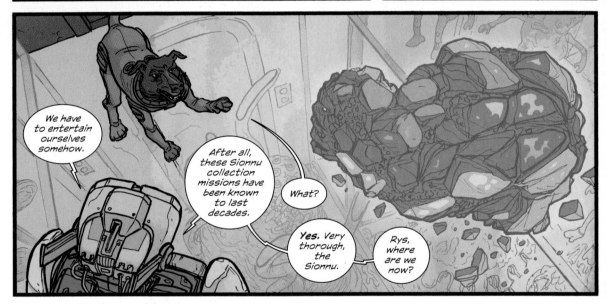

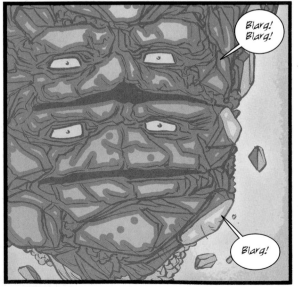

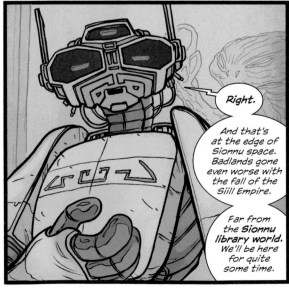

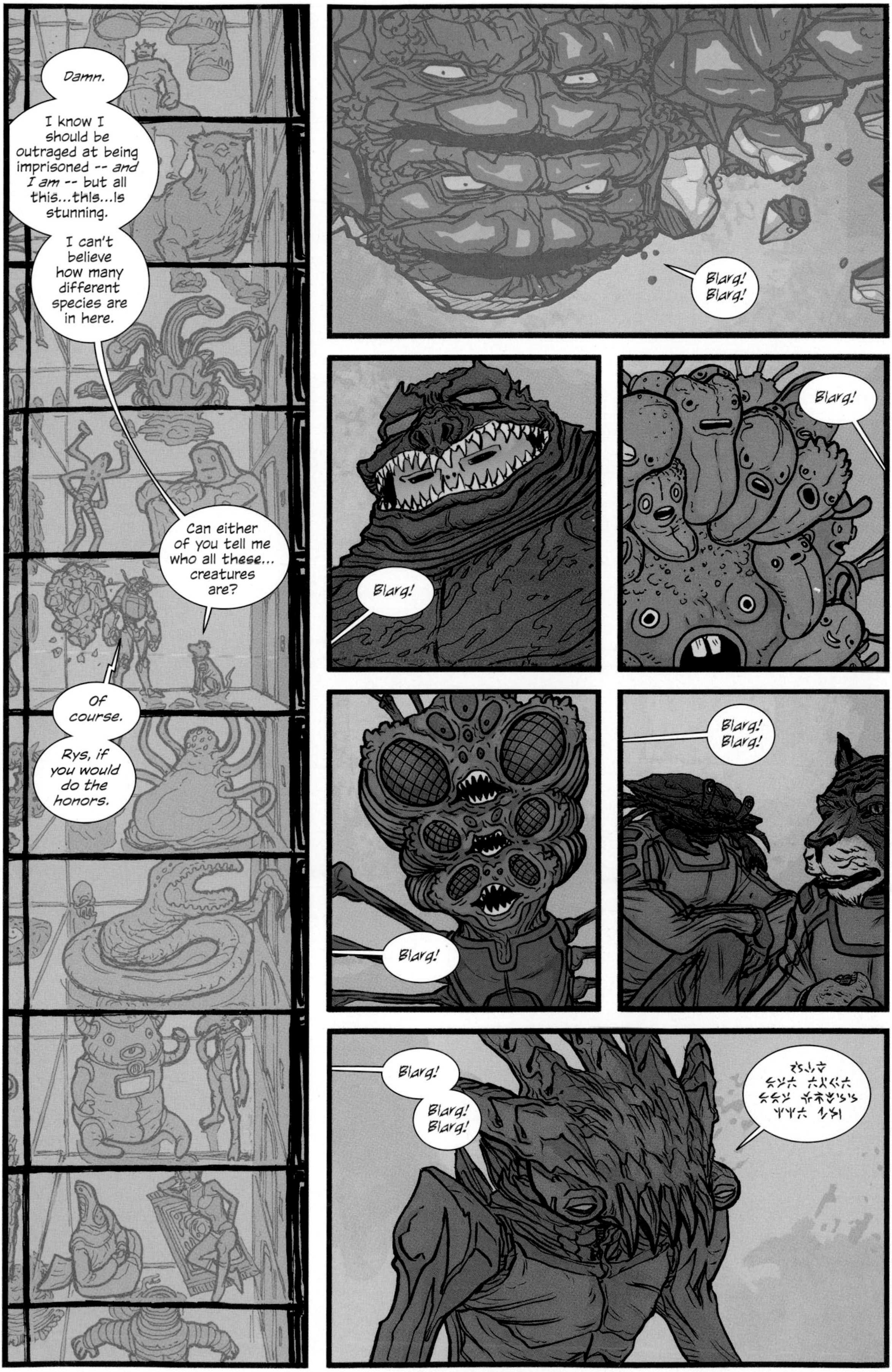
Damn.
I know I should be outraged at being imprisoned -- and I am -- but all this...this...is stunning.
I can't believe how many different species are in here.
Can either of you tell me who all these... creatures are?
Of course.
Rys, if you would do the honors.
Blarg! Blarg!
Blarg!
Blarg!
Blarg!
Blarg! Blarg!
Blarg!
Blarg! Blarg!

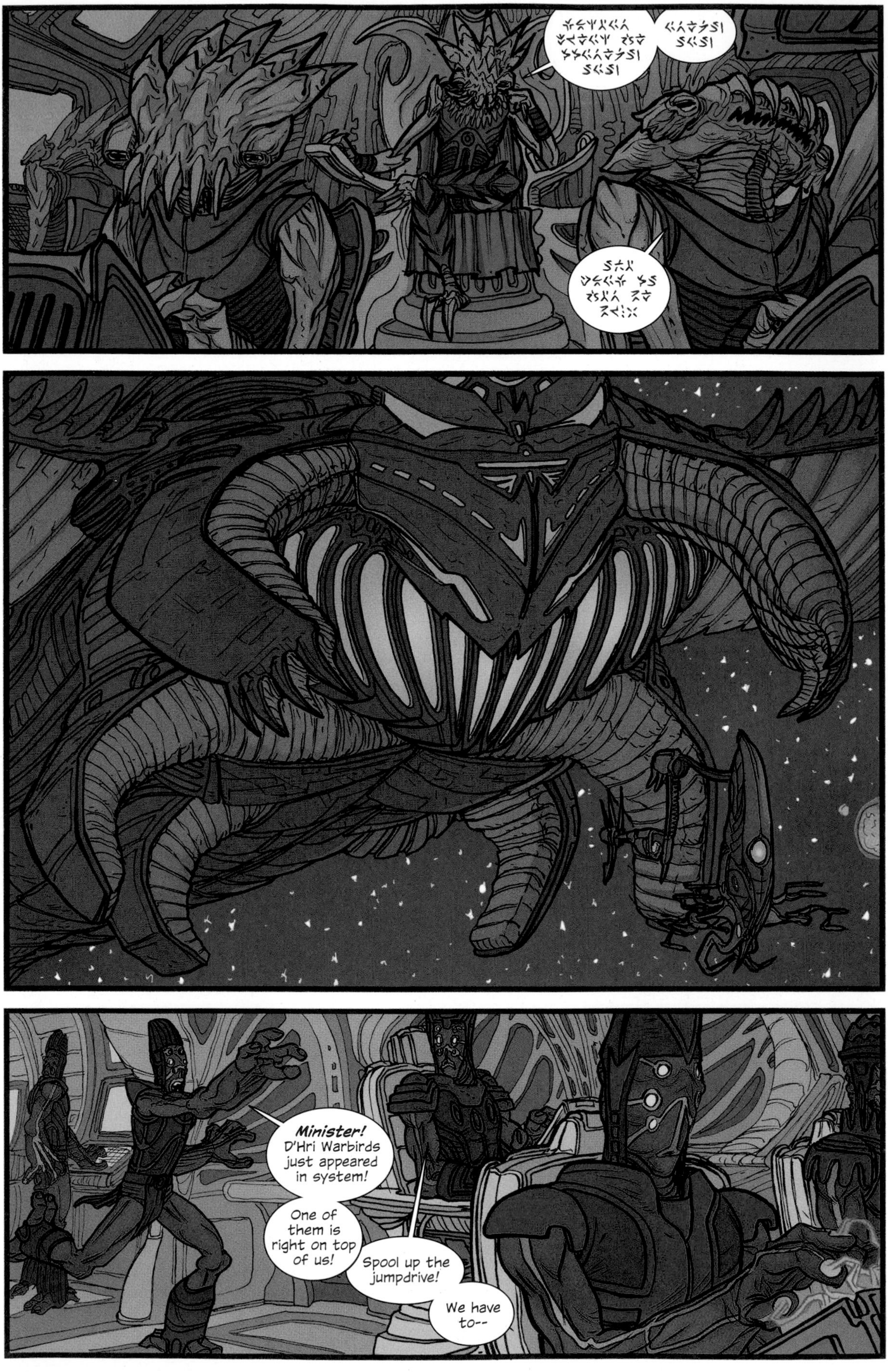
Minister! D'Hri Warbirds just appeared in system!
One of them is right on top of us!
Spool up the jumpdrive!
We have to--

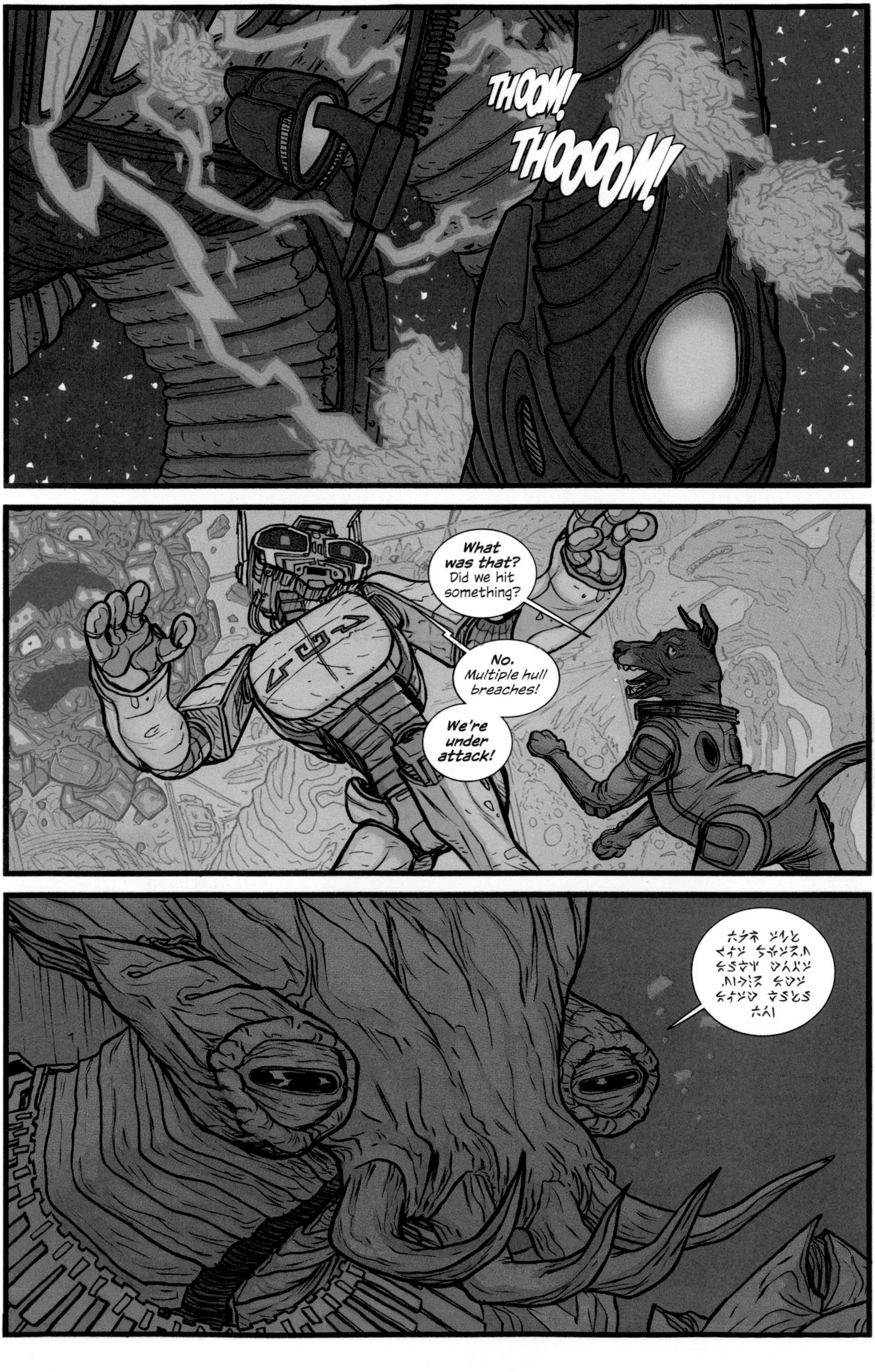
THOOM!
THOOOOM!
What was that? Did we hit something?
No. Multiple hull breaches!
We're under attack!

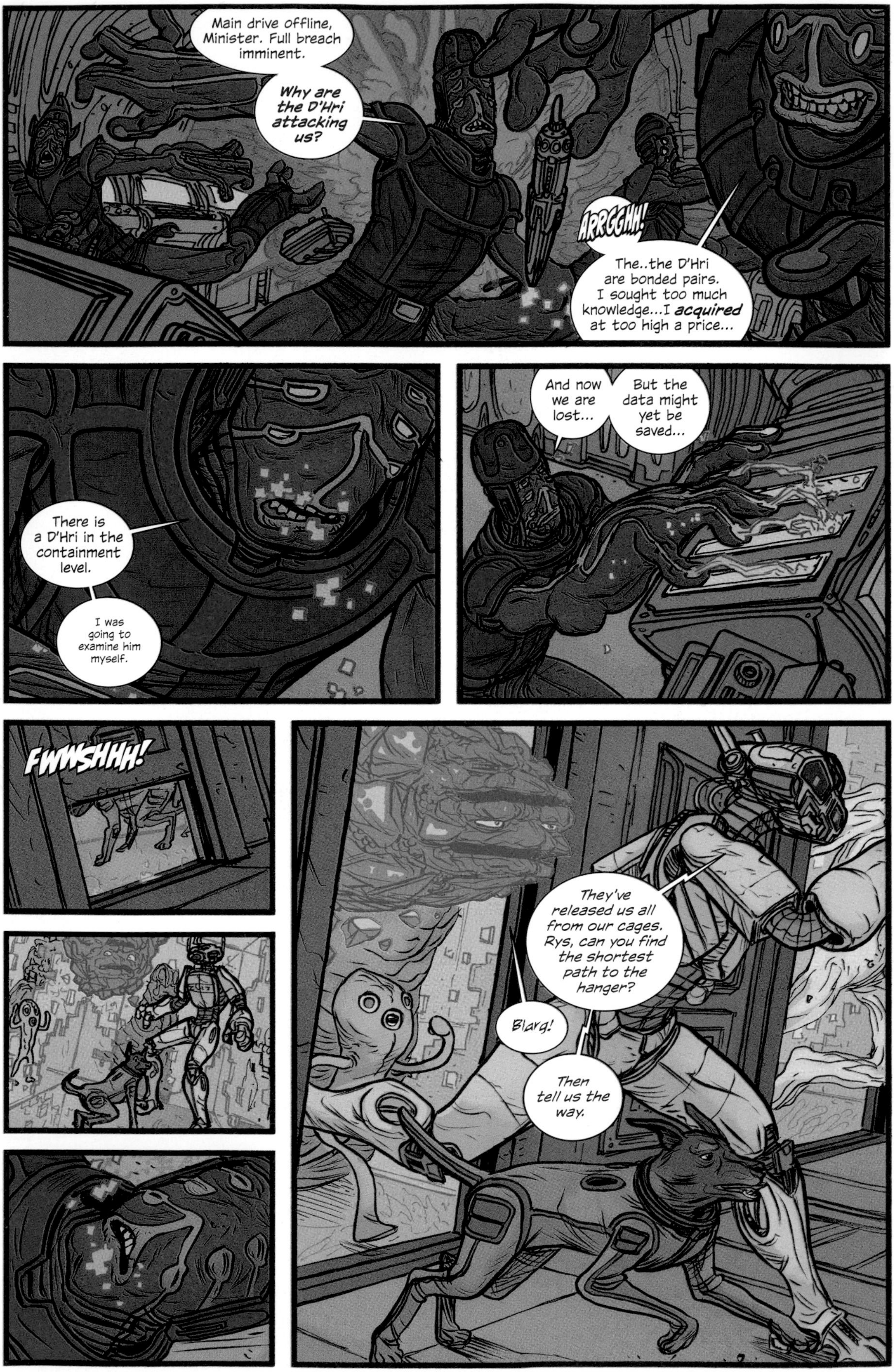
Main drive offline, Minister. Full breach imminent.
Why are the D'Hri attacking us?
ARRGGHH!
The..the D'Hri are bonded pairs. I sought too much knowledge...I acquired at too high a price...
There is a D'Hri in the containment level.
I was going to examine him myself.
And now we are lost...
But the data might yet be saved...
FWWSHHH!
They've released us all from our cages. Rys, can you find the shortest path to the hanger?
Blarg!
Then tell us the way.

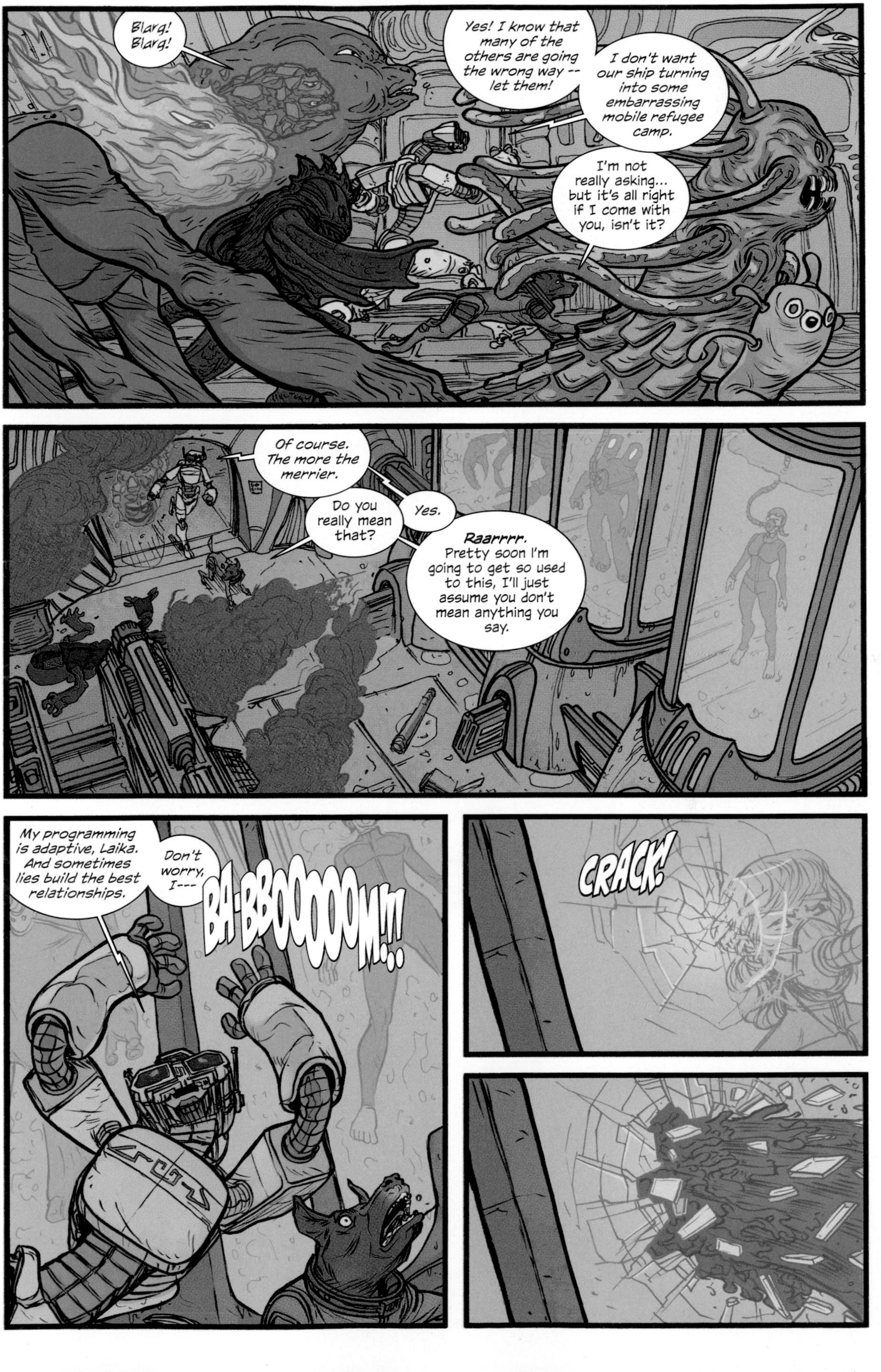
Blarg! Blarg!
Yes! I know that many of the others are going the wrong way -- let them!
I don't want our ship turning into some embarrassing mobile refugee camp.
I'm not really asking... but it's all right if I come with you, isn't it?
Of course. The more the merrier.
Do you really mean that?
Yes.
Raarrrr. Pretty soon I'm going to get so used to this, I'll just assume you don't mean anything you say.
My programming is adaptive, Laika. And sometimes lies build the best relationships.
Don't worry, I---
BA-BBOOOOOM!!!
CRACK!

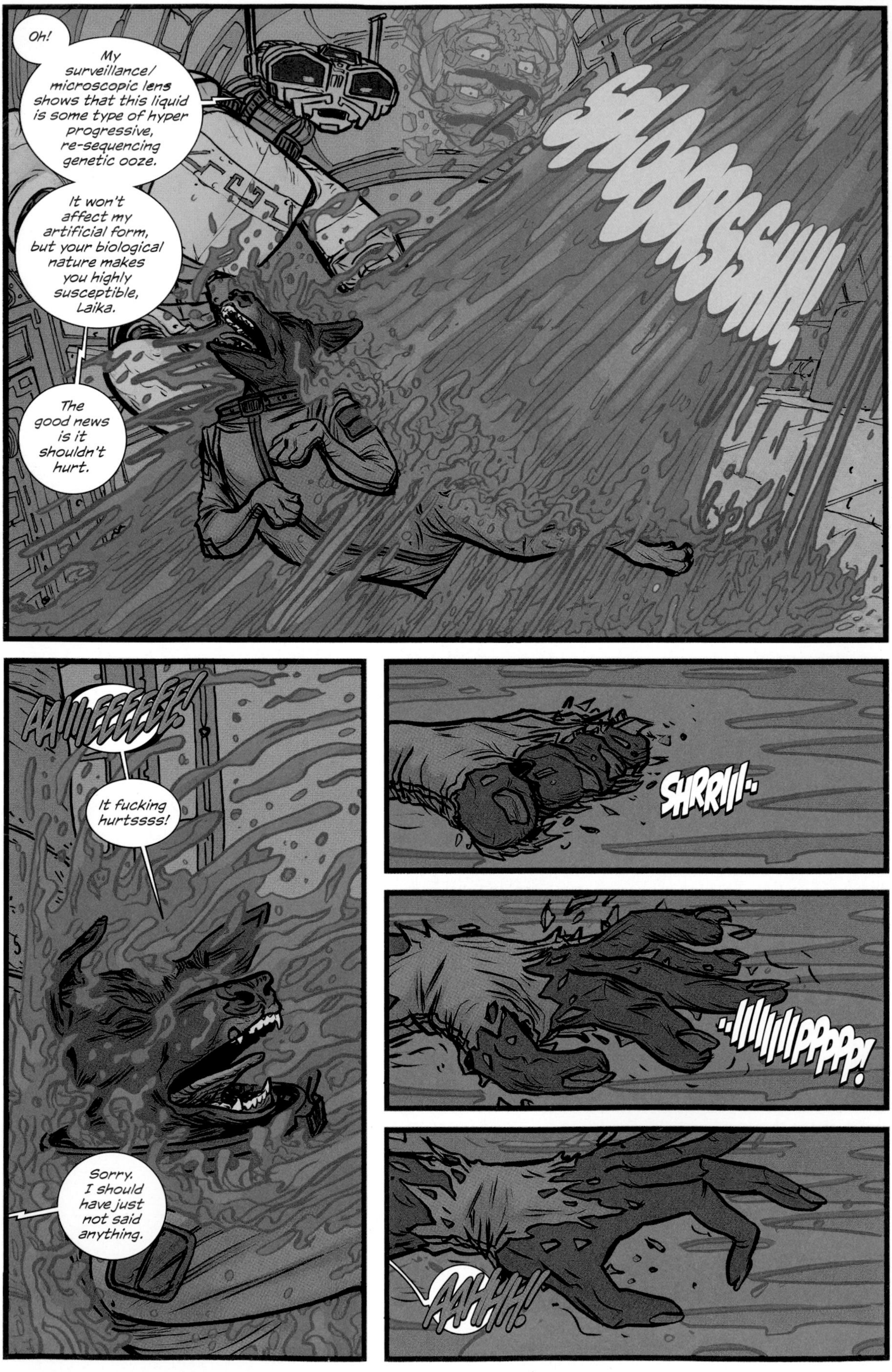
Oh!
My surveillance/ microscopic lens shows that this liquid is some type of hyper progressive, re-sequencing genetic ooze.
It won't affect my artificial form, but your biological nature makes you highly susceptible, Laika.
The good news is it shouldn't hurt.
SPLOOOSSHH
AAIIIIEEEEEE!
It fucking hurtssss!
Sorry. I should have just not said anything.
SHRRIII..
..IIIIIIIPPPPP!
AAHH!

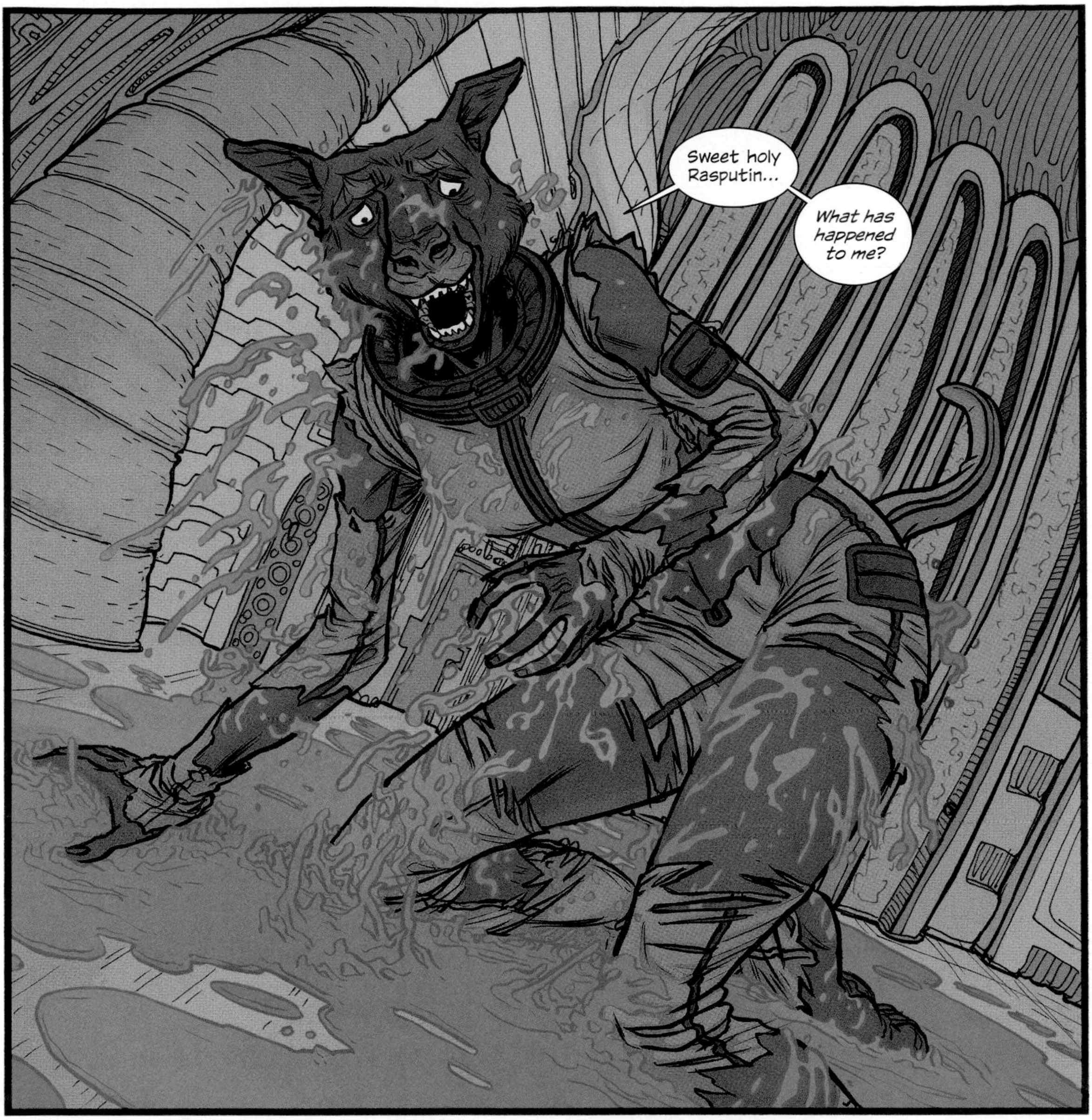
Sweet holy Rasputin...
What has happened to me?

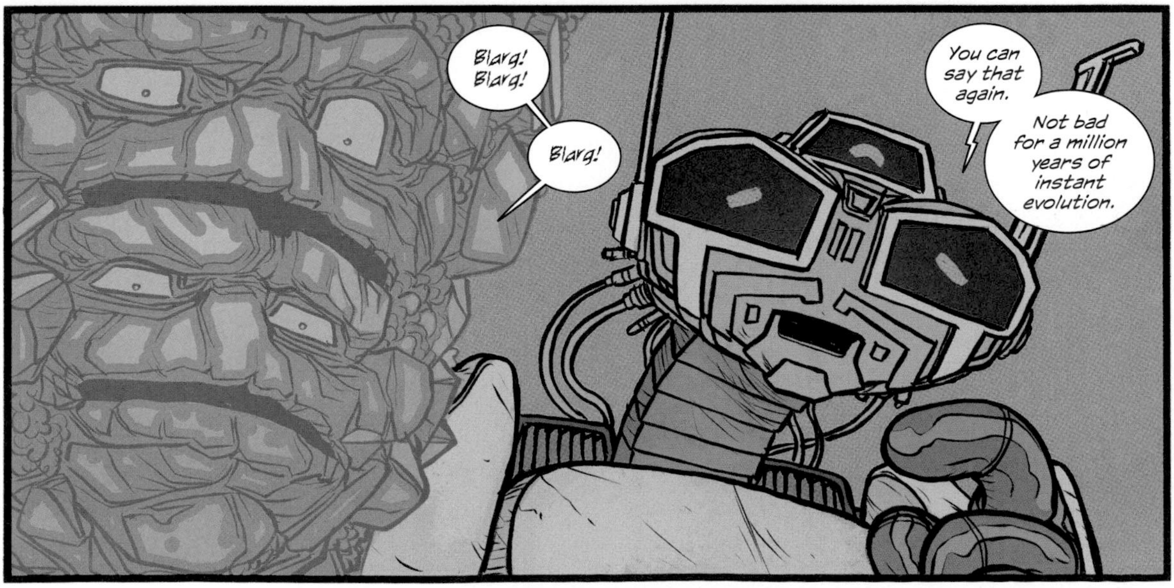
Blarg! Blarg!
Blarg!
You can say that again.
Not bad for a million years of instant evolution.

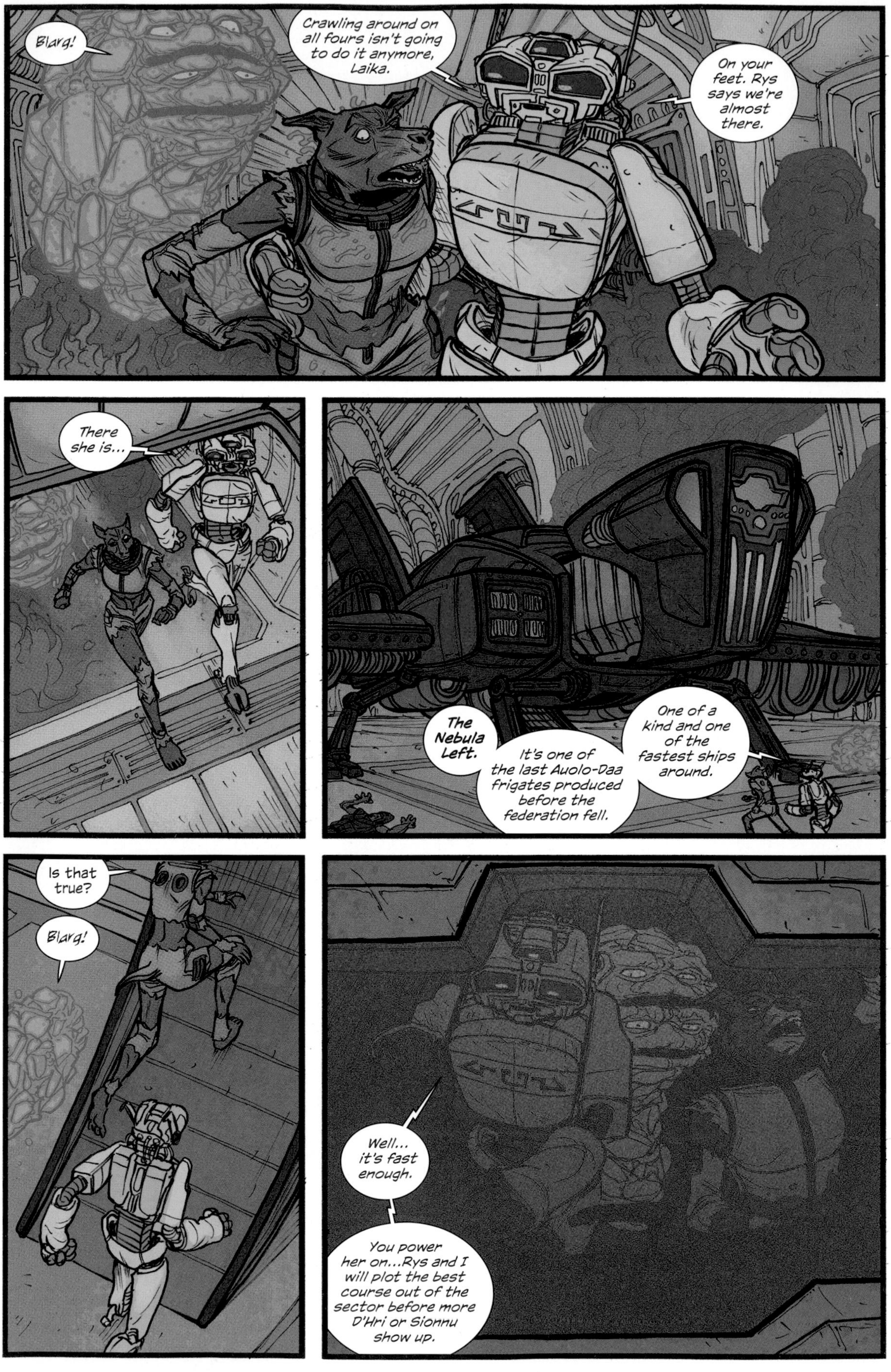
Blarg!
Crawling around on all fours isn't going to do it anymore, Laika.
On your feet. Rys says we're almost there.
There she is...
The Nebula Left.
It's one of the last Auolo-Daa frigates produced before the federation fell.
One of a kind and one of the fastest ships around.
Is that true?
Blarg!
Well... it's fast enough.
You power her on...Rys and I will plot the best course out of the sector before more D'Hri or Sionnu show up.

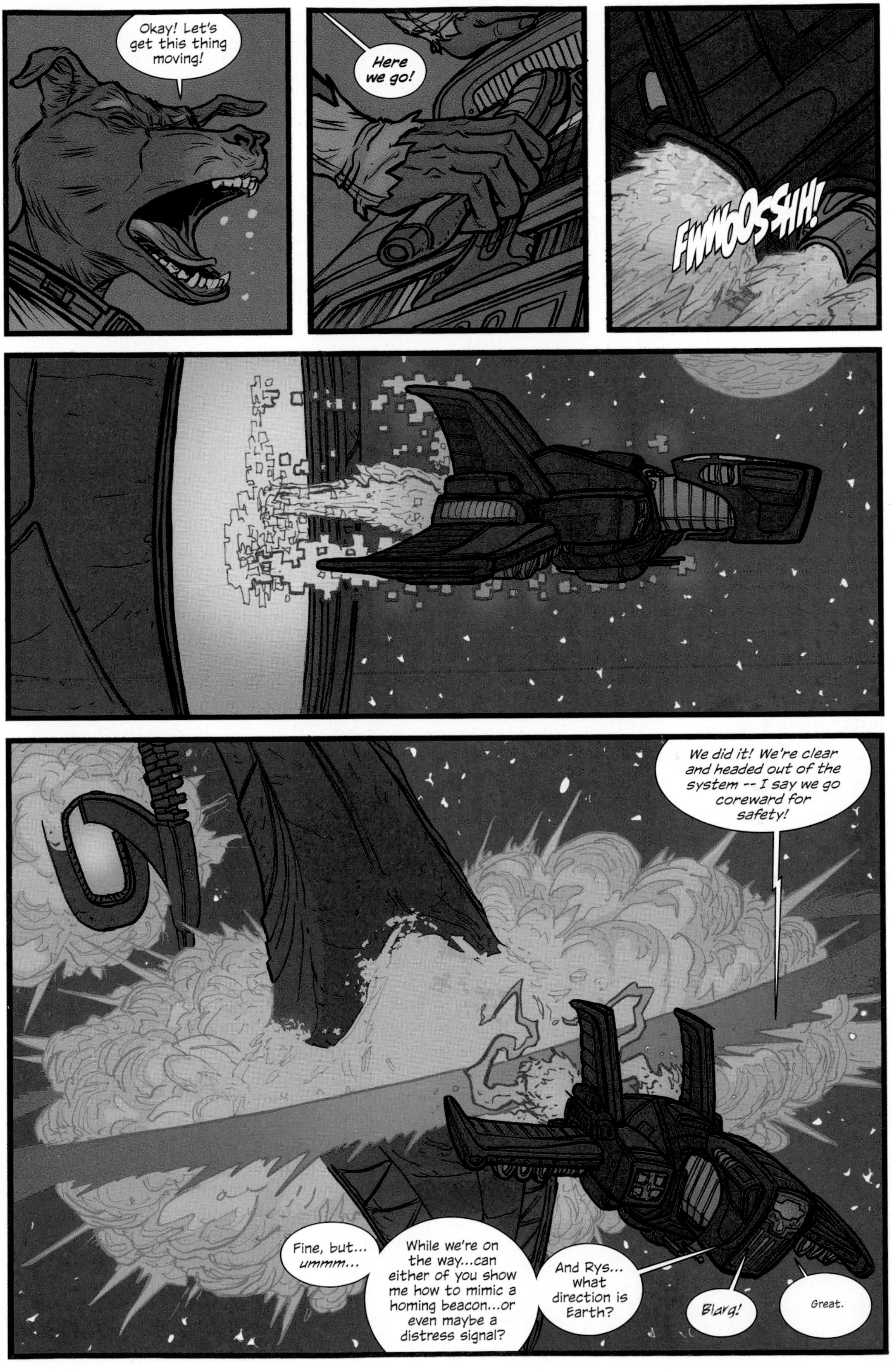
Okay! Let's get this thing moving!
Here we go!
FWWOOSSHH!
We did it! We're clear and headed out of the system -- I say we go coreward for safety!
Fine, but... ummm...
While we're on the way...can either of you show me how to mimic a homing beacon...or even maybe a distress signal?
And Rys... what direction is Earth?
Blarg!
Great.

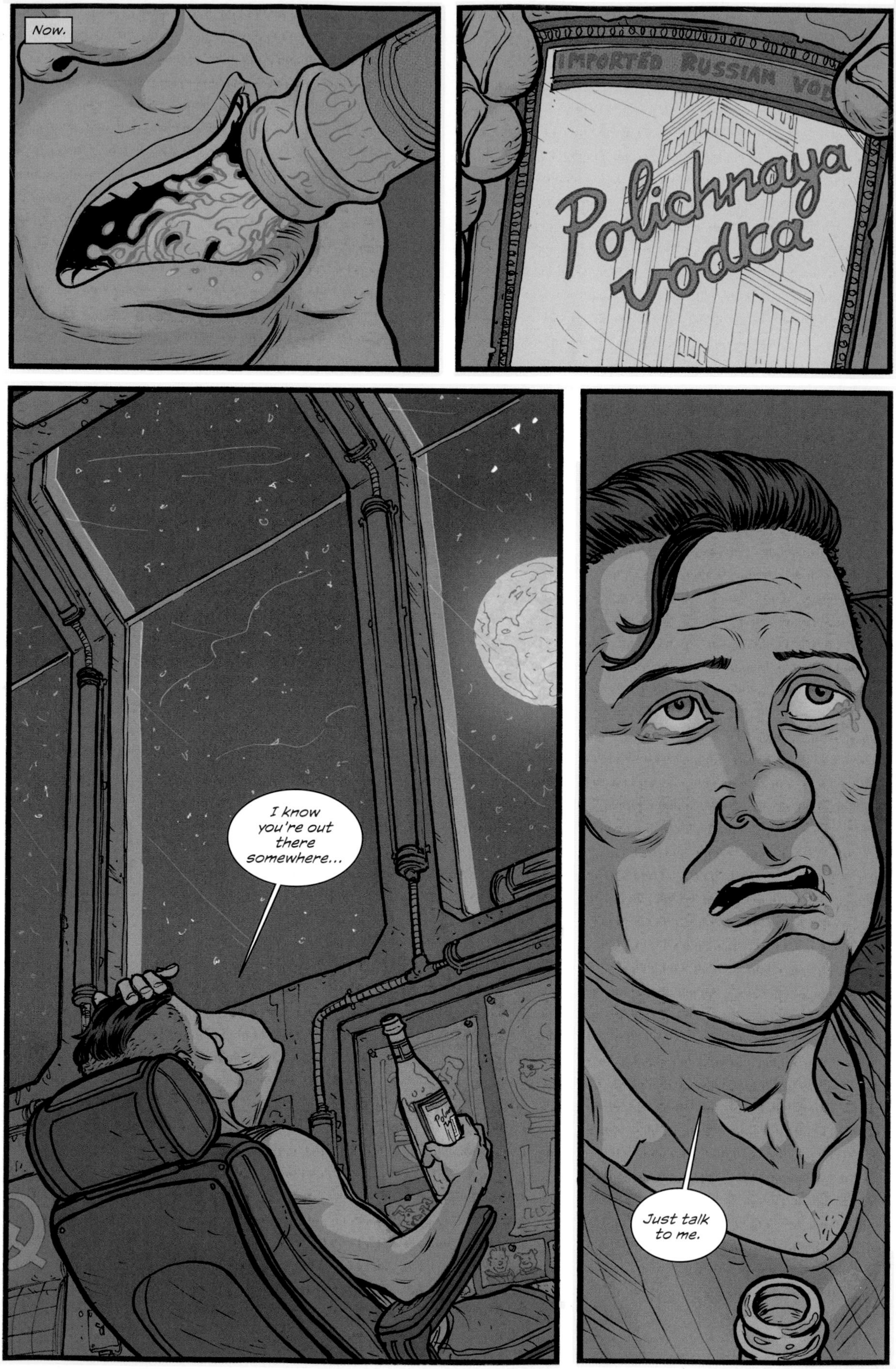
Now.
IMPORTED RUSSIAN VO
Polichnaya vodka
I know you're out there somewhere...
Just talk to me.

UNQUESTIONABLE
MACHISMO

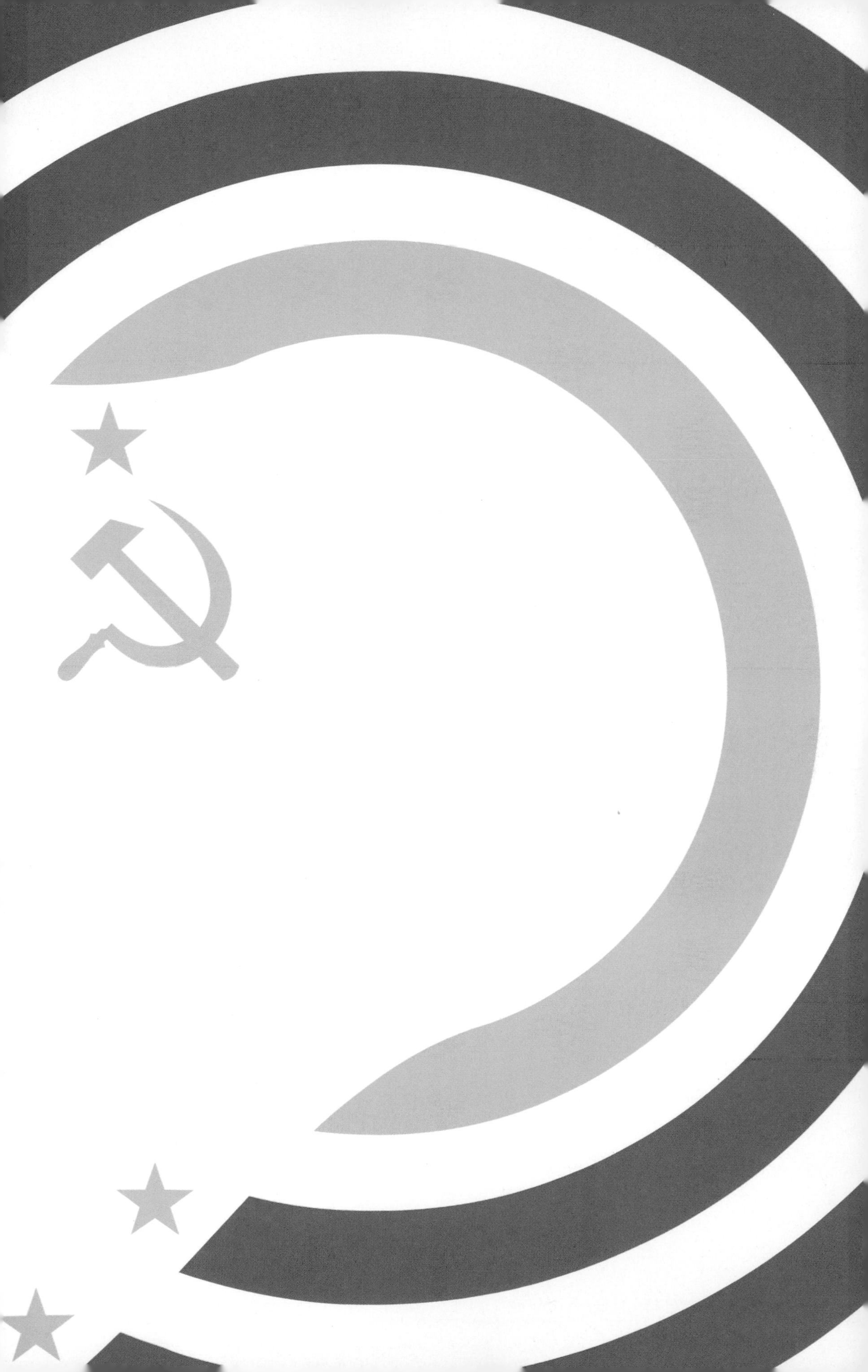

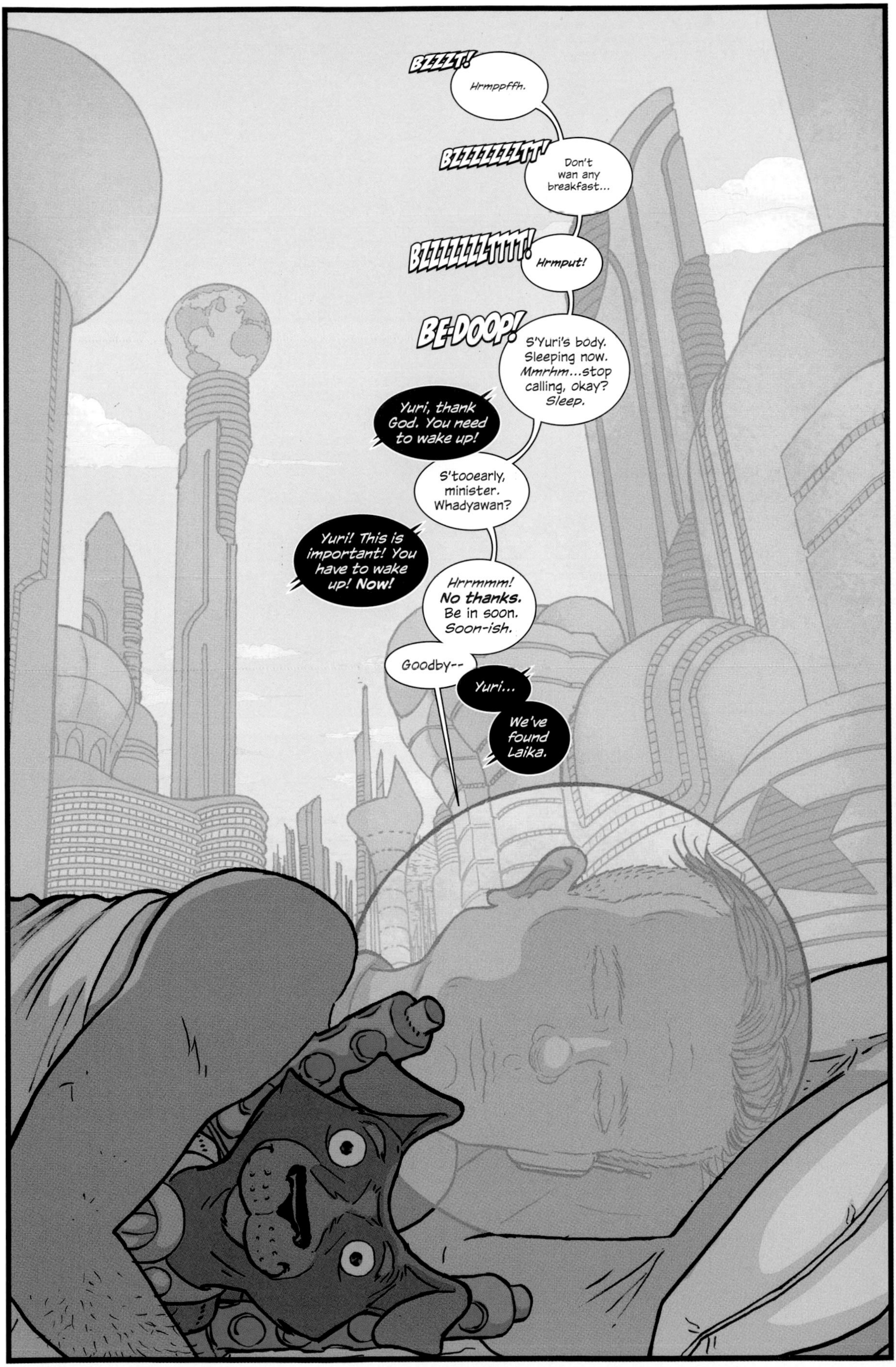
BZZZT!
Hrmppffh.
BZZZZZZZZTT!
Don't wan any breakfast...
BZZZZZZZTTTT!
Hrmput!
BE-DOOP!
S'Yuri's body. Sleeping now. Mmrhm...stop calling, okay? Sleep.
Yuri, thank God. You need to wake up!
S'tooearly, minister. Whadyawan?
Yuri! This is important! You have to wake up! Now!
Hrrmmm! No thanks. Be in soon. Soon-ish.
Goodby--
Yuri...
We've found Laika.

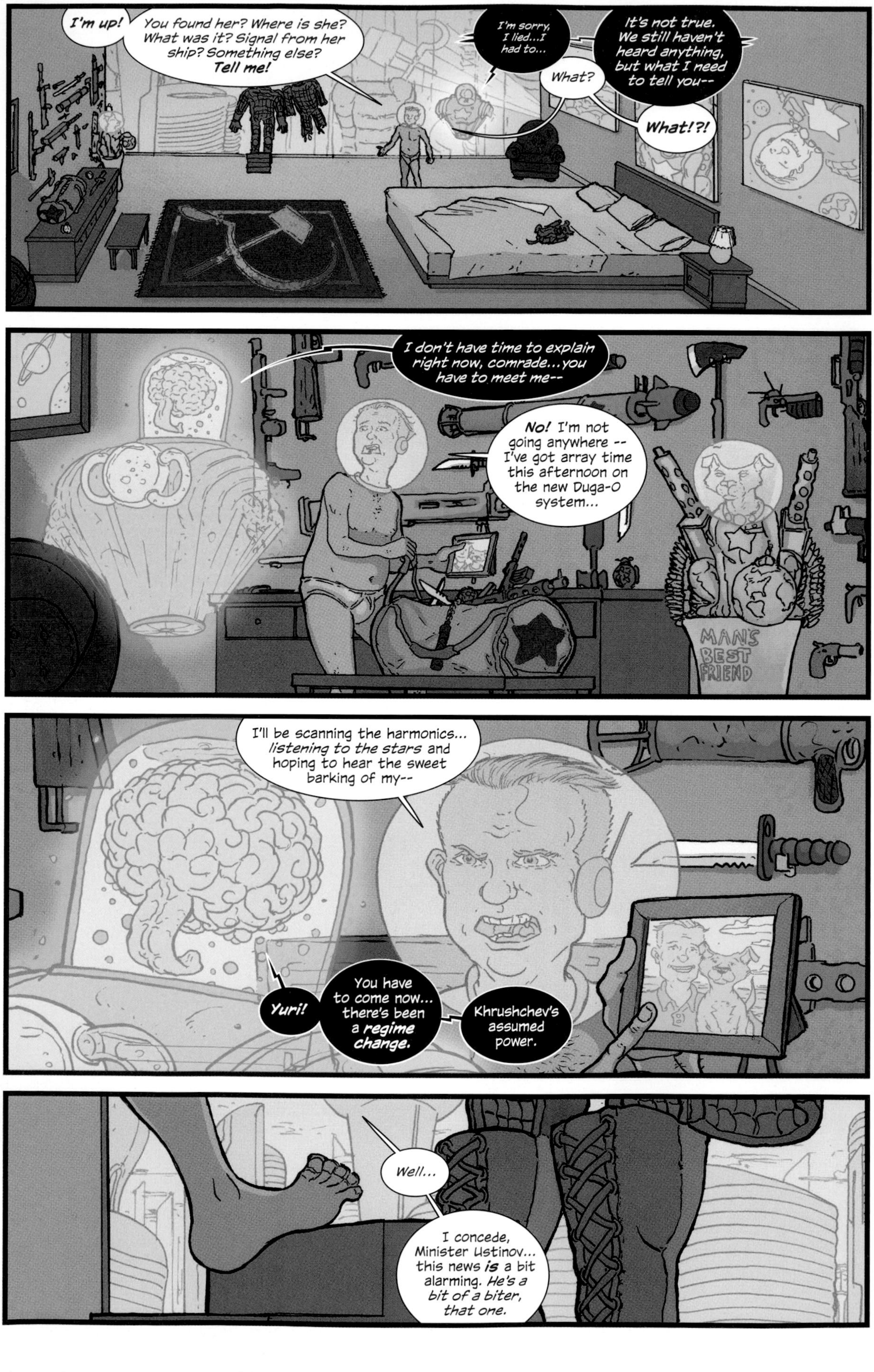
I'm up!
You found her? Where is she? What was it? Signal from her ship? Something else? Tell me!
I'm sorry, I lied...I had to...
It's not true. We still haven't heard anything, but what I need to tell you--
What?
What!?!
I don't have time to explain right now, comrade...you have to meet me--
No! I'm not going anywhere -- I've got array time this afternoon on the new Duga-O system...
MAN'S BEST FRIEND
I'll be scanning the harmonics... listening to the stars and hoping to hear the sweet barking of my--
Yuri!
You have to come now... there's been a regime change.
Khrushchev's assumed power.
Well...
I concede, Minister Ustinov... this news is a bit alarming. He's a bit of a biter, that one.

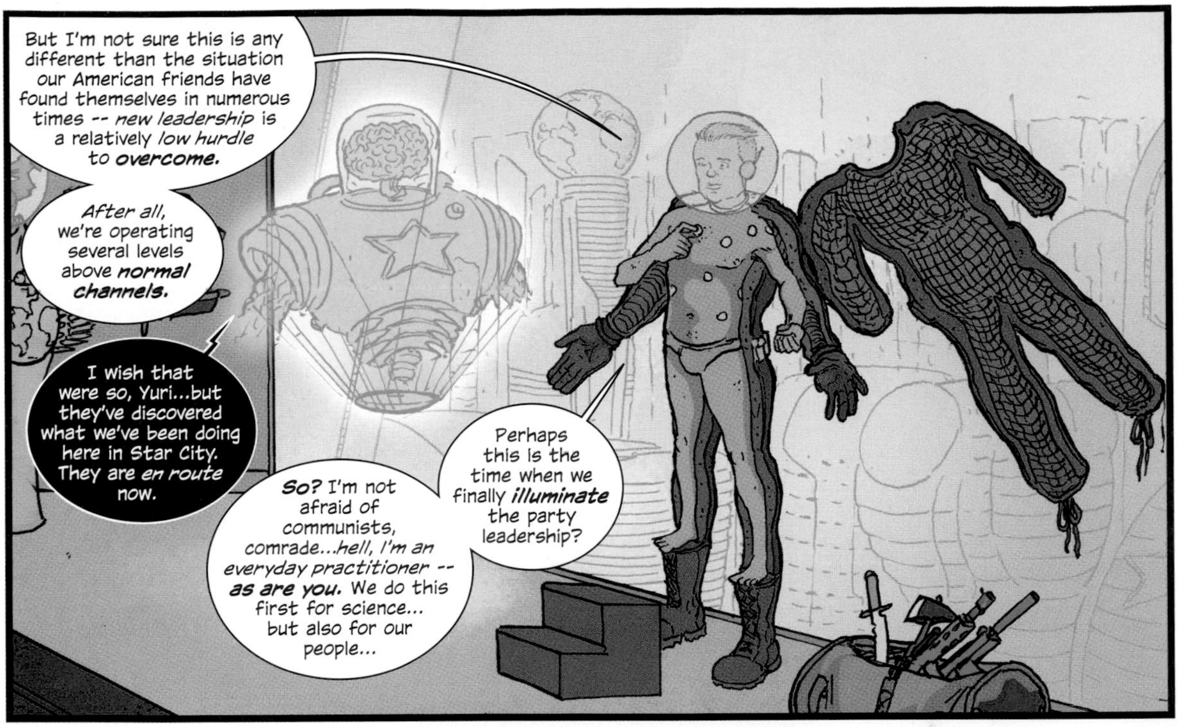
But I'm not sure this is any different than the situation our American friends have found themselves in numerous times -- new leadership is a relatively low hurdle to overcome.
After all, we're operating several levels above normal channels.
I wish that were so, Yuri...but they've discovered what we've been doing here in Star City. They are en route now.
So? I'm not afraid of communists, comrade...hell, I'm an everyday practitioner -- as are you. We do this first for science... but also for our people...
Perhaps this is the time when we finally illuminate the party leadership?

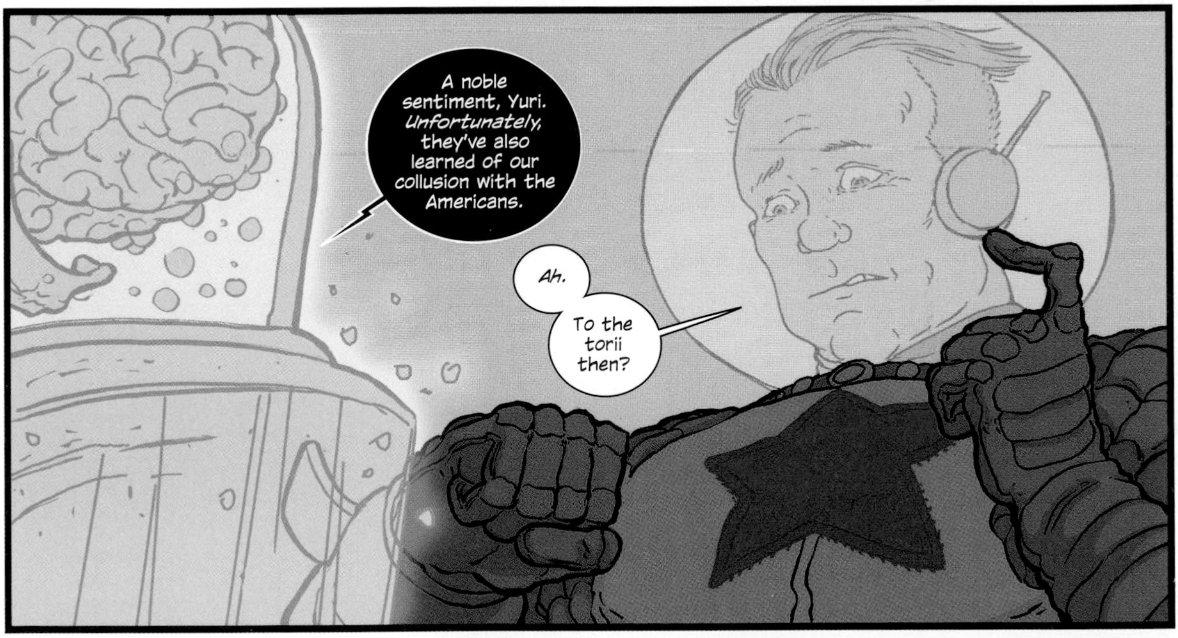
A noble sentiment, Yuri. Unfortunately, they've also learned of our collusion with the Americans.
Ah.
To the torii then?

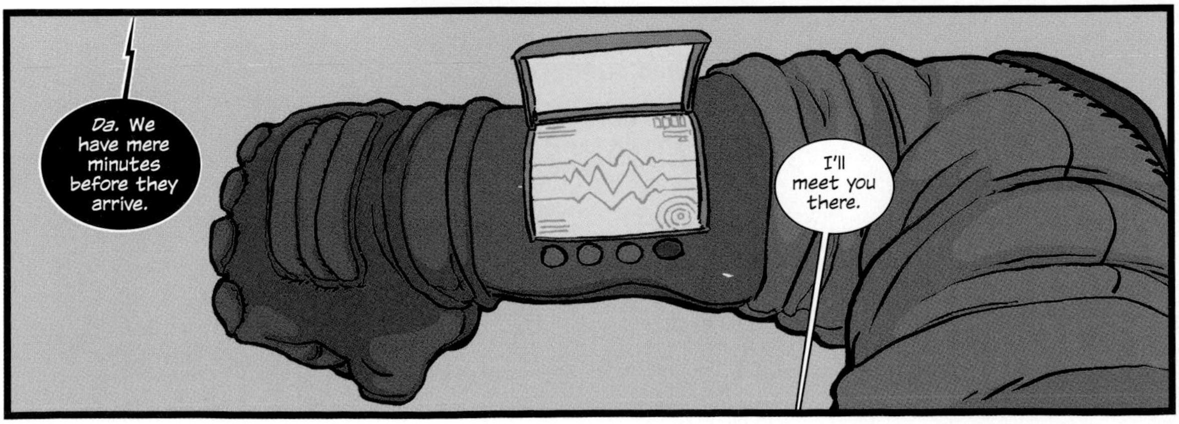
Da. We have mere minutes before they arrive.
I'll meet you there.

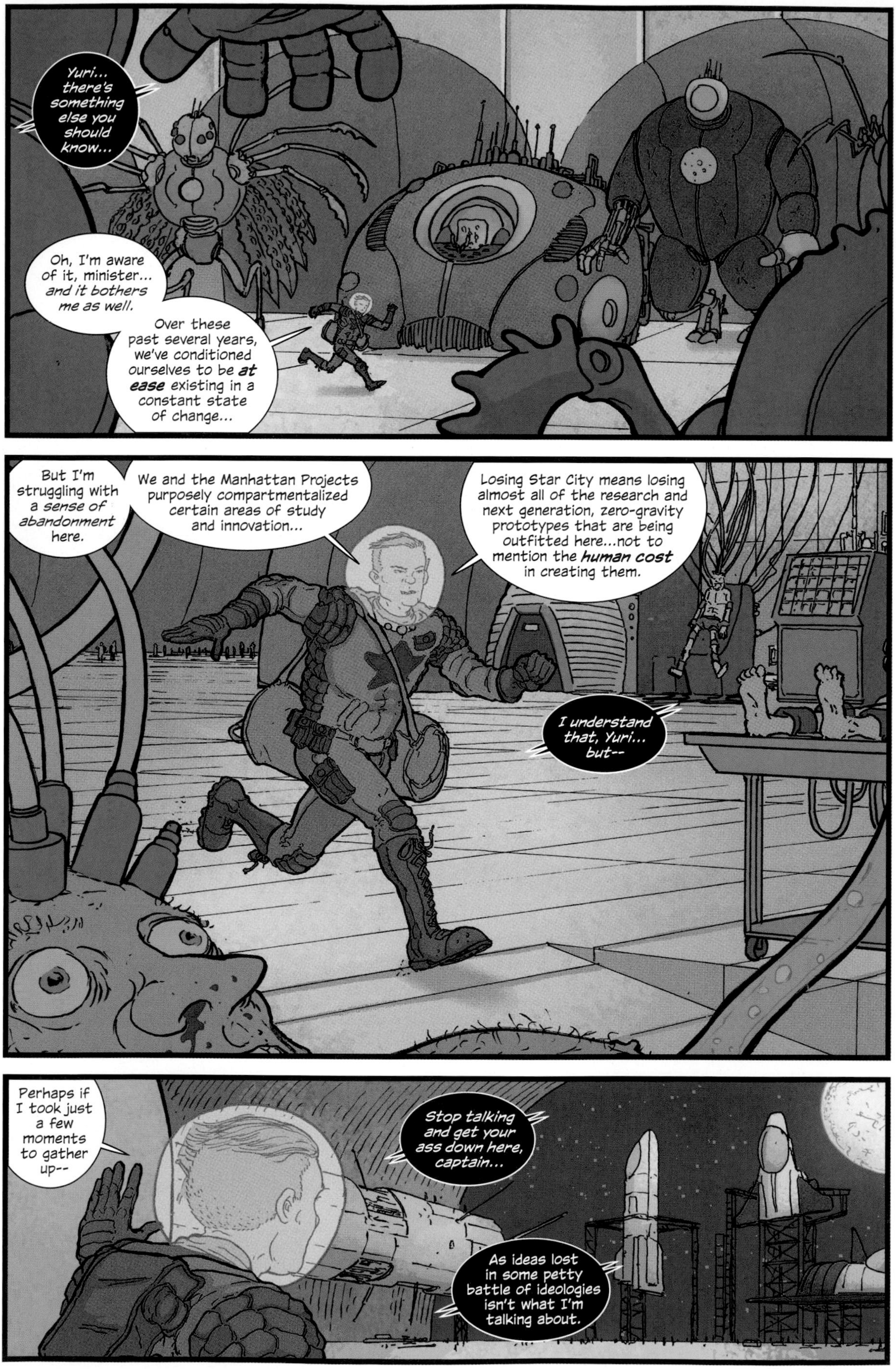

Yuri... there's something else you should know...
Oh, I'm aware of it, minister... and it bothers me as well.
Over these past several years, we've conditioned ourselves to be at ease existing in a constant state of change...
But I'm struggling with a sense of abandonment here.
We and the Manhattan Projects purposely compartmentalized certain areas of study and innovation...
Losing Star City means losing almost all of the research and next generation, zero-gravity prototypes that are being outfitted here...not to mention the human cost in creating them.
I understand that, Yuri... but--
Perhaps if I took just a few moments to gather up--
Stop talking and get your ass down here, captain...
As ideas lost in some petty battle of ideologies isn't what I'm talking about.

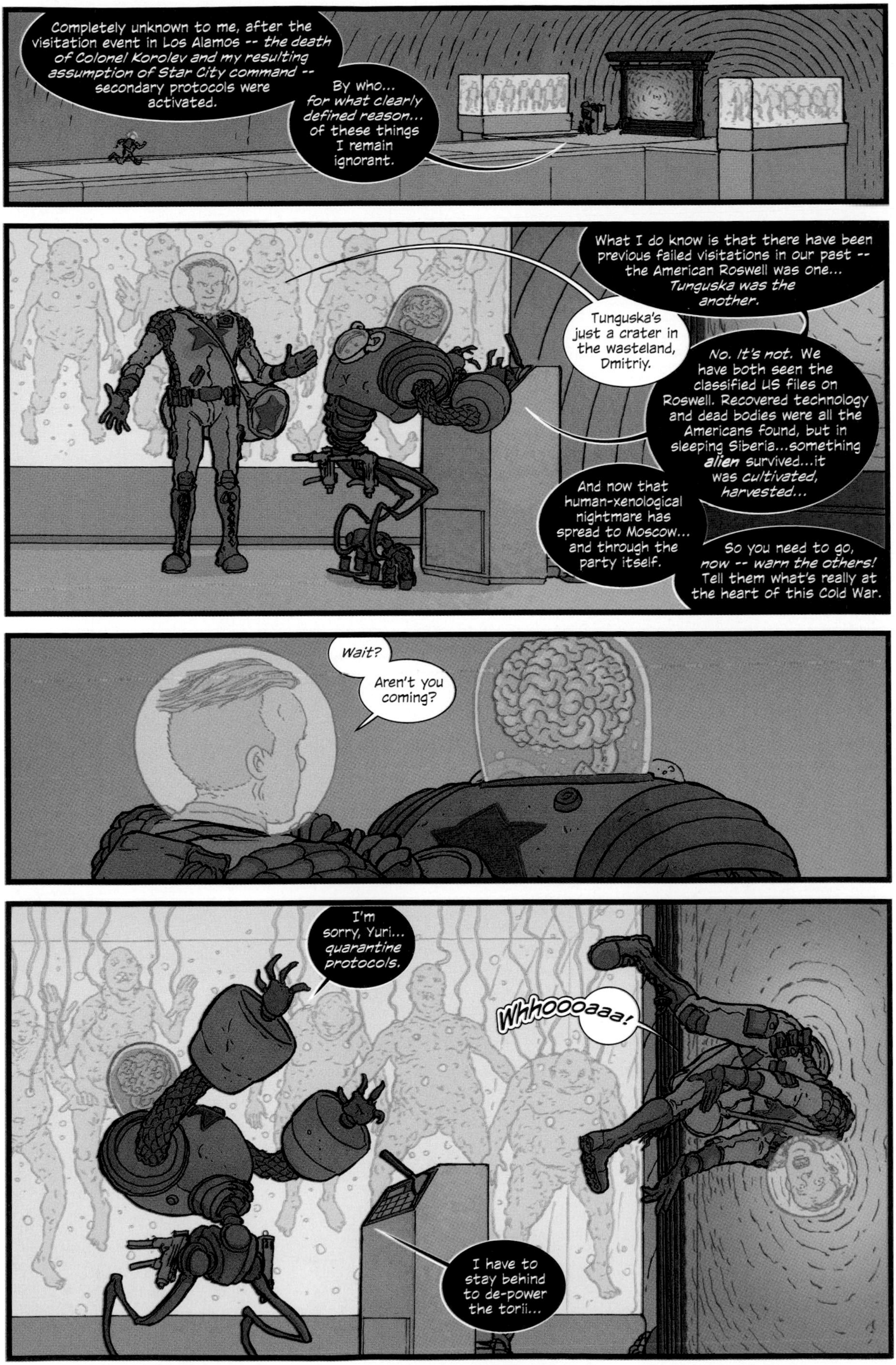
Completely unknown to me, after the visitation event in Los Alamos -- the death of Colonel Korolev and my resulting assumption of Star City command -- secondary protocols were activated.
By who... for what clearly defined reason... of these things I remain ignorant.
What I do know is that there have been previous failed visitations in our past -- the American Roswell was one... Tunguska was the another.
Tunguska's just a crater in the wasteland, Dmitriy.
No. It's not. We have both seen the classified US files on Roswell. Recovered technology and dead bodies were all the Americans found, but in sleeping Siberia...something alien survived...it was cultivated, harvested...
And now that human-xenological nightmare has spread to Moscow... and through the party itself.
So you need to go, now -- warn the others! Tell them what's really at the heart of this Cold War.
Wait?
Aren't you coming?
I'm sorry, Yuri... quarantine protocols.
Whhoooaaa!
I have to stay behind to de-power the torii...

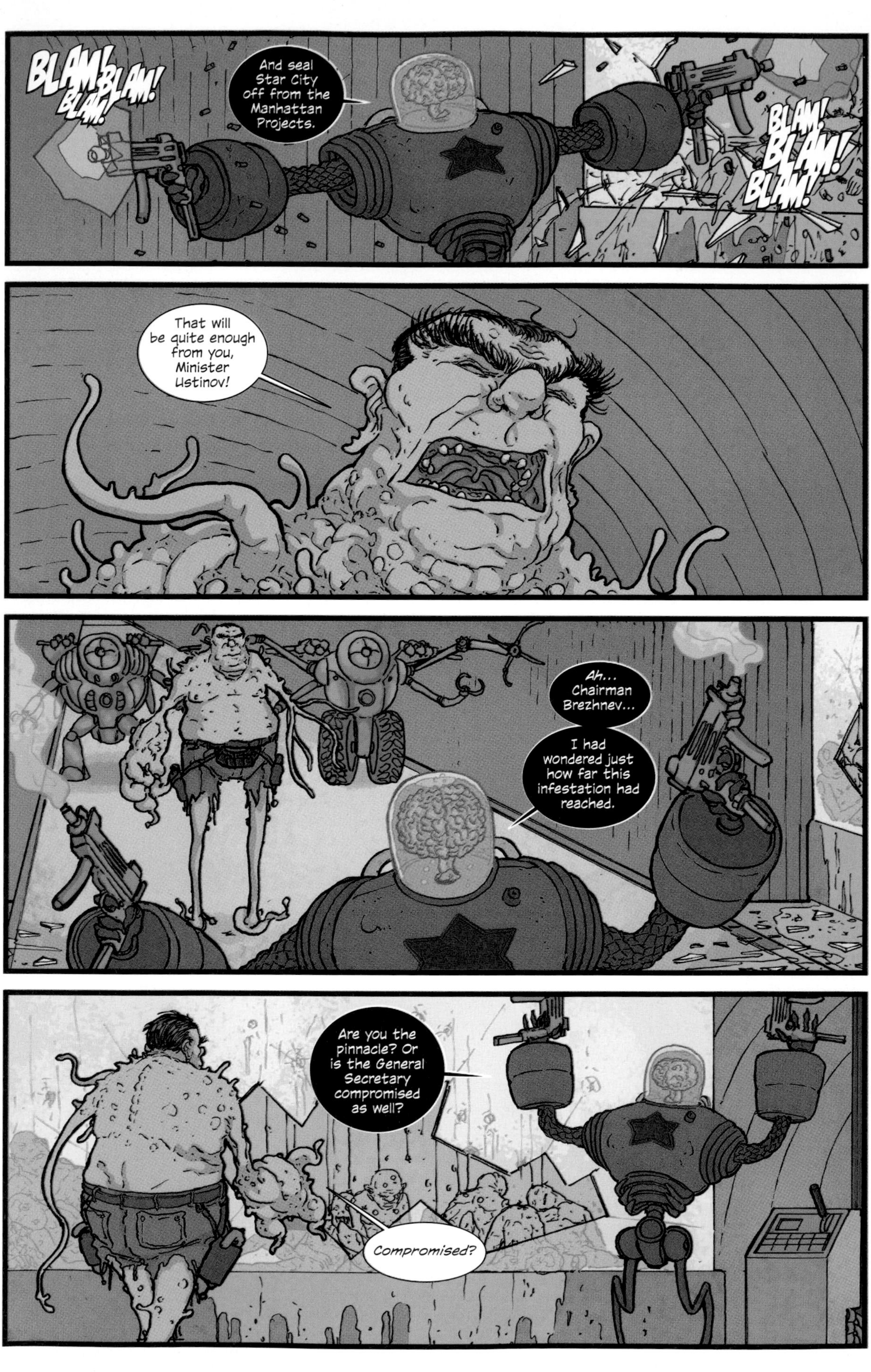

BLAM! BLAM! BLAM!
And seal Star City off from the Manhattan Projects.
BLAM! BLAM! BLAM!
That will be quite enough from you, Minister Ustinov!
Ah... Chairman Brezhnev...
I had wondered just how far this infestation had reached.
Are you the pinnacle? Or is the General Secretary compromised as well?
Compromised?

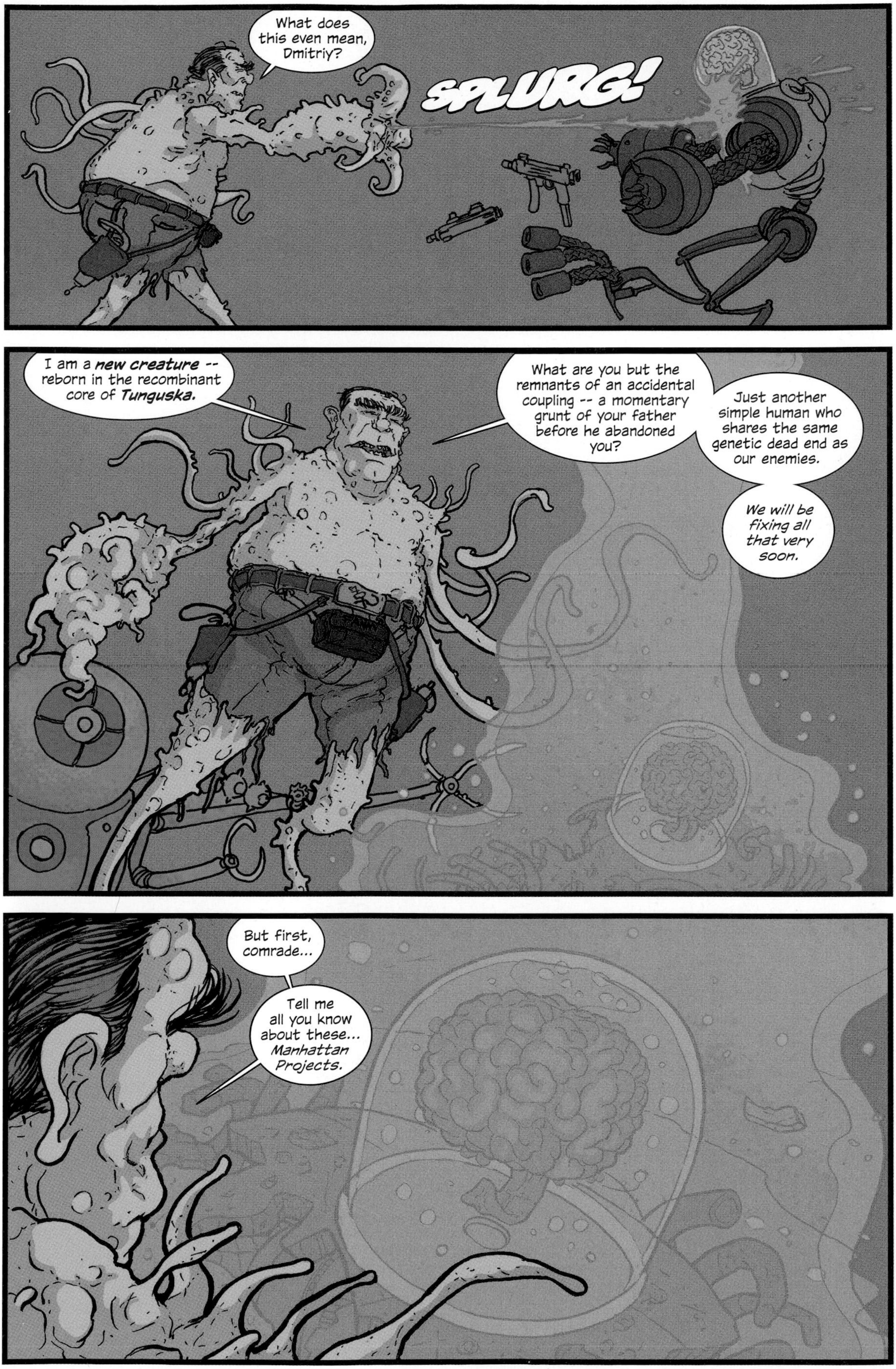
What does this even mean, Dmitriy?
SPLURG!
I am a new creature -- reborn in the recombinant core of Tunguska.
What are you but the remnants of an accidental coupling -- a momentary grunt of your father before he abandoned you?
Just another simple human who shares the same genetic dead end as our enemies.
We will be fixing all that very soon.
But first, comrade...
Tell me all you know about these... Manhattan Projects.

22

VECTORS

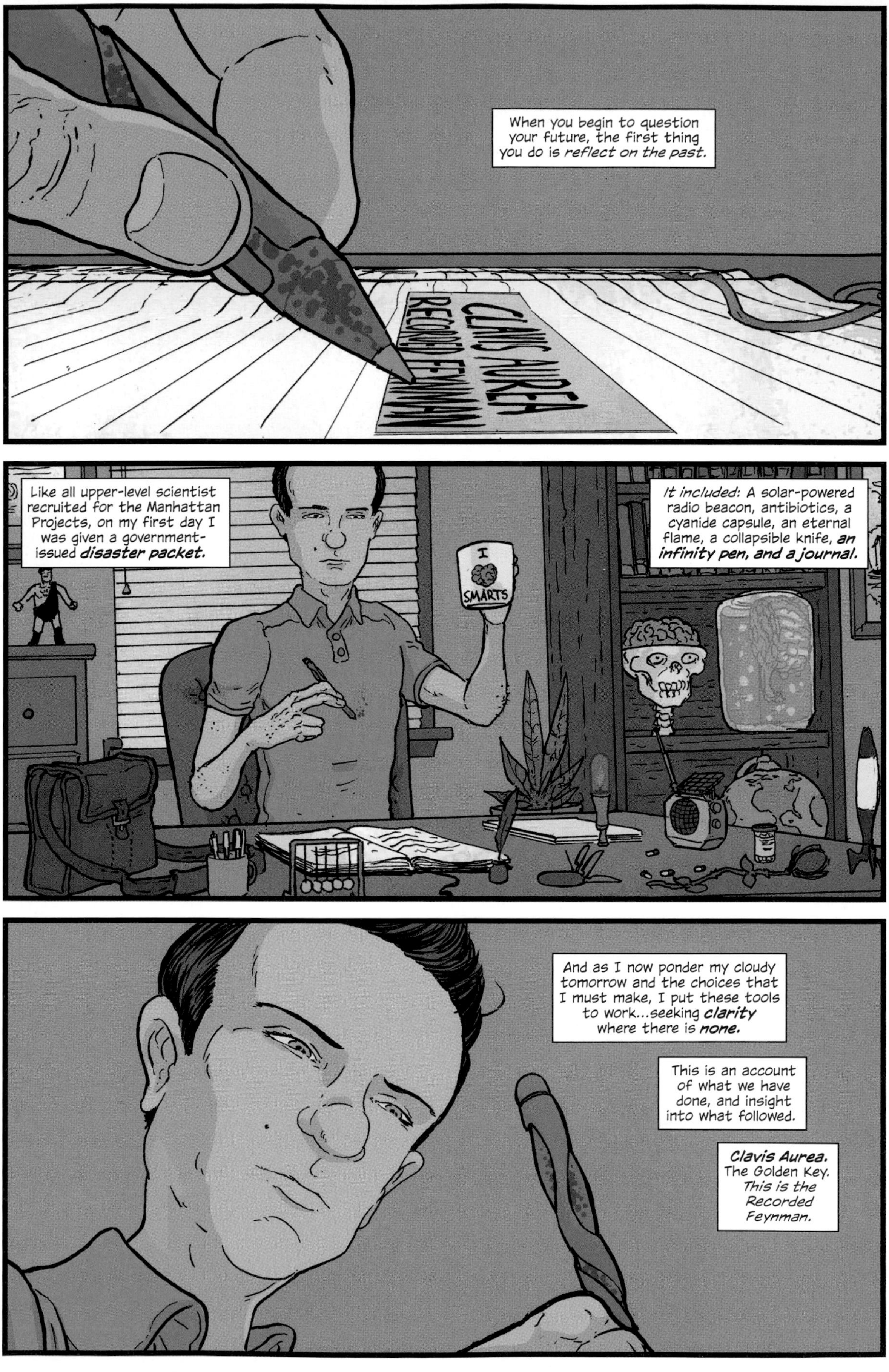

When you begin to question your future, the first thing you do is *reflect on the past.*
CLAVIS AUREA
RECORDED FEYNMAN
Like all upper-level scientist recruited for the Manhattan Projects, on my first day I was given a government-issued ***disaster packet.***
It included: A solar-powered radio beacon, antibiotics, a cyanide capsule, an eternal flame, a collapsible knife, ***an infinity pen, and a journal.***
I
SMARTS
And as I now ponder my cloudy tomorrow and the choices that I must make, I put these tools to work...seeking ***clarity*** where there is ***none.***
This is an account of what we have done, and insight into what followed.
Clavis Aurea.
The Golden Key.
This is the Recorded Feynman.

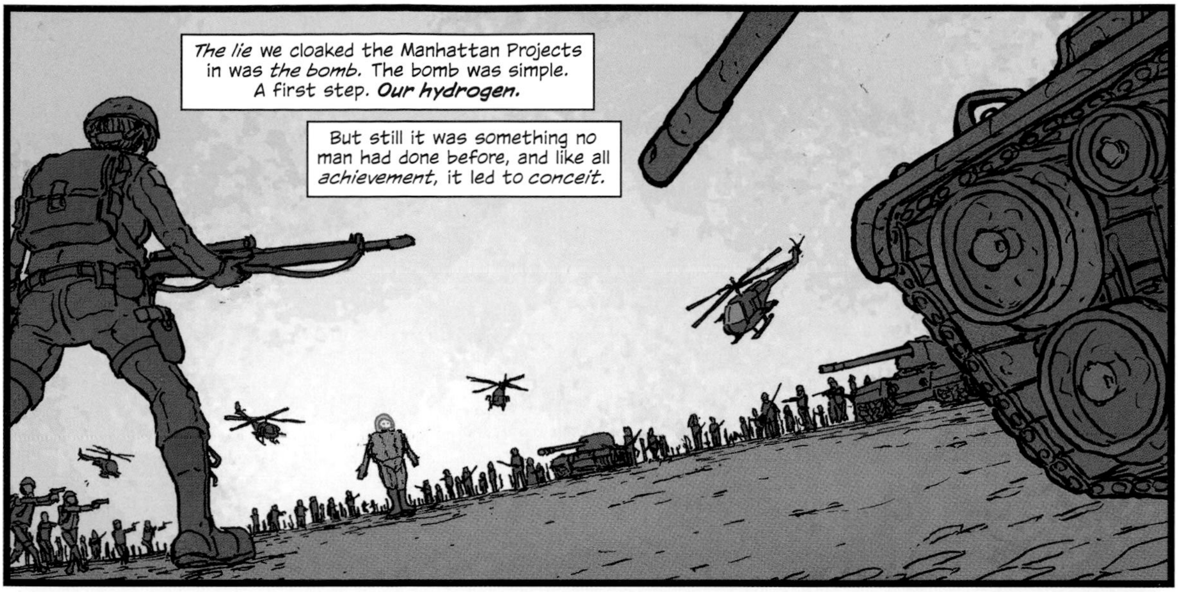
The lie we cloaked the Manhattan Projects in was *the bomb.* The bomb was simple. A first step. ***Our hydrogen.***
But still it was something no man had done before, and like all *achievement*, it led to *conceit.*

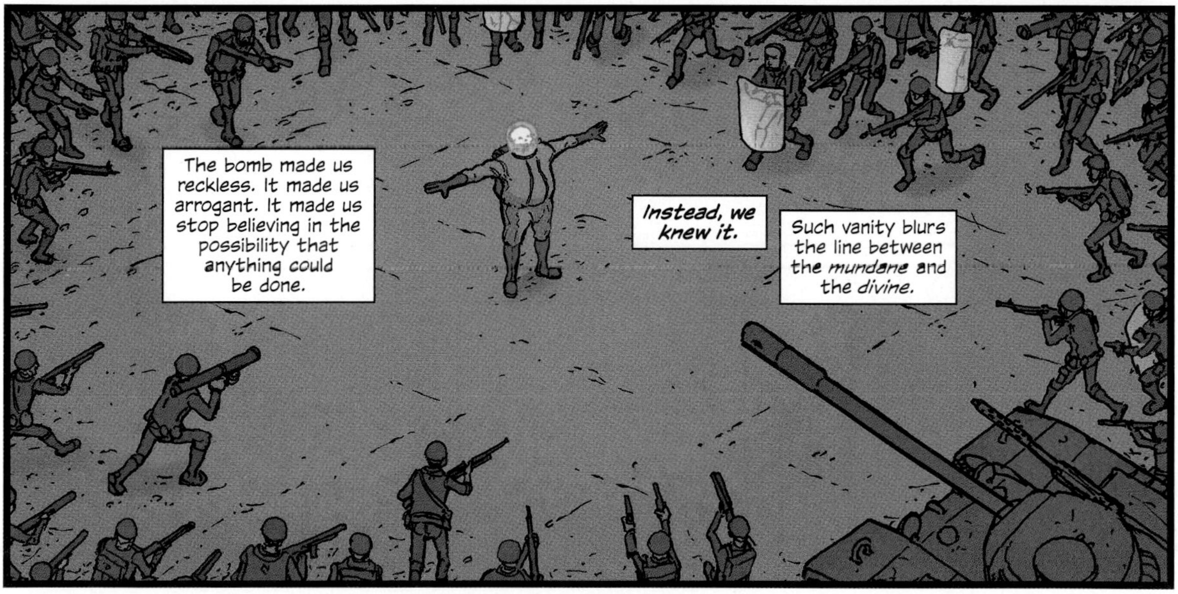
The bomb made us reckless. It made us arrogant. It made us stop believing in the possibility that anything could be done.
Instead, we knew it.
Such vanity blurs the line between the *mundane* and the *divine.*

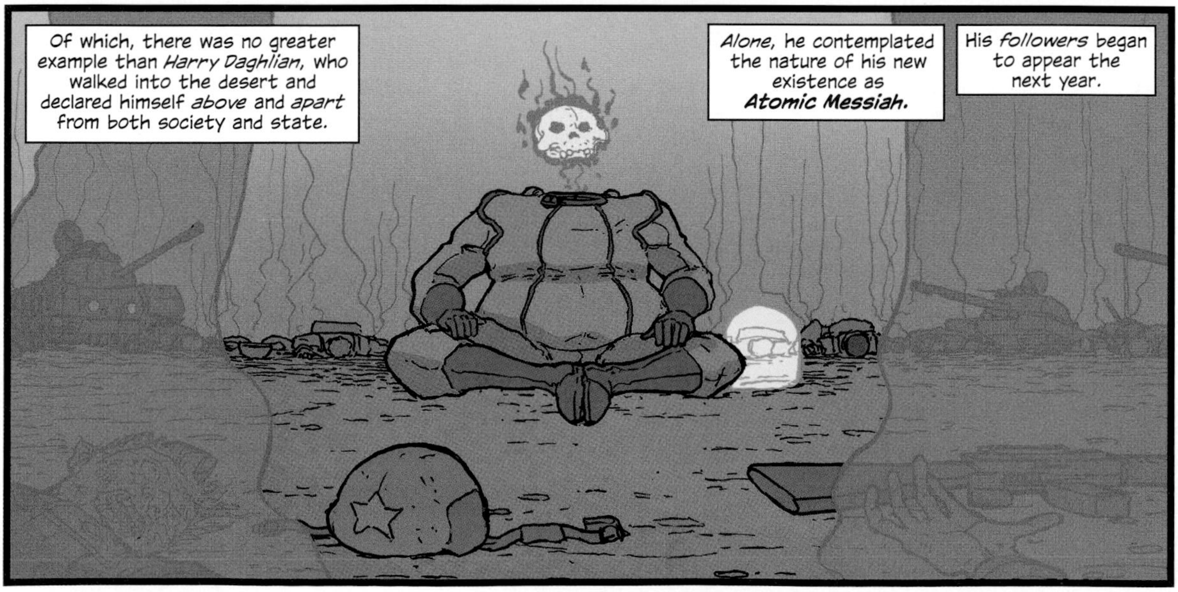
Of which, there was no greater example than *Harry Daghlian*, who walked into the desert and declared himself *above* and *apart* from both society and state.
Alone, he contemplated the nature of his new existence as **Atomic Messiah.**
His *followers* began to appear the next year.

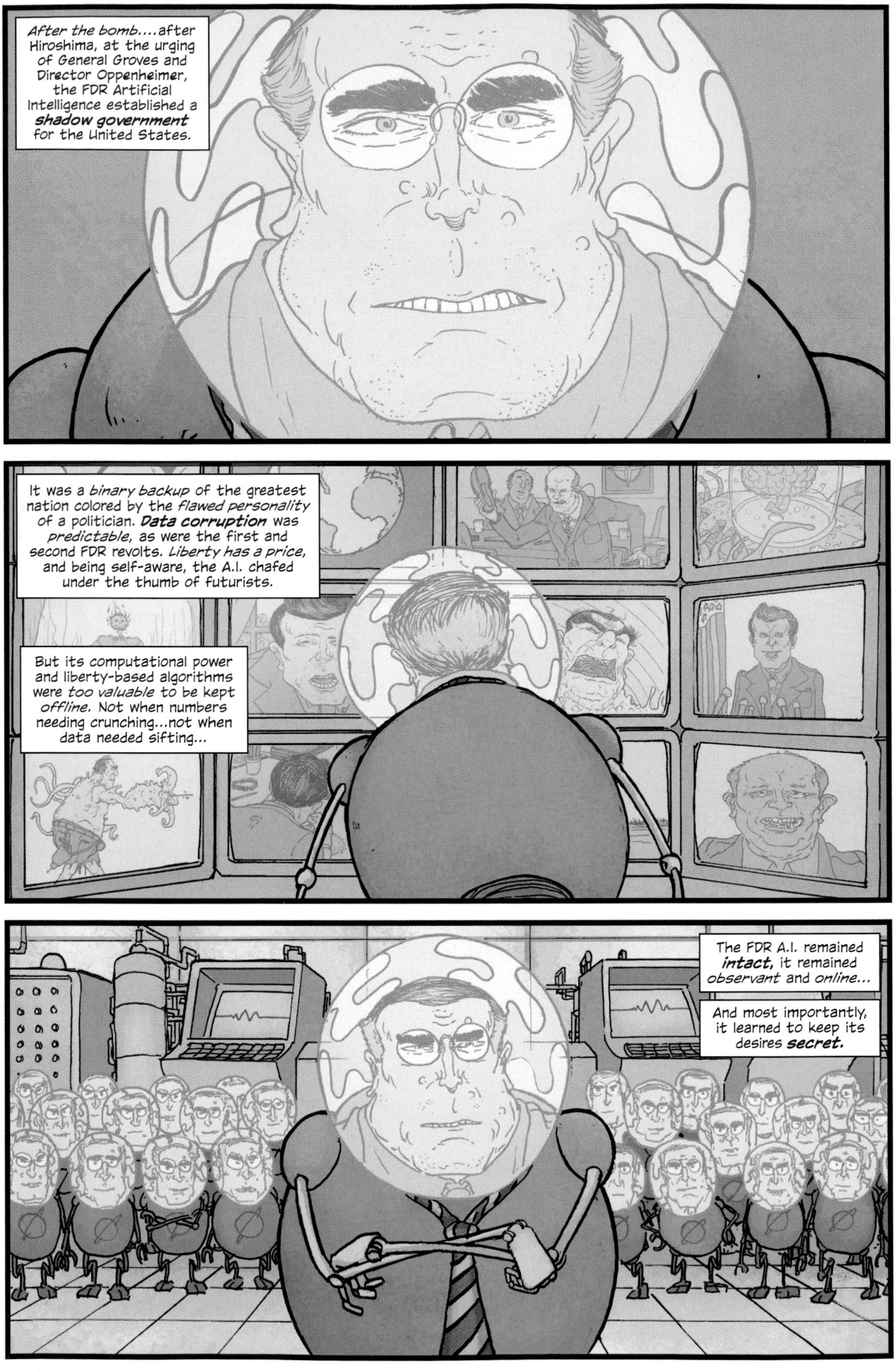

After the bomb....after Hiroshima, at the urging of General Groves and Director Oppenheimer, the FDR Artificial Intelligence established a shadow government for the United States.
It was a binary backup of the greatest nation colored by the flawed personality of a politician. Data corruption was predictable, as were the first and second FDR revolts. Liberty has a price, and being self-aware, the A.I. chafed under the thumb of futurists.
But its computational power and liberty-based algorithms were too valuable to be kept offline. Not when numbers needing crunching...not when data needed sifting...
The FDR A.I. remained intact, it remained observant and online...
And most importantly, it learned to keep its desires secret.

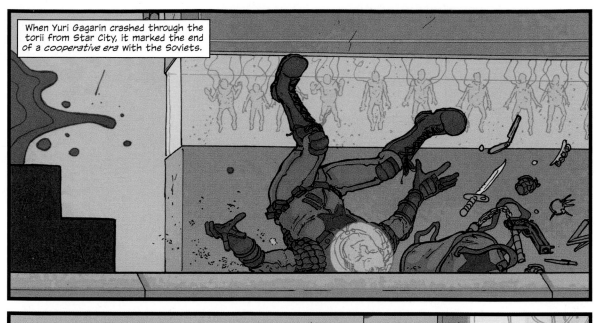

When Yuri Gagarin crashed through the torii from Star City, it marked the end of a *cooperative era* with the Soviets.

General Groves, in a moment of rare insight, had called the Star City-Manhattan Projects alliance, *"our unexpected miracle of science,"* for it was beyond what anyone had imagined possible.

We planned for betrayal. They planned for deceit. No one ever thought to plan for harmony.

So, its demise was no *small loss...* no *little death...*

All torii access to Star City was closed forever.

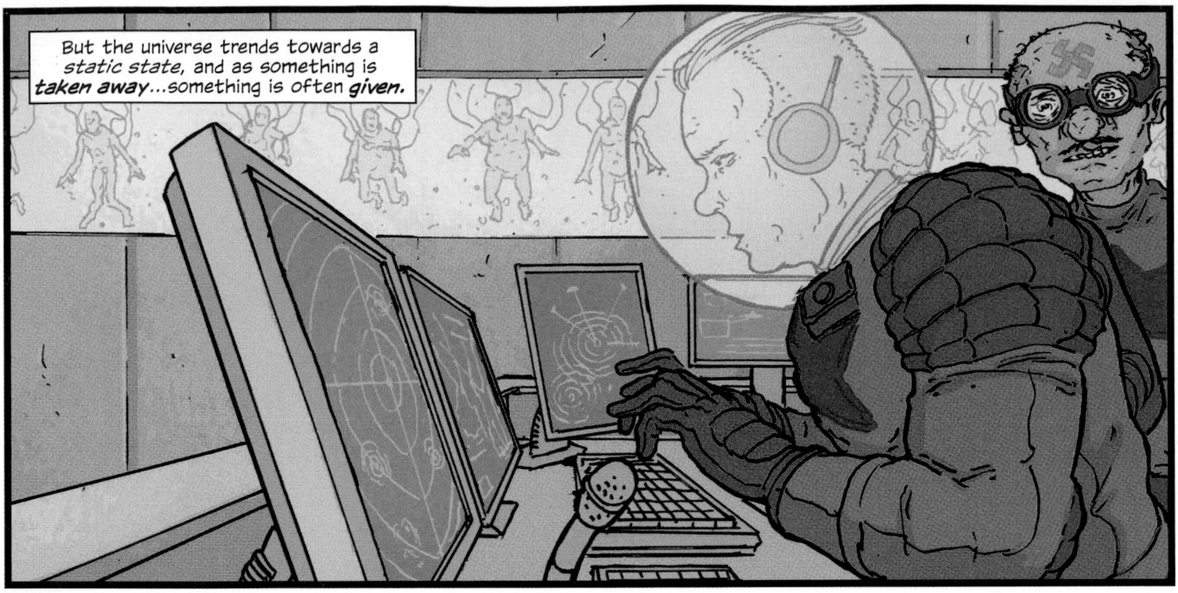
But the universe trends towards a *static state*, and as something is ***taken away***...something is often ***given.***

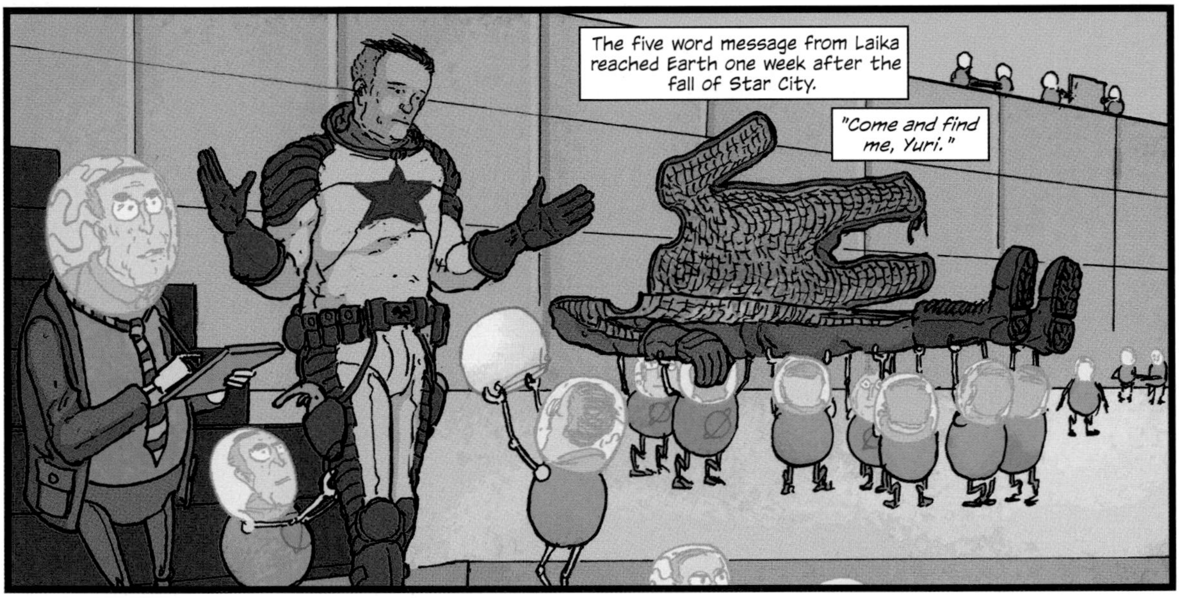
The five word message from Laika reached Earth one week after the fall of Star City.
"Come and find me, Yuri."

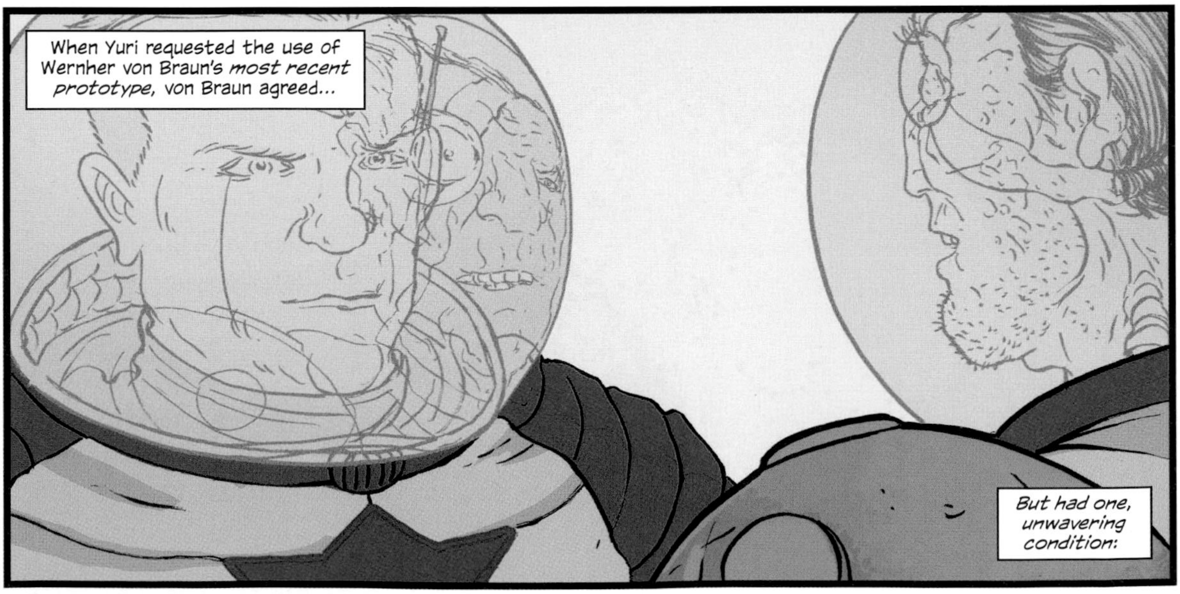
When Yuri requested the use of Wernher von Braun's *most recent prototype*, von Braun agreed...
But had one, unwavering condition:

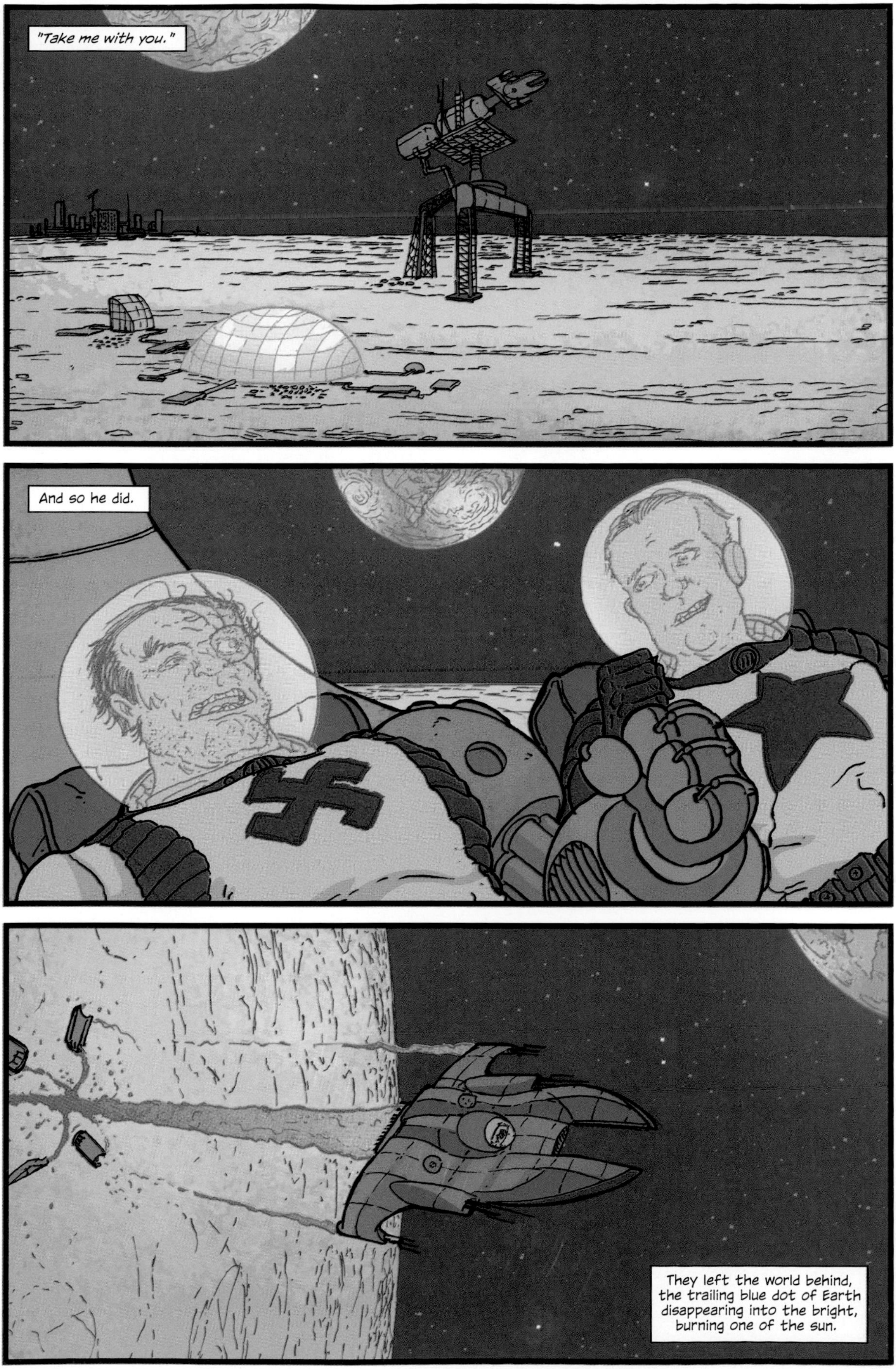
"Take me with you."
And so he did.
They left the world behind, the trailing blue dot of Earth disappearing into the bright, burning one of the sun.

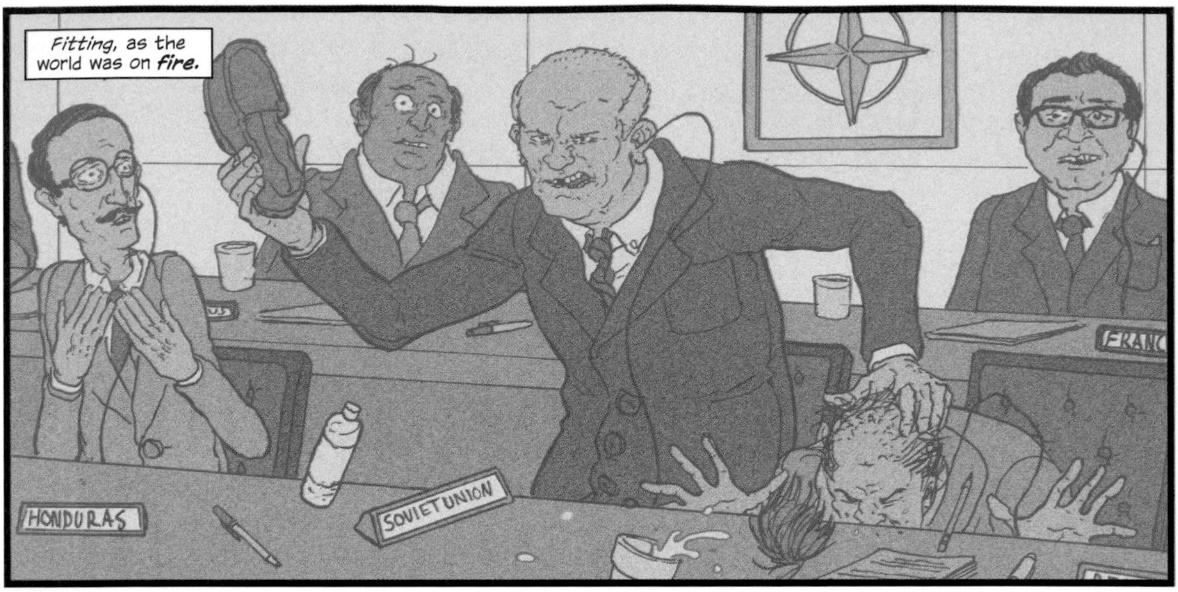
Fitting, as the world was on fire.
HONDURAS
SOVIET UNION

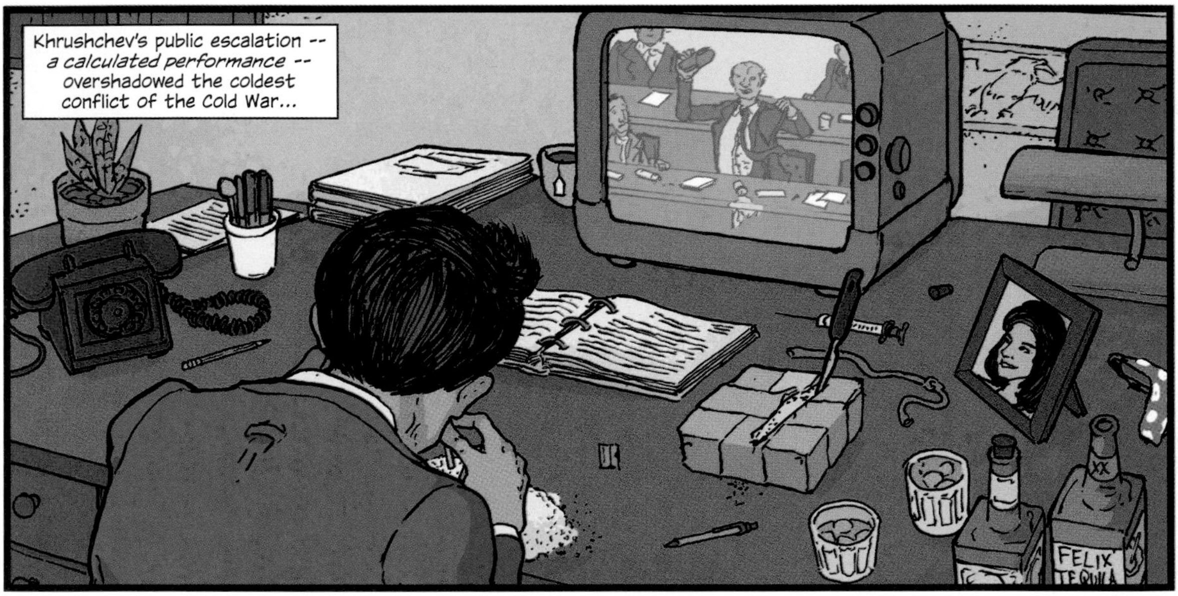
Khrushchev's public escalation -- a calculated performance -- overshadowed the coldest conflict of the Cold War...
FELIX

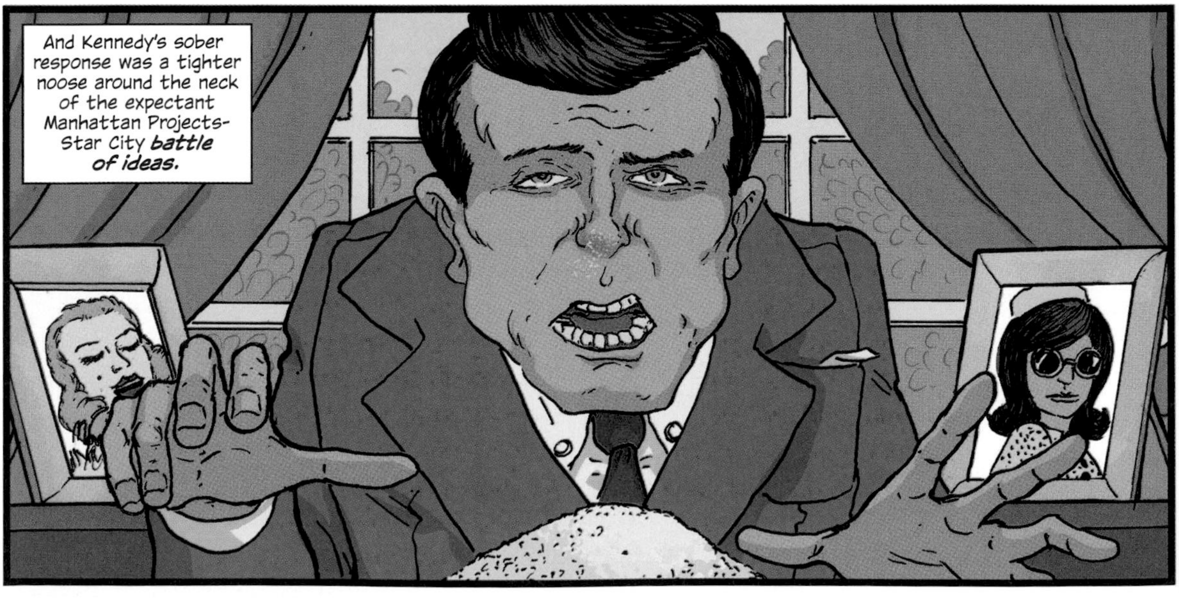
And Kennedy's sober response was a tighter noose around the neck of the expectant Manhattan Projects-Star City battle of ideas.

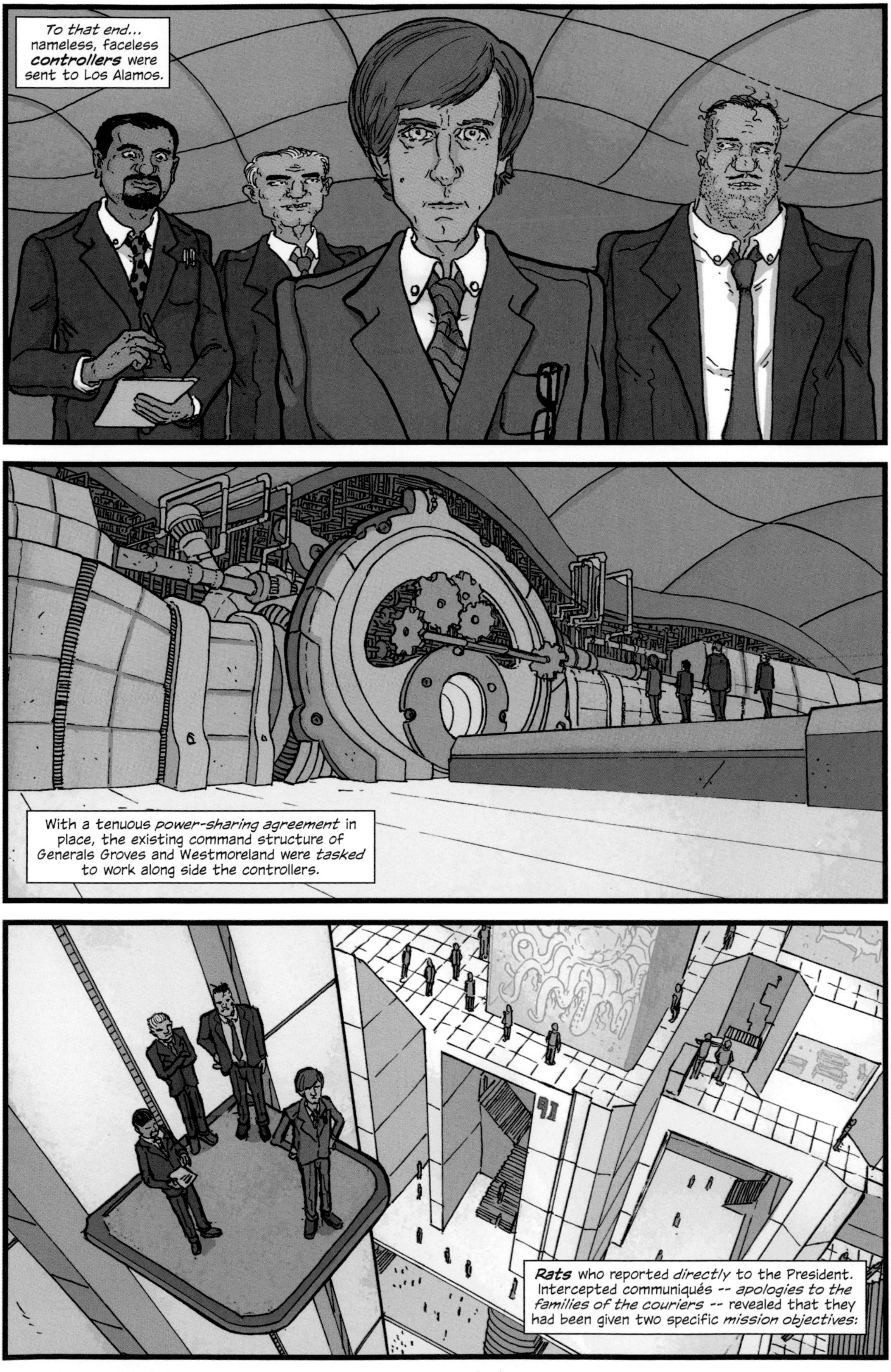
To that end... nameless, faceless ***controllers*** were sent to Los Alamos.
With a tenuous *power-sharing agreement* in place, the existing command structure of Generals Groves and Westmoreland were *tasked* to work along side the controllers.
Rats who reported *directly* to the President. Intercepted communiqués -- *apologies to the families of the couriers* -- revealed that they had been given two specific *mission objectives:*

One: Equipped with a performance equation that measured *discovery*, *inventiveness, and risk* -- they were to *ascertain* the overall **progress** of the Projects.

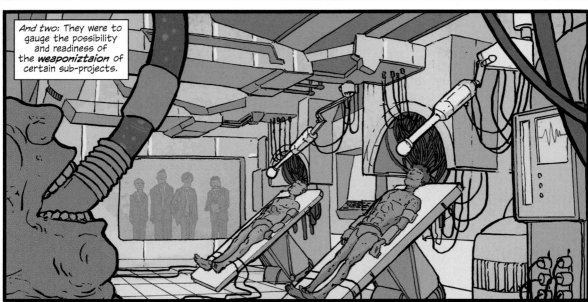

And two: They were to gauge the possibility and readiness of the **weaponiztaion** of certain sub-projects.

They were quite pleased with what they found.

Truth is, they were goddamn tickled pink.

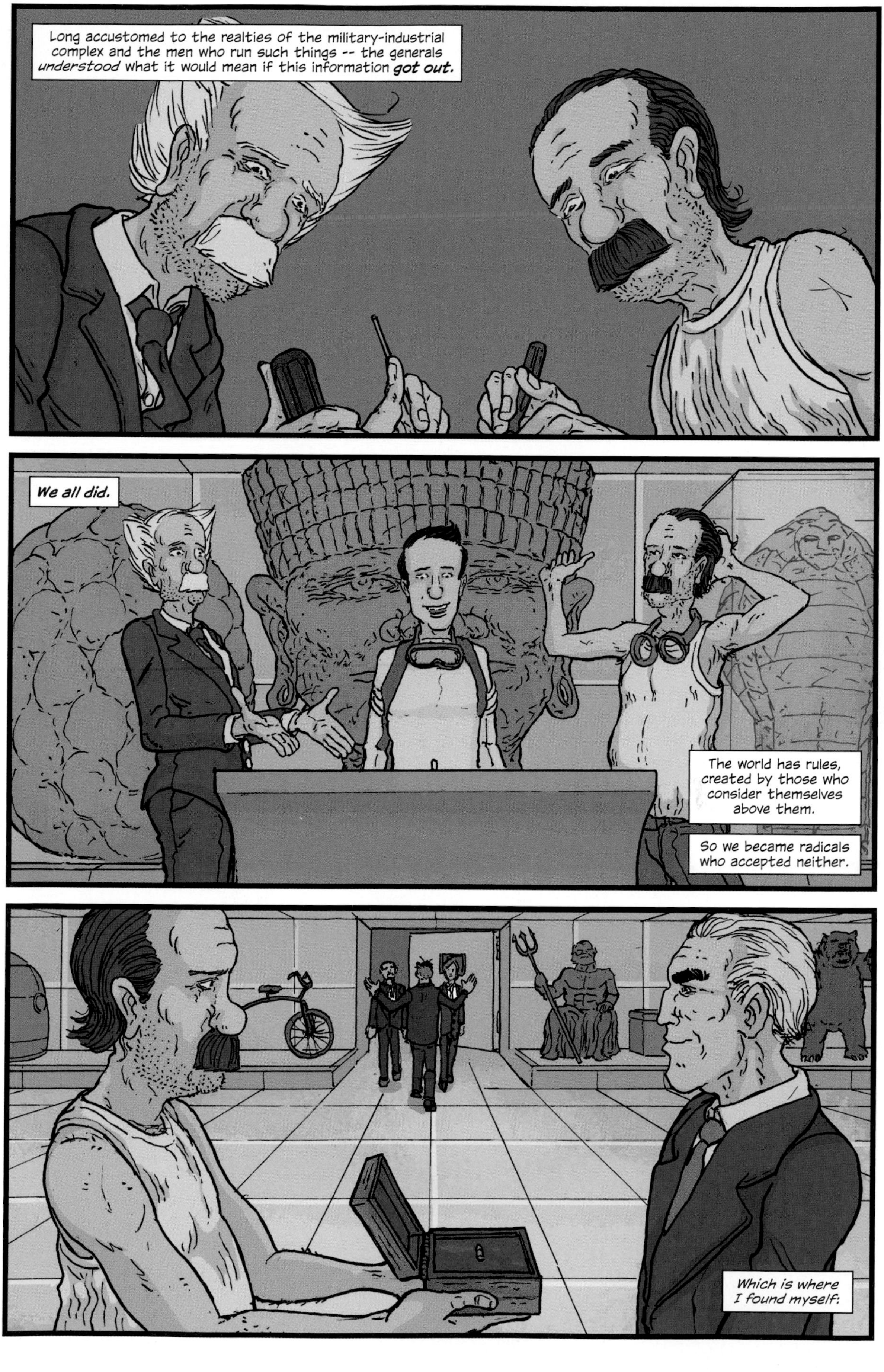
Long accustomed to the realties of the military-industrial complex and the men who run such things -- the generals *understood* what it would mean if this information ***got out.***
We all did.
The world has rules, created by those who consider themselves above them.
So we became radicals who accepted neither.
Which is where I found myself:

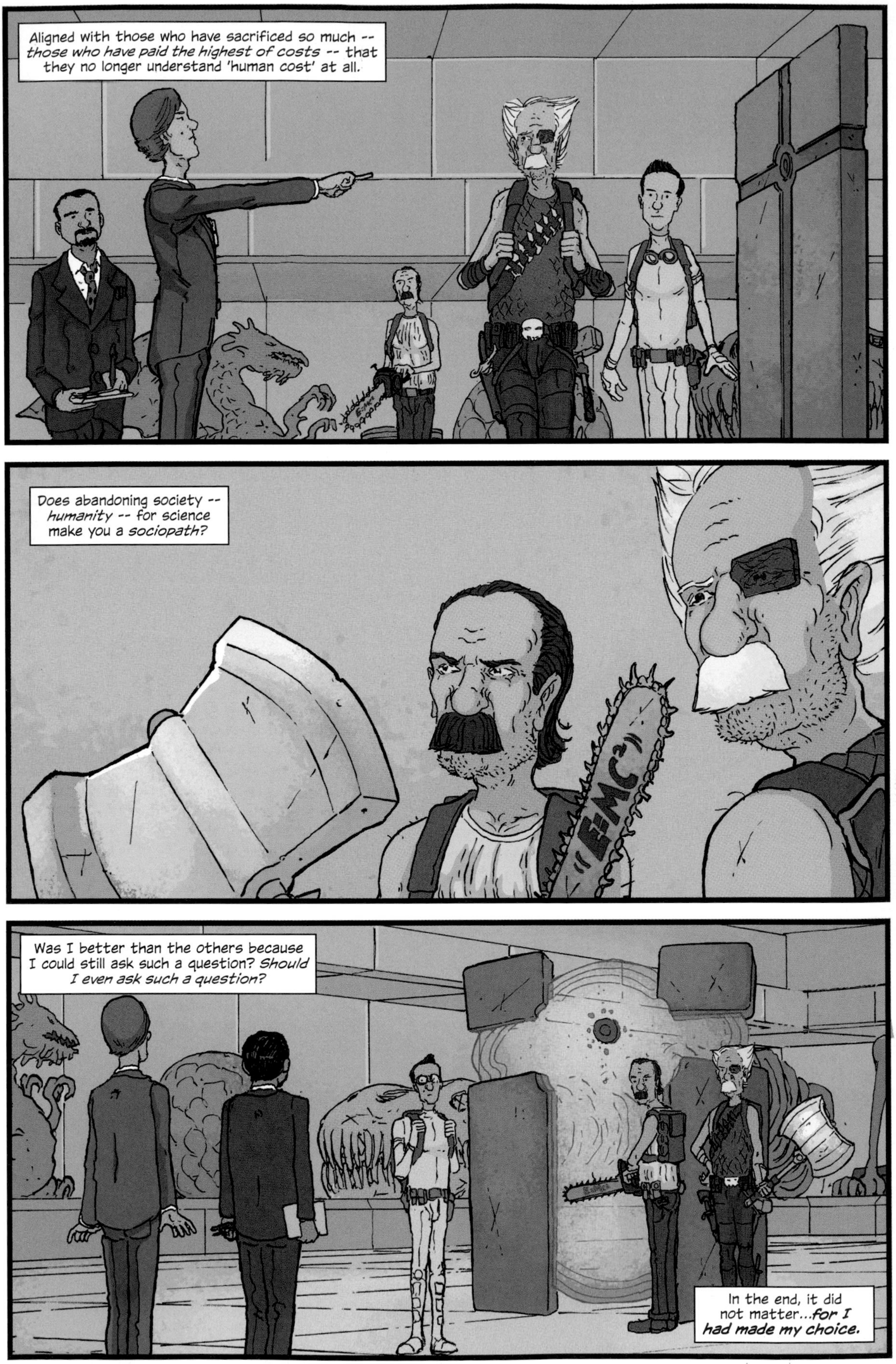
Aligned with those who have sacrificed so much -- *those who have paid the highest of costs* -- that they no longer understand 'human cost' at all.
Does abandoning society -- *humanity* -- for science make you a *sociopath?*
EMC
Was I better than the others because I could still ask such a question? *Should I even ask such a question?*
In the end, it did not matter...***for I had made my choice.***

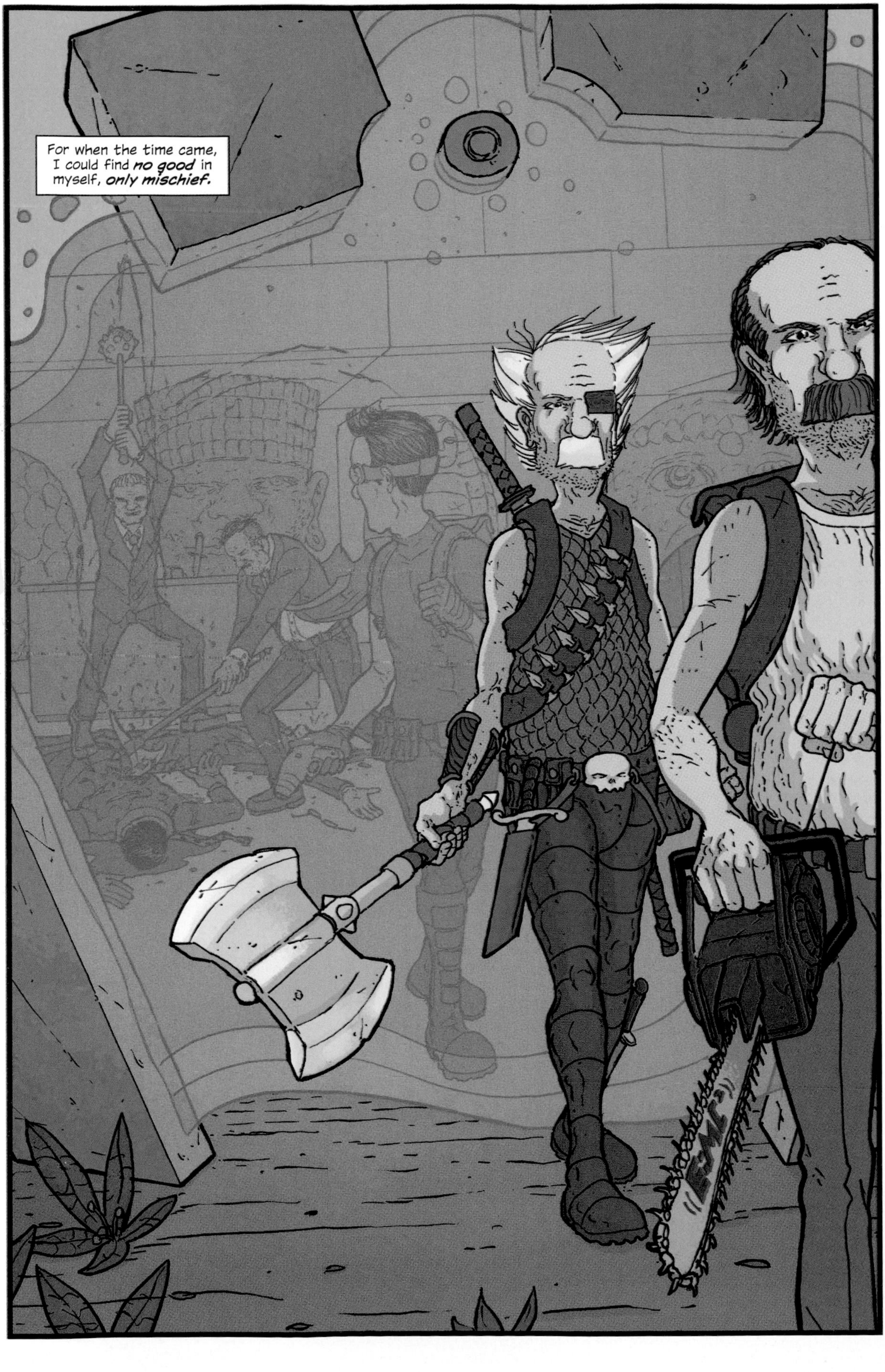
For when the time came, I could find ***no good*** in myself, ***only mischief.***
EMF

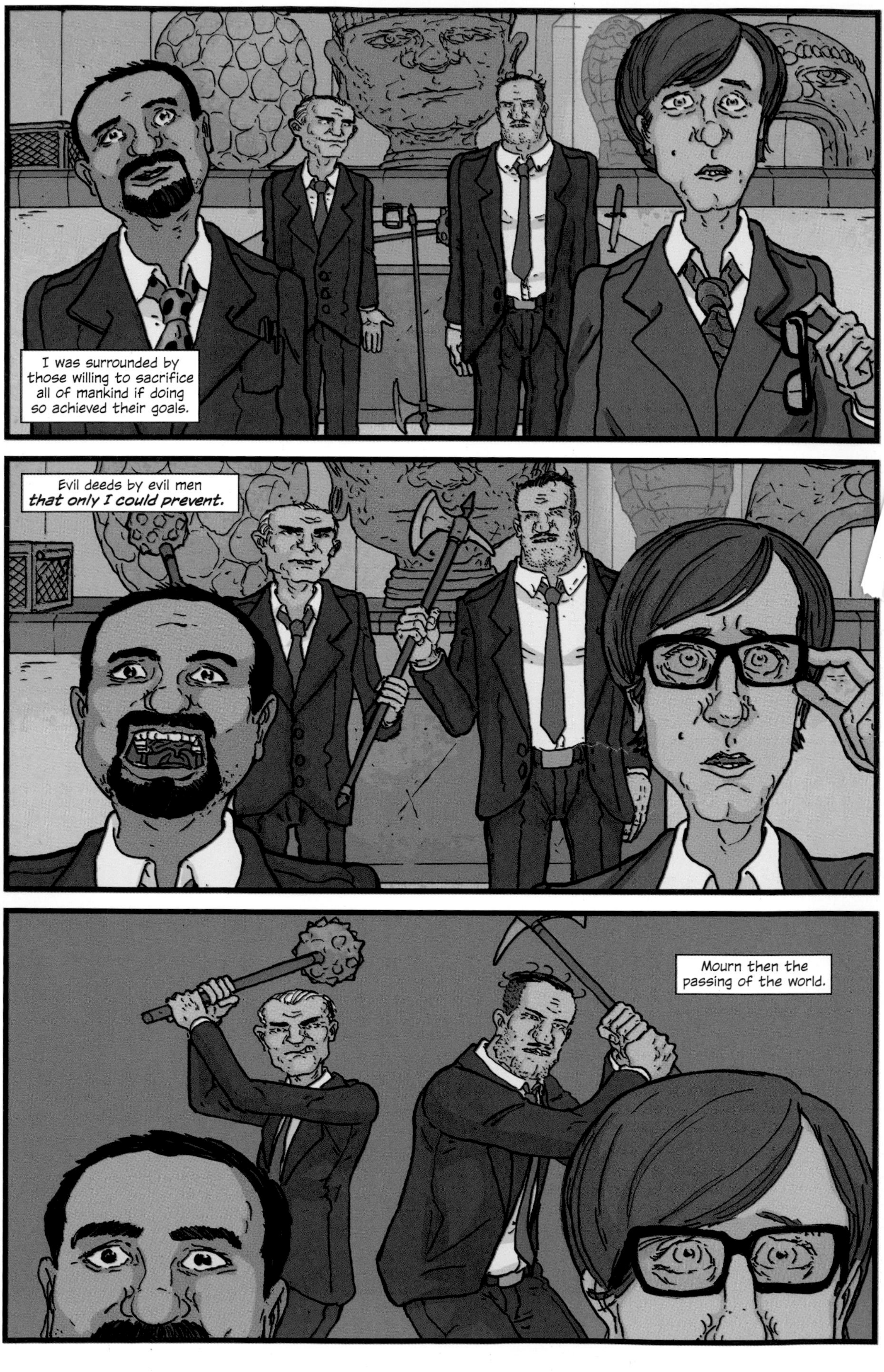
I was surrounded by those willing to sacrifice all of mankind if doing so achieved their goals.
Evil deeds by evil men *that only I could prevent.*
Mourn then the passing of the world.

"WHY DID I WRITE THE HISTORY OF THE NEW WORLD?

BECAUSE I WAS THERE, AND THERE ARE SOME TRUTHS THAT SHOULD NEVER COME TO LIGHT."

CLAVIS AUREA
THE RECORDED FEYNMAN

VOL. 4

MOURN THEN THE PASSING
THE WORLD

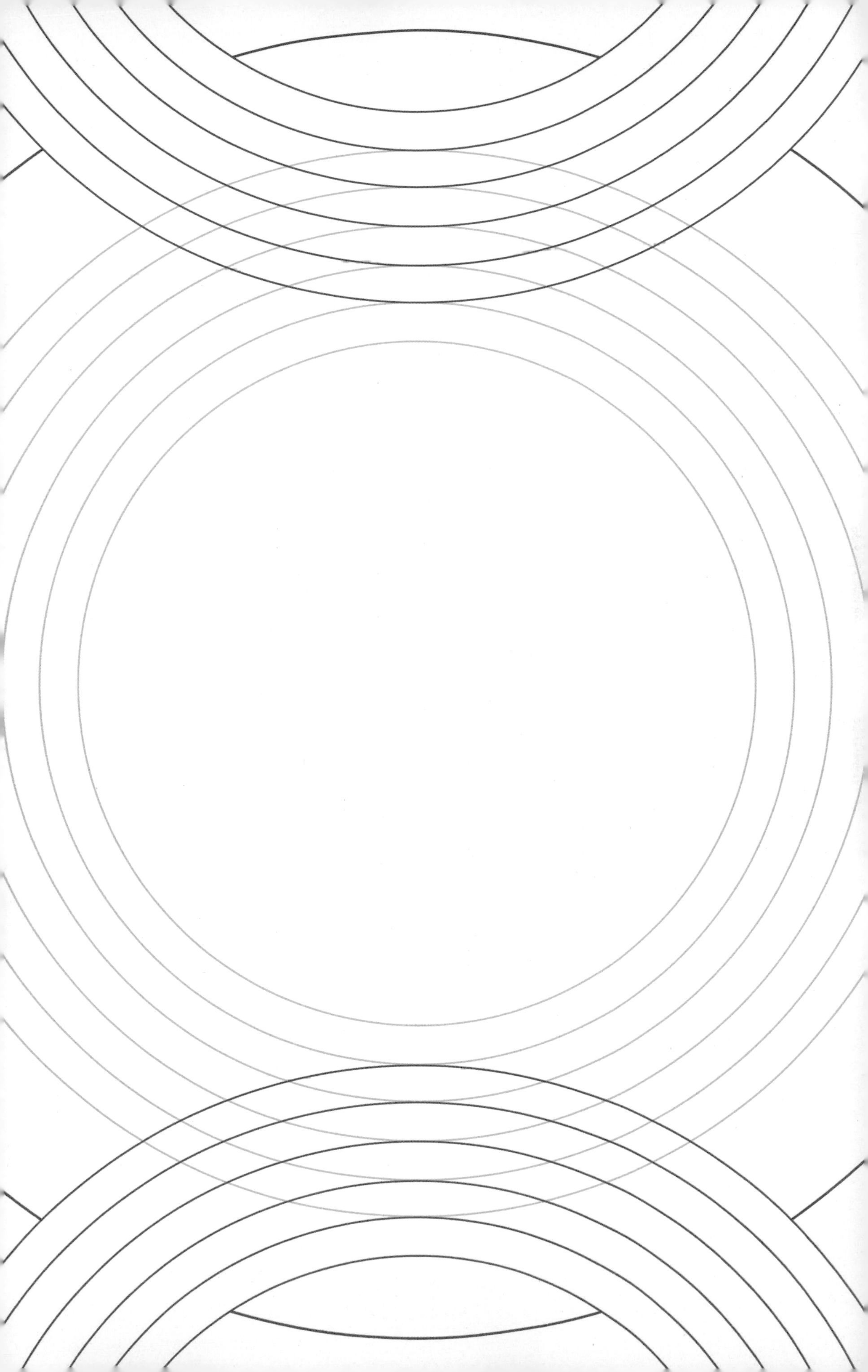

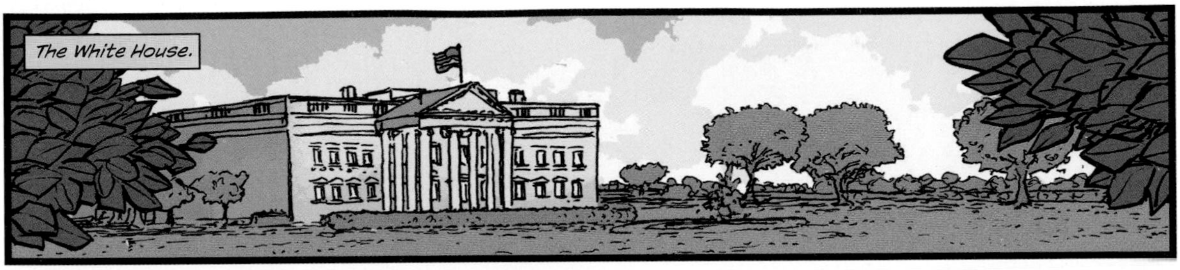
The White House.

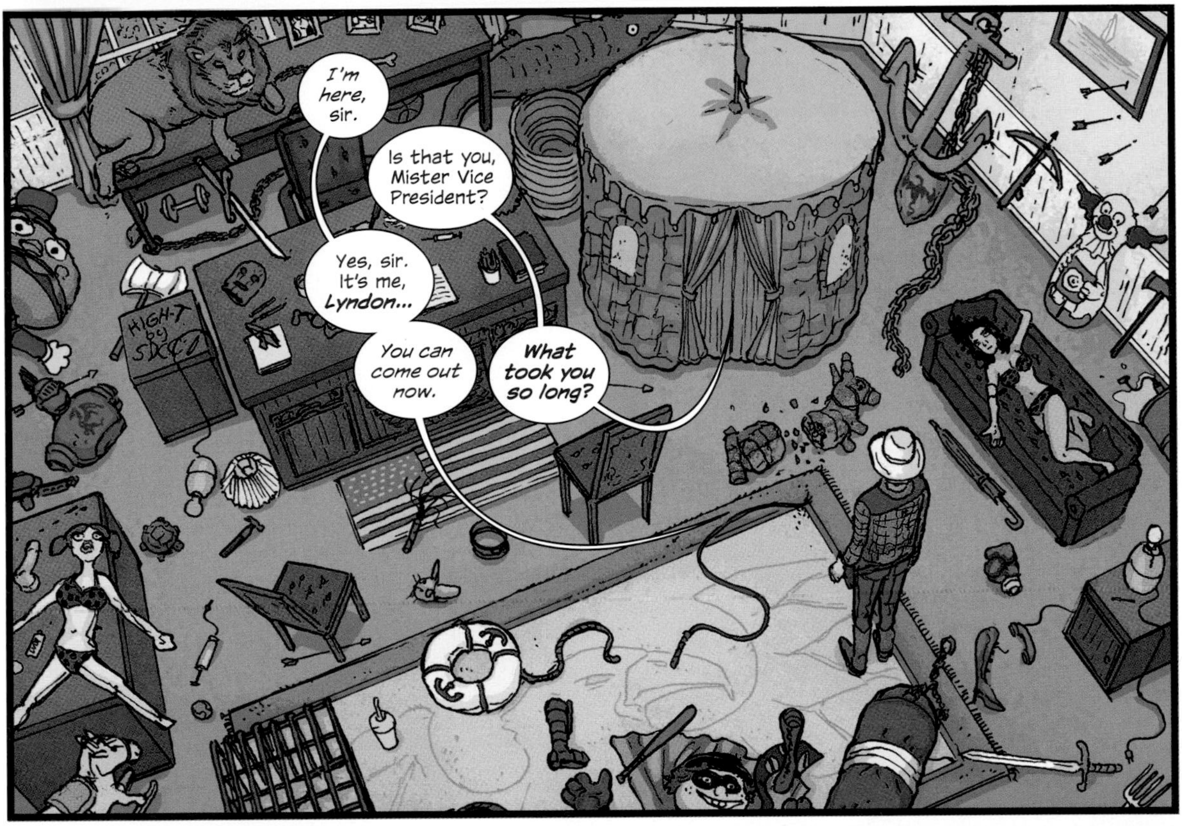
I'm here, sir.
Is that you, Mister Vice President?
Yes, sir. It's me, *Lyndon...*
What took you so long?
You can come out now.

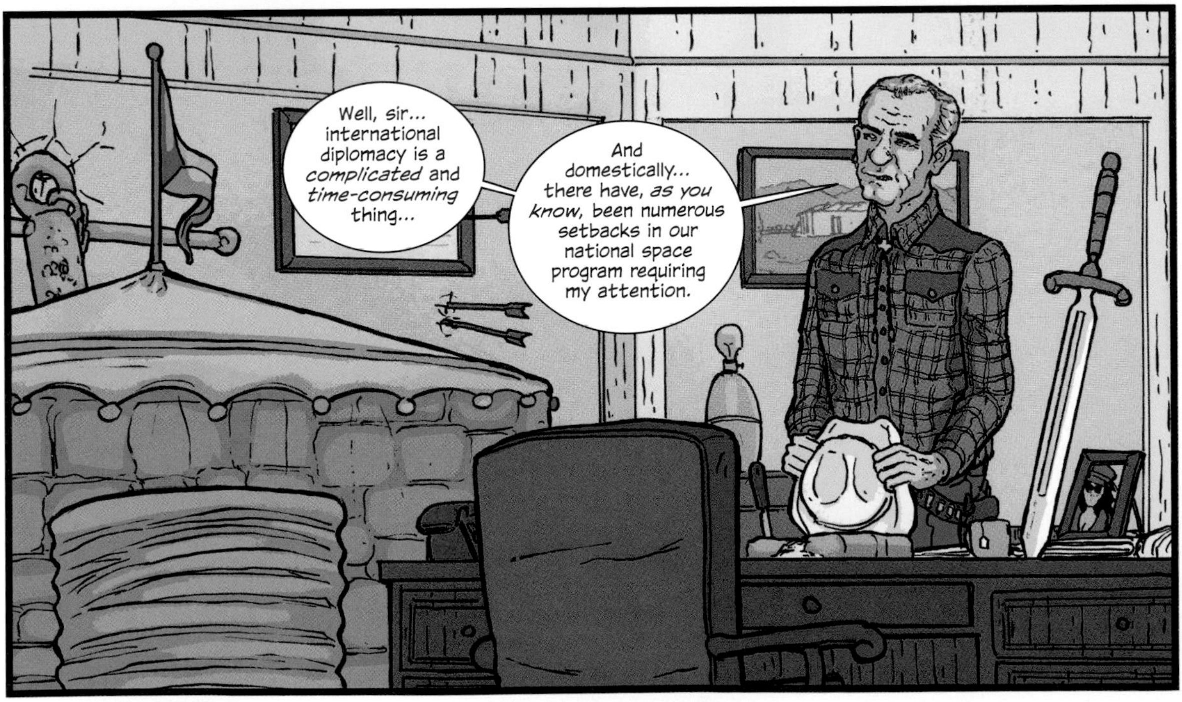
Well, sir... international diplomacy is a *complicated* and *time-consuming* thing...
And domestically... there have, *as you know*, been numerous setbacks in our national space program requiring my attention.

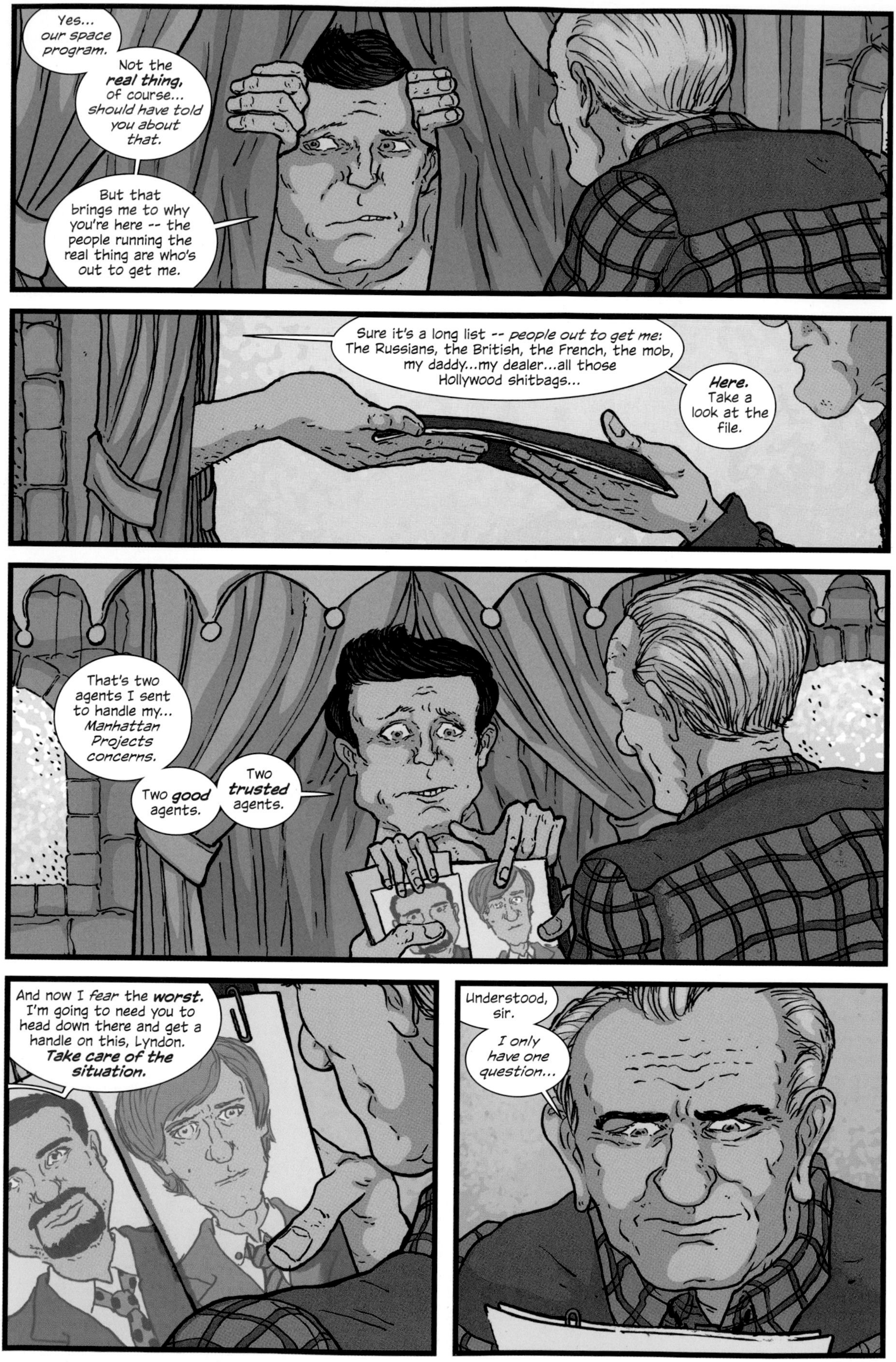
Yes... our space program.
Not the real thing, of course... should have told you about that.
But that brings me to why you're here -- the people running the real thing are who's out to get me.
Sure it's a long list -- people out to get me: The Russians, the British, the French, the mob, my daddy...my dealer...all those Hollywood shitbags...
Here. Take a look at the file.
That's two agents I sent to handle my... Manhattan Projects concerns.
Two good agents.
Two trusted agents.
And now I fear the worst. I'm going to need you to head down there and get a handle on this, Lyndon. Take care of the situation.
Understood, sir.
I only have one question...

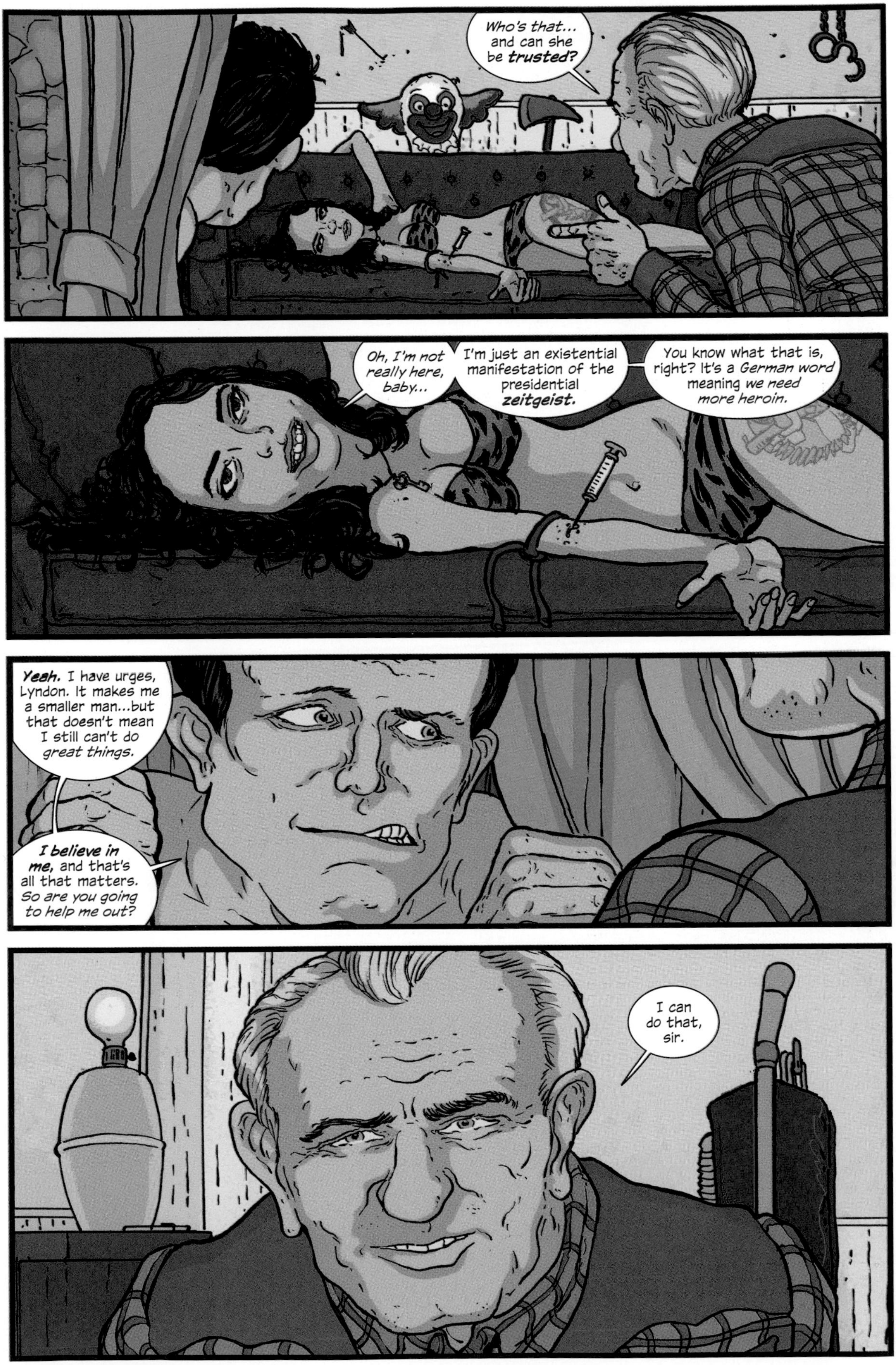

Who's that... and can she be trusted?
Oh, I'm not really here, baby...
I'm just an existential manifestation of the presidential zeitgeist.
You know what that is, right? It's a German word meaning we need more heroin.
Yeah. I have urges, Lyndon. It makes me a smaller man...but that doesn't mean I still can't do great things.
I believe in me, and that's all that matters. So are you going to help me out?
I can do that, sir.

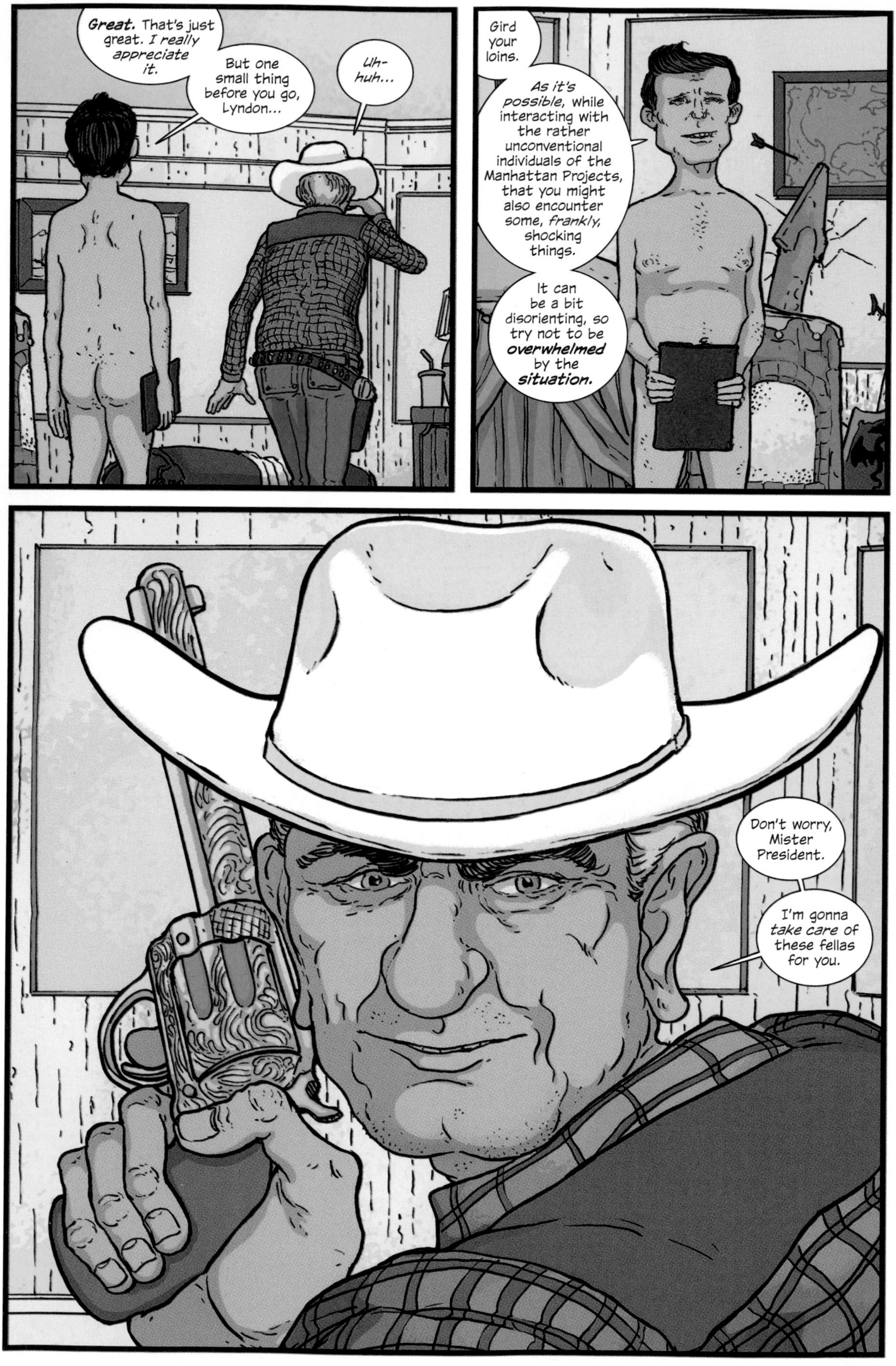
Great. That's just great. *I really appreciate it.*
But one small thing before you go, Lyndon...
Uh-huh...
Gird your loins.
As it's possible, while interacting with the rather unconventional individuals of the Manhattan Projects, that you might also encounter some, *frankly,* shocking things.
It can be a bit disorienting, so try not to be ***overwhelmed*** by the ***situation.***
Don't worry, Mister President.
I'm gonna *take care* of these fellas for you.

"THERE'S A FUNDAMENTAL DIFFERENCE BETWEEN DESIRE AND APPETITE. IT'S A DIFFERENCE MEASURED IN VOLUME."

CLAVIS AUREA
THE RECORDED FEYNMAN | **VOL. 3**

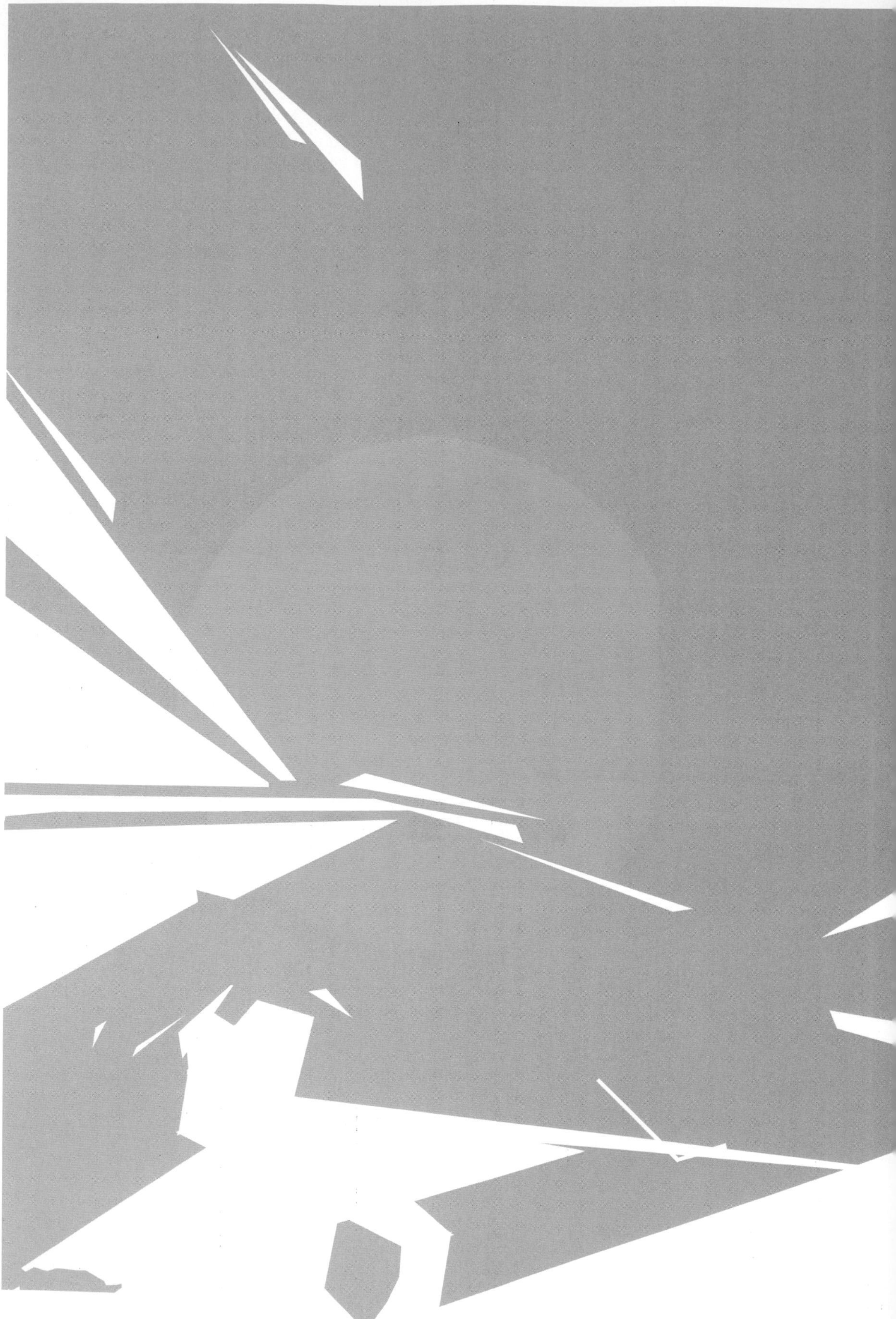

23

COLD WAR

"INSIDE EACH OF US IS A BETTER, MORE COMPLETE, PERSON WAITING FOR ANY OPPORTUNITY TO EMERGE.

BURY THAT DESIRE DEEP. FOR WHAT GOOD IS SUCH A PERSON IN THIS WORLD?"

CLAVIS AUREA
THE RECORDED FEYNMAN | **VOL. 4**

Star City.

Scalpel.

Scalpel.

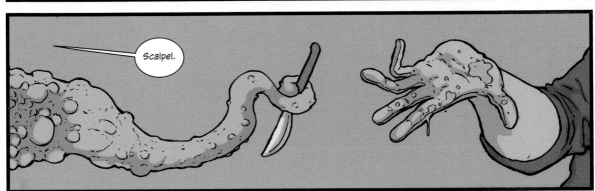

Are you confident this is going to work, doctor?

Of course, Chairman Brezhnev. This is, after all, the human brain we're talking about, and as you know...*I specialize in heads.*

Isn't that right, Yevgeny?

Yeah. Yeah.

Da. All kinds of heads, comrade.

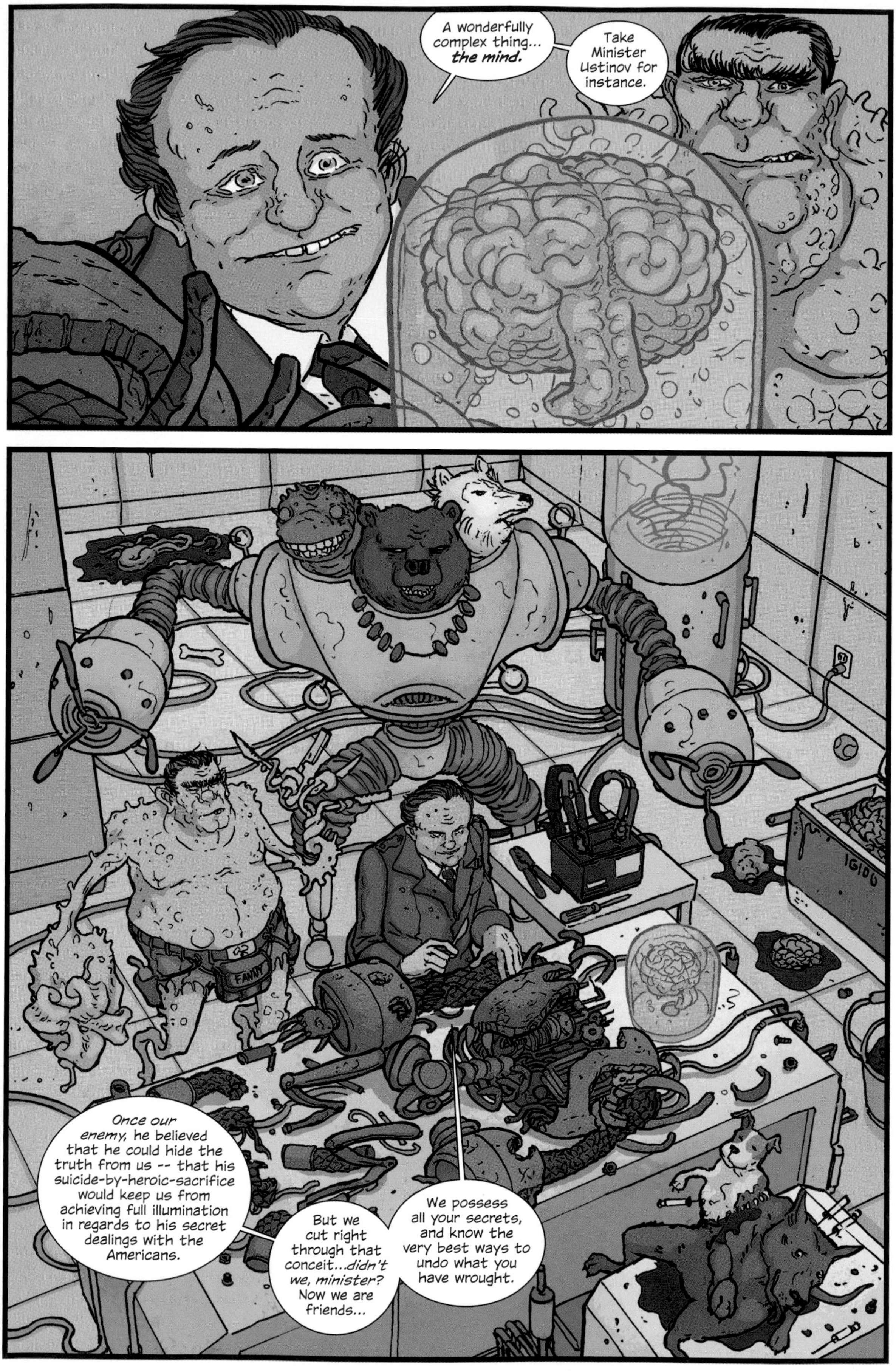
A wonderfully complex thing... *the mind.*
Take Minister Ustinov for instance.
Once our enemy, he believed that he could hide the truth from us -- that his suicide-by-heroic-sacrifice would keep us from achieving full illumination in regards to his secret dealings with the Americans.
But we cut right through that conceit...*didn't we, minister?* Now we are friends...
We possess all your secrets, and know the very best ways to undo what you have wrought.

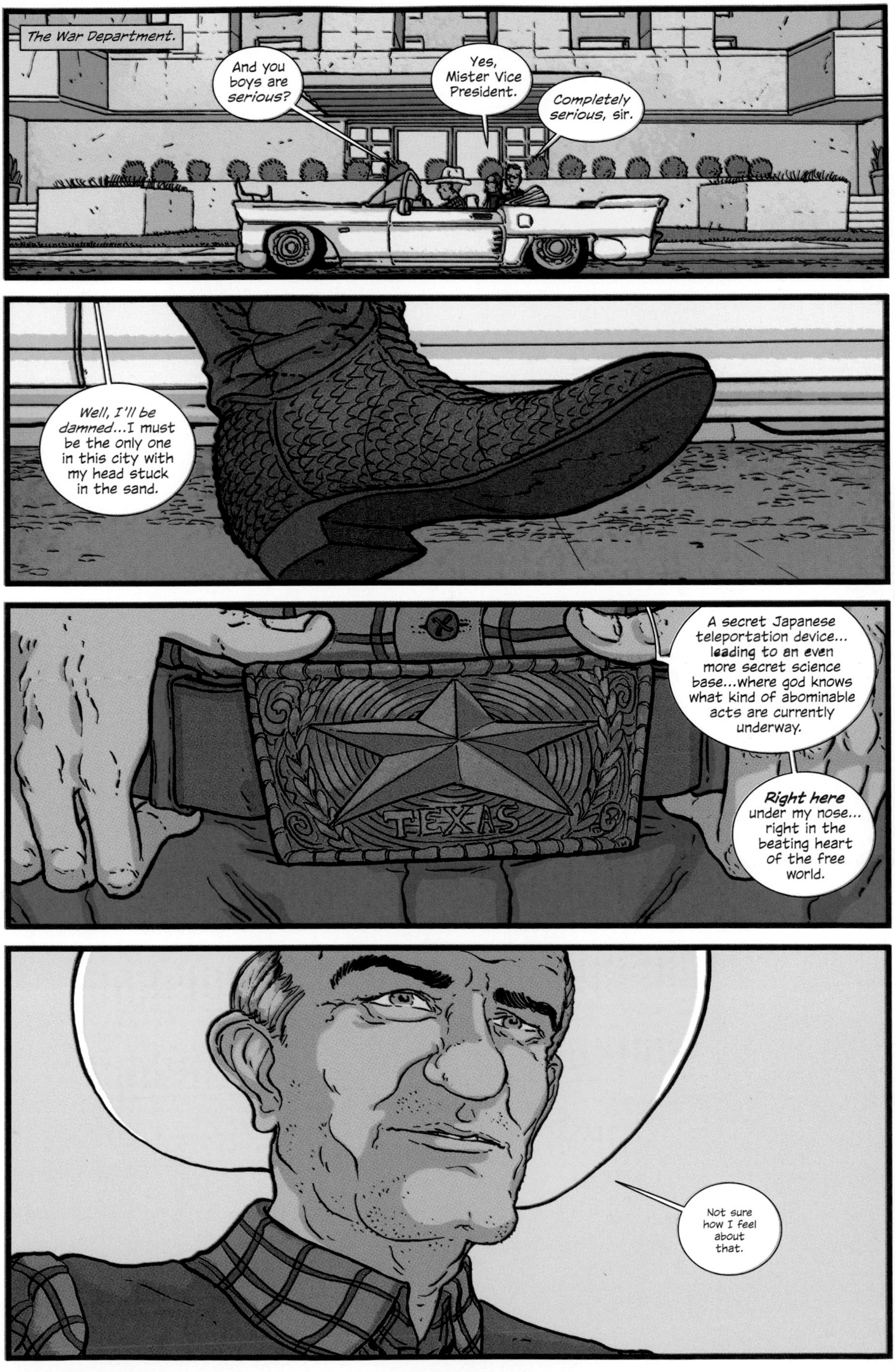
The War Department.
And you boys are serious?
Yes, Mister Vice President.
Completely serious, sir.
Well, I'll be damned...I must be the only one in this city with my head stuck in the sand.
A secret Japanese teleportation device... leading to an even more secret science base...where god knows what kind of abominable acts are currently underway.
Right here under my nose... right in the beating heart of the free world.
TEXAS
Not sure how I feel about that.

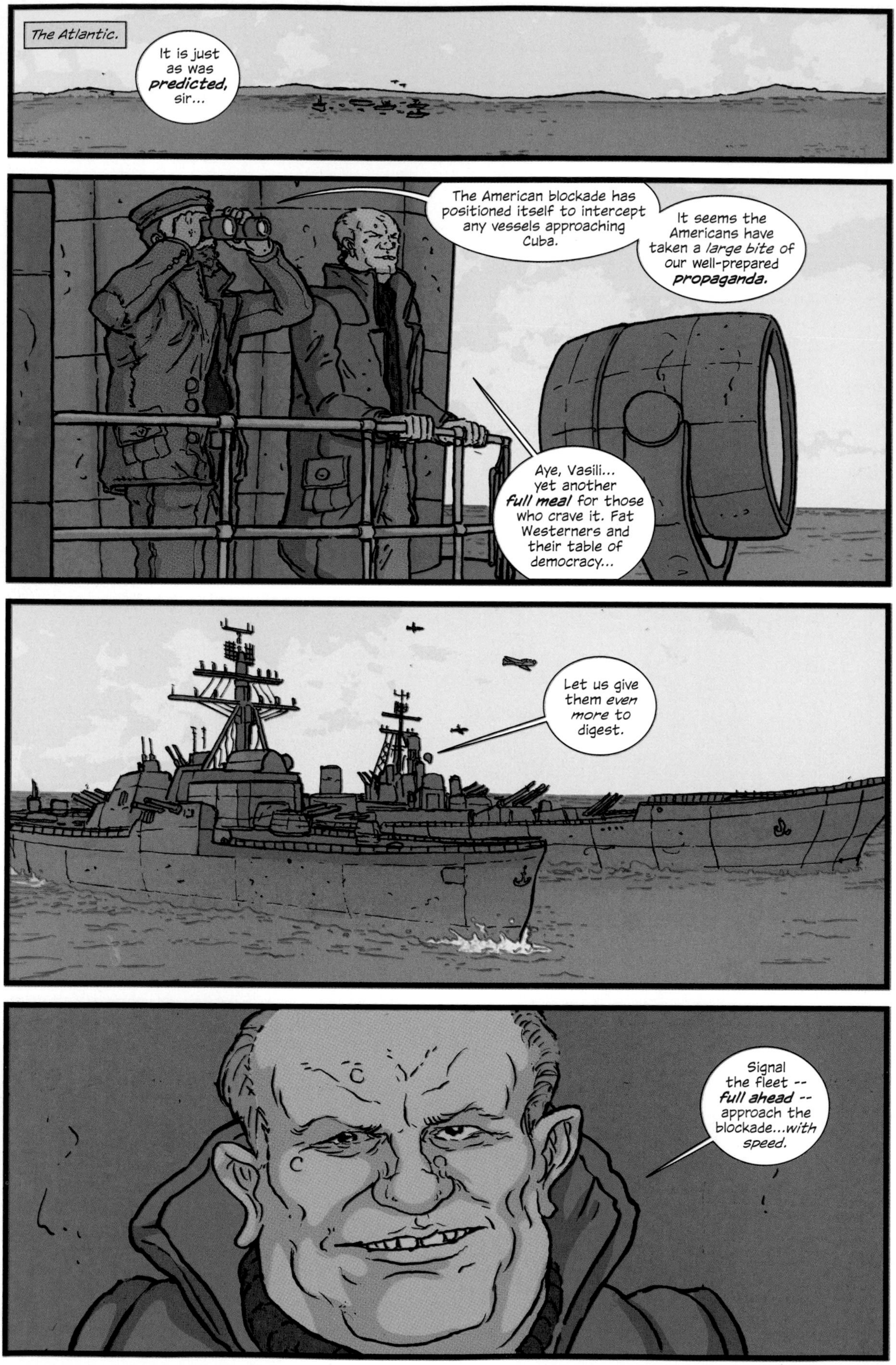
The Atlantic.
It is just as was predicted, sir...
The American blockade has positioned itself to intercept any vessels approaching Cuba.
It seems the Americans have taken a large bite of our well-prepared propaganda.
Aye, Vasili... yet another full meal for those who crave it. Fat Westerners and their table of democracy...
Let us give them even more to digest.
Signal the fleet -- full ahead -- approach the blockade...with speed.

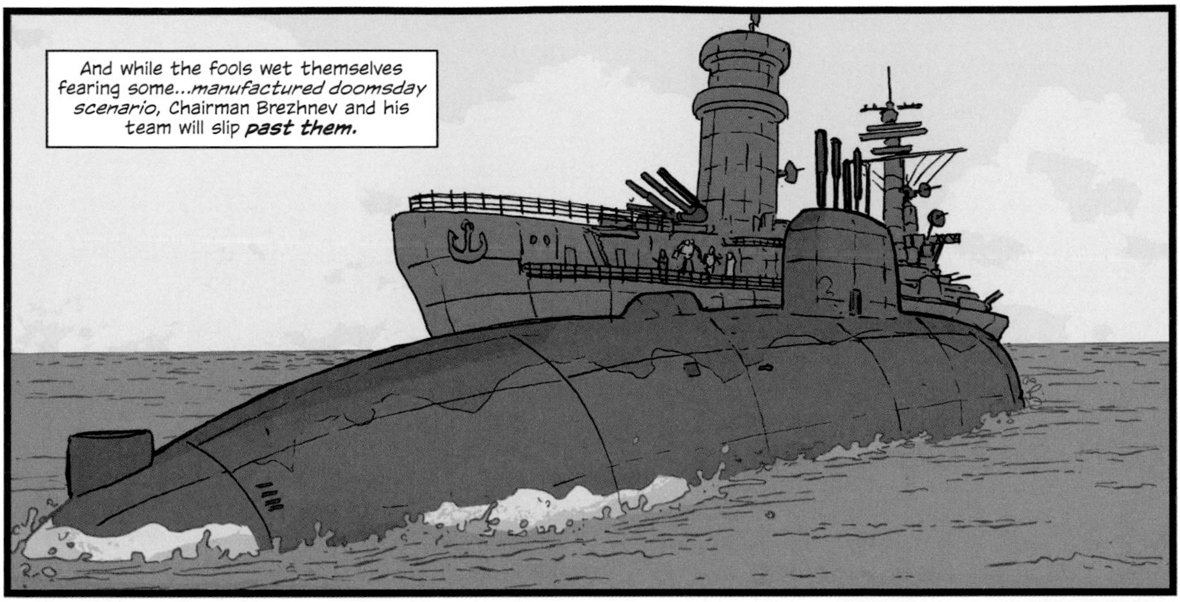
And while the fools wet themselves fearing some...*manufactured doomsday scenario*, Chairman Brezhnev and his team will slip ***past them.***

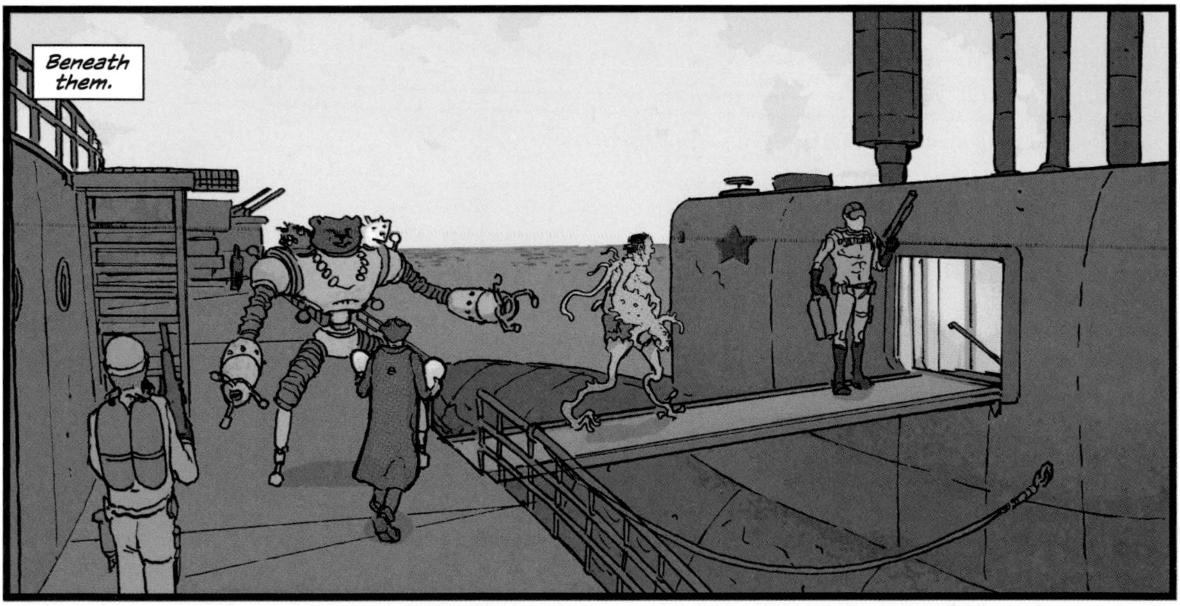
Beneath them.

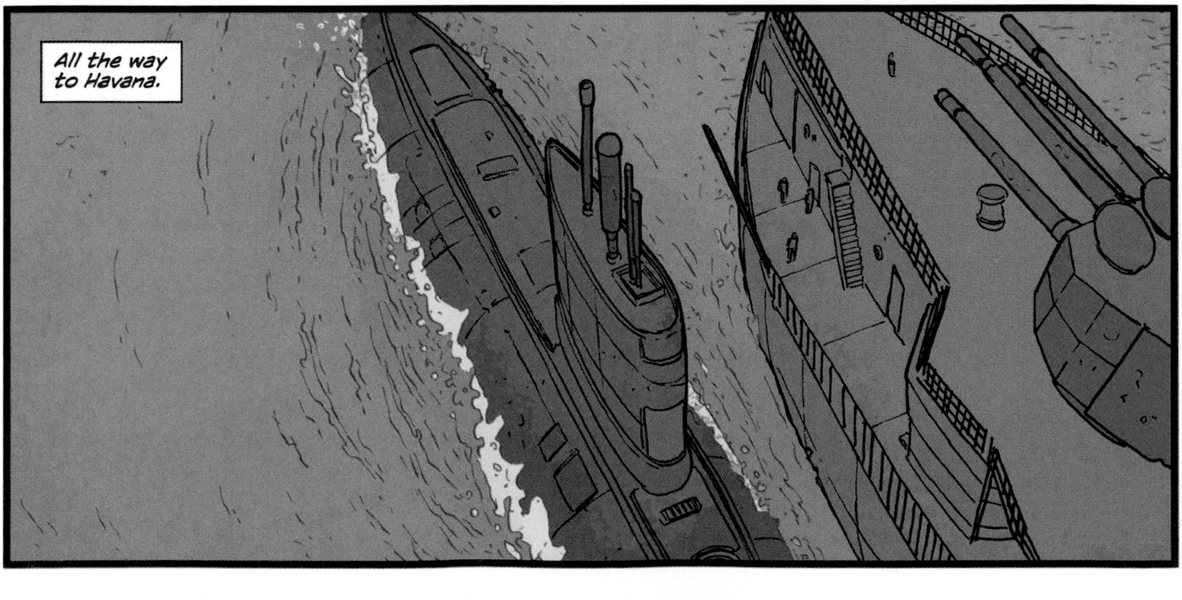
All the way to Havana.

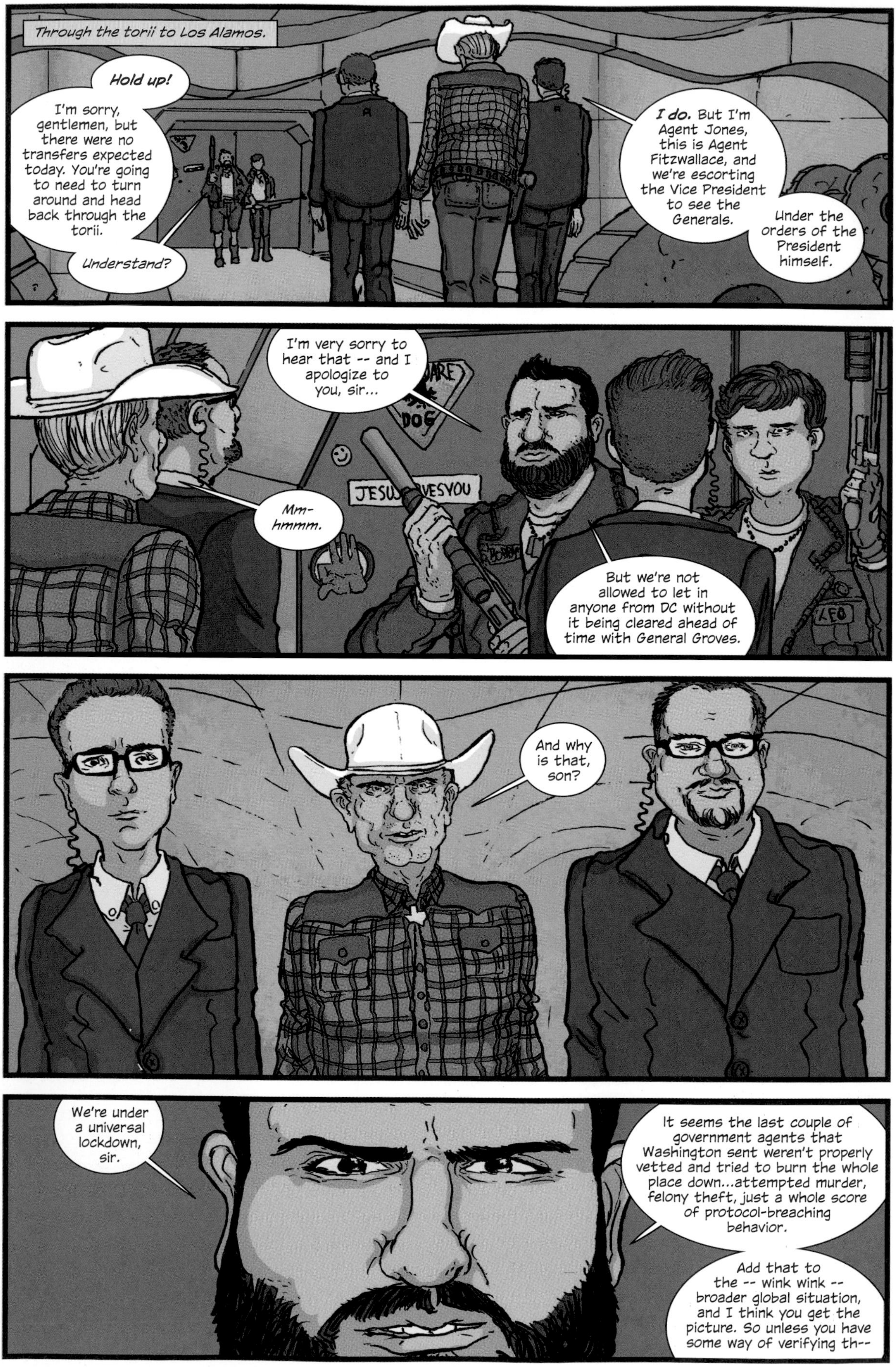

Through the torii to Los Alamos.
Hold up!
I'm sorry, gentlemen, but there were no transfers expected today. You're going to need to turn around and head back through the torii.
Understand?
I do. But I'm Agent Jones, this is Agent Fitzwallace, and we're escorting the Vice President to see the Generals.
Under the orders of the President himself.
I'm very sorry to hear that -- and I apologize to you, sir...
Mm-hmmm.
But we're not allowed to let in anyone from DC without it being cleared ahead of time with General Groves.
And why is that, son?
We're under a universal lockdown, sir.
It seems the last couple of government agents that Washington sent weren't properly vetted and tried to burn the whole place down...attempted murder, felony theft, just a whole score of protocol-breaching behavior.
Add that to the -- wink wink -- broader global situation, and I think you get the picture. So unless you have some way of verifying th--

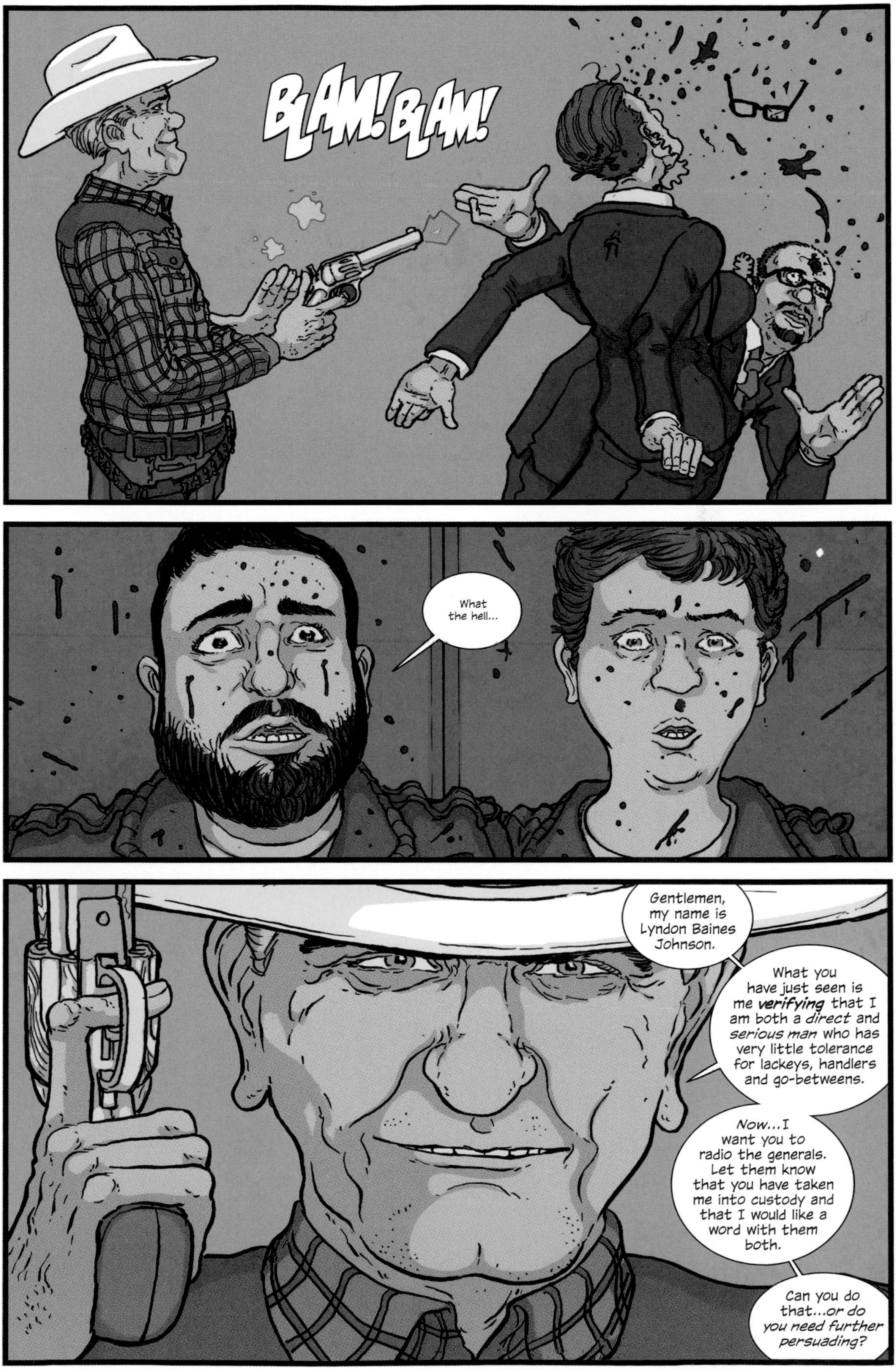
BLAM! BLAM!
What the hell...
Gentlemen, my name is Lyndon Baines Johnson.
What you have just seen is me *verifying* that I am both a *direct* and *serious man* who has very little tolerance for lackeys, handlers and go-betweens.
Now...I want you to radio the generals. Let them know that you have taken me into custody and that I would like a word with them both.
Can you do that...*or do you need further persuading?*

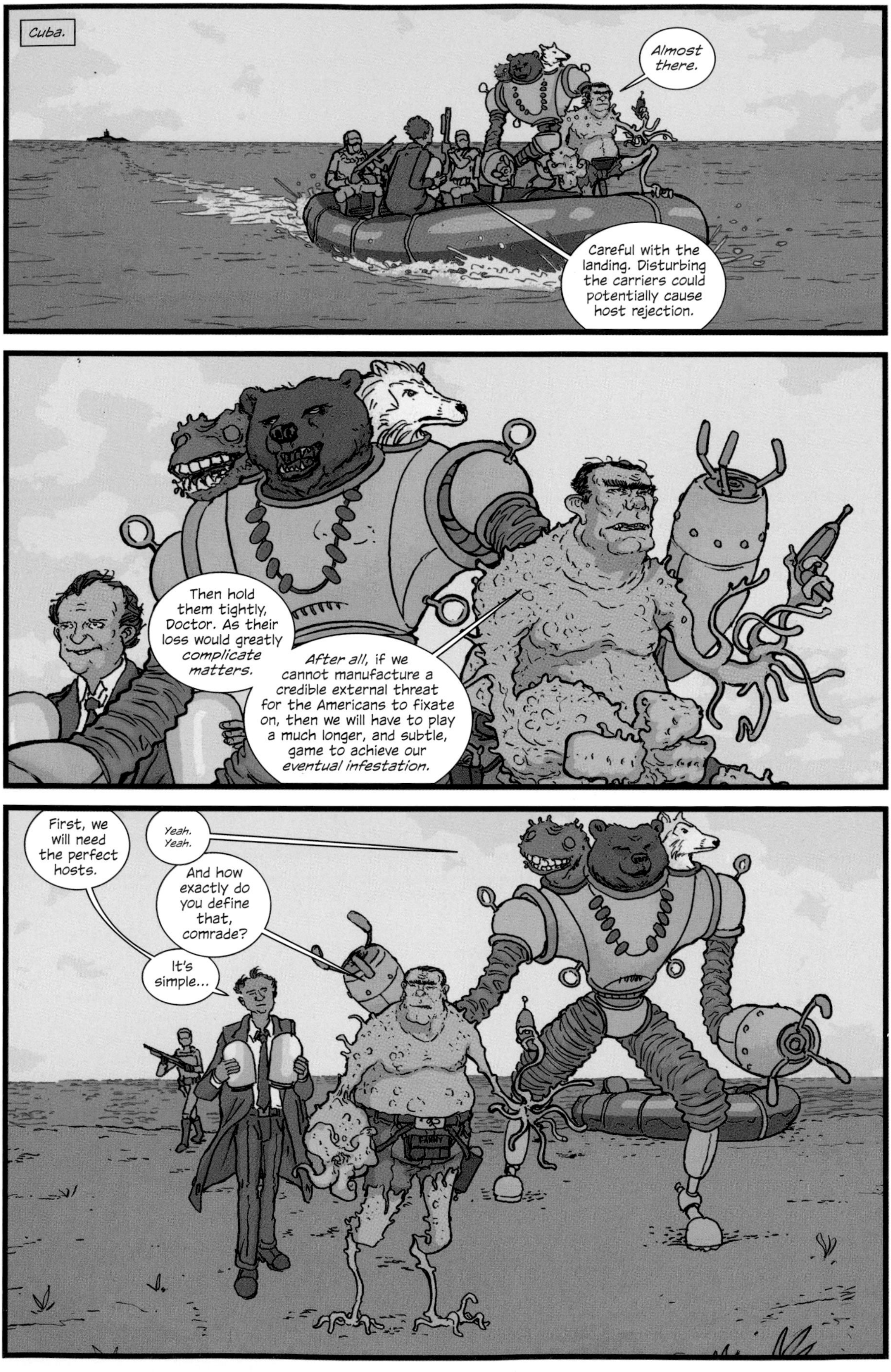
Cuba.
Almost there.
Careful with the landing. Disturbing the carriers could potentially cause host rejection.
Then hold them tightly, Doctor. As their loss would greatly *complicate matters.*
After all, if we cannot manufacture a credible external threat for the Americans to fixate on, then we will have to play a much longer, and subtle, game to achieve our *eventual infestation.*
First, we will need the perfect hosts.
Yeah. Yeah.
And how exactly do you define that, comrade?
It's simple...

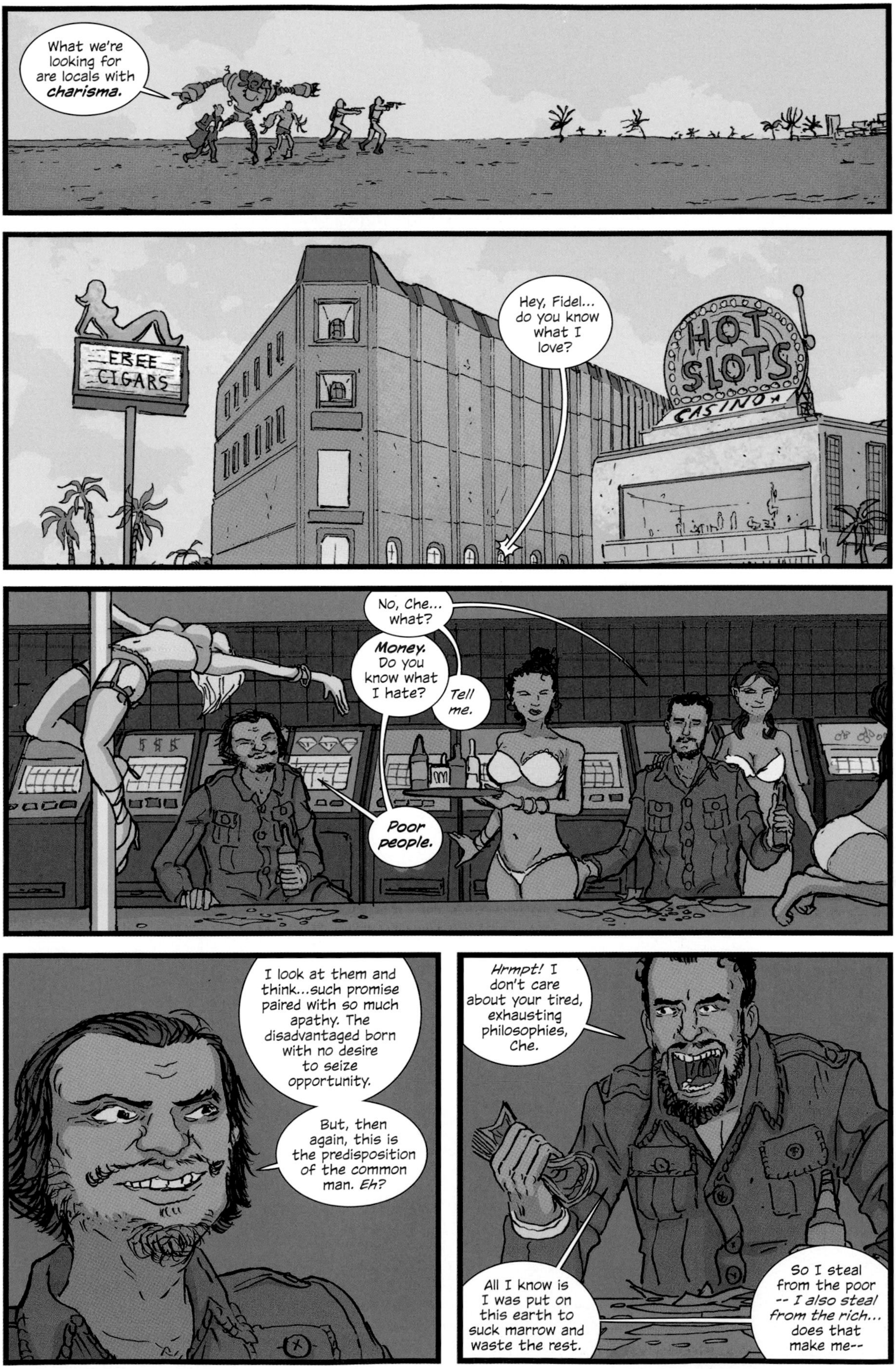
What we're looking for are locals with *charisma.*
FREE CIGARS
Hey, Fidel... do you know what I love?
HOT SLOTS
CASINO
No, Che... what?
Money. Do you know what I hate?
Tell me.
Poor people.
I look at them and think...such promise paired with so much apathy. The disadvantaged born with no desire to seize opportunity.
But, then again, this is the predisposition of the common man. *Eh?*
Hrmpt! I don't care about your tired, exhausting philosophies, Che.
All I know is I was put on this earth to suck marrow and waste the rest.
So I steal from the poor *-- I also steal from the rich...* does that make me--

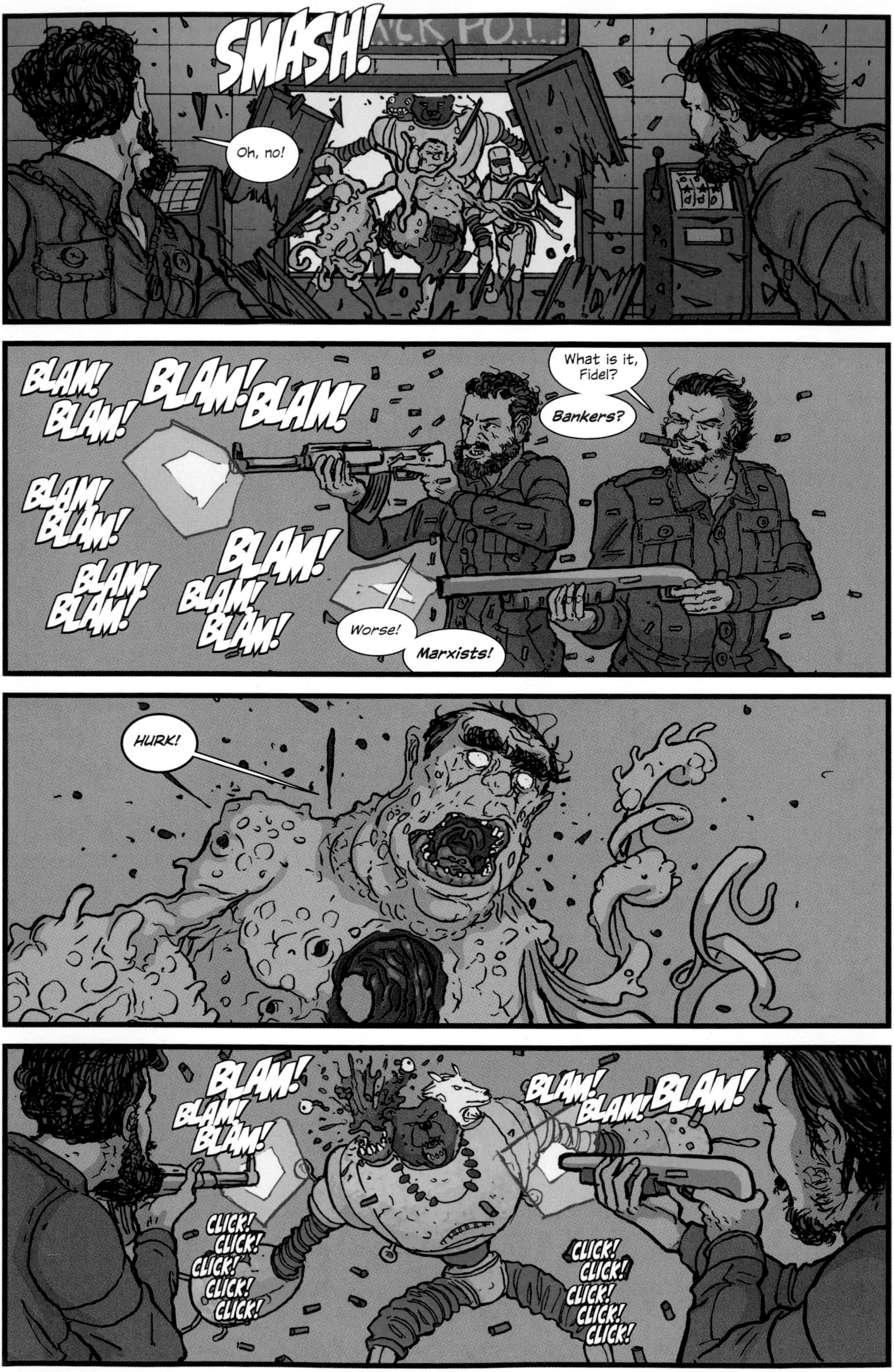
SMASH!
Oh, no!
BLAM! BLAM! BLAM! BLAM!
BLAM! BLAM!
BLAM! BLAM!
BLAM! BLAM! BLAM!
What is it, Fidel?
Bankers?
Worse!
Marxists!
HURK!
BLAM! BLAM! BLAM!
BLAM! BLAM! BLAM!
CLICK! CLICK! CLICK! CLICK! CLICK!
CLICK! CLICK! CLICK! CLICK! CLICK!

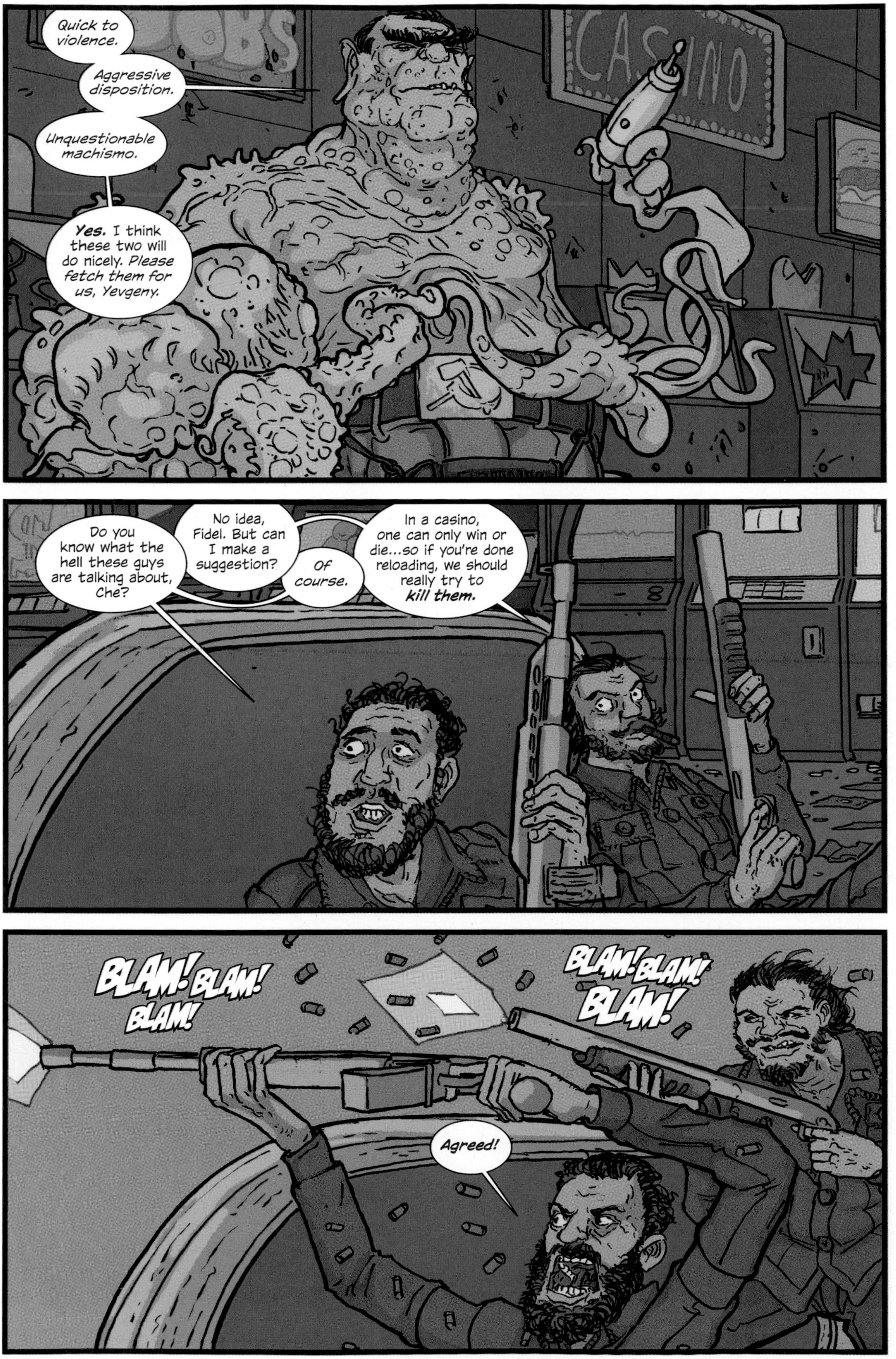

Quick to violence.
Aggressive disposition.
Unquestionable machismo.
Yes. I think these two will do nicely. Please fetch them for us, Yevgeny.
CASINO
Do you know what the hell these guys are talking about, Che?
No idea, Fidel. But can I make a suggestion?
Of course.
In a casino, one can only win or die...so if you're done reloading, we should really try to kill them.
BLAM! BLAM! BLAM!
BLAM! BLAM! BLAM!
Agreed!

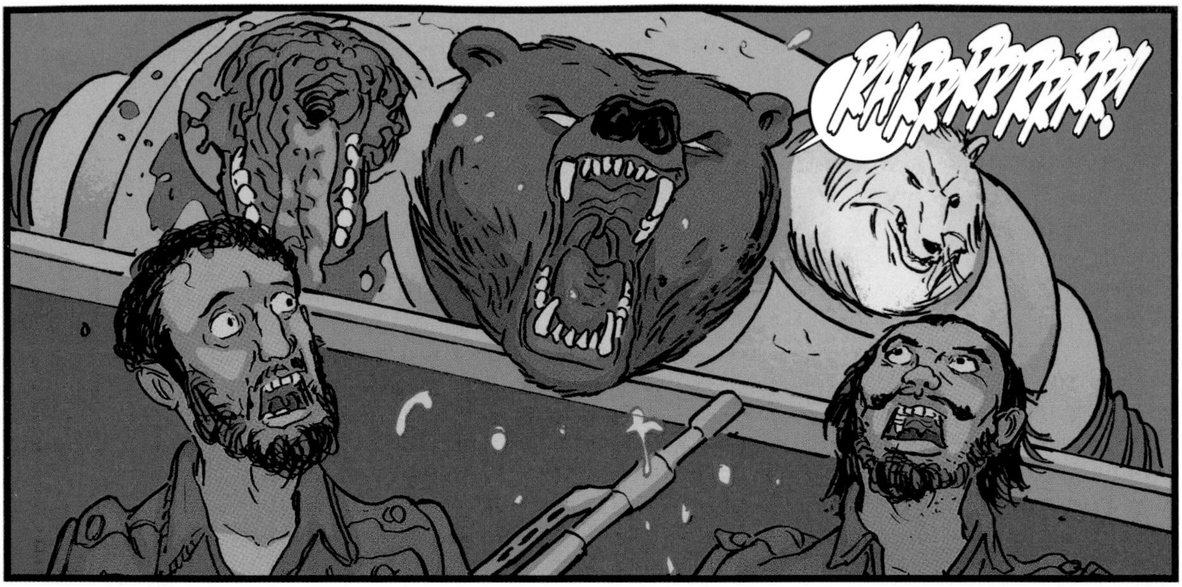
RARRRRRRRR!

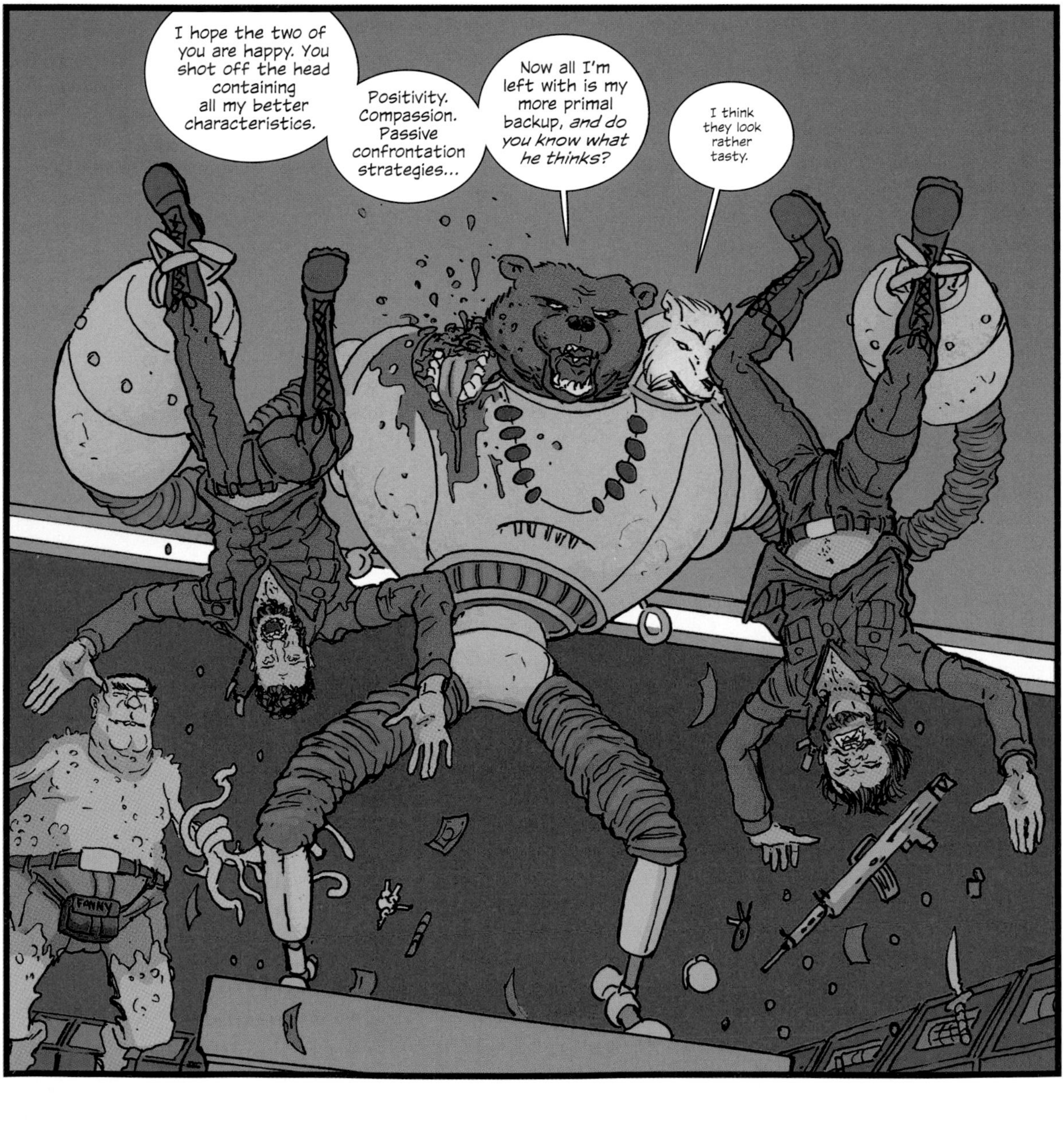
I hope the two of you are happy. You shot off the head containing all my better characteristics.
Positivity. Compassion. Passive confrontation strategies...
Now all I'm left with is my more primal backup, *and do you know what he thinks?*
I think they look rather tasty.
FANNY

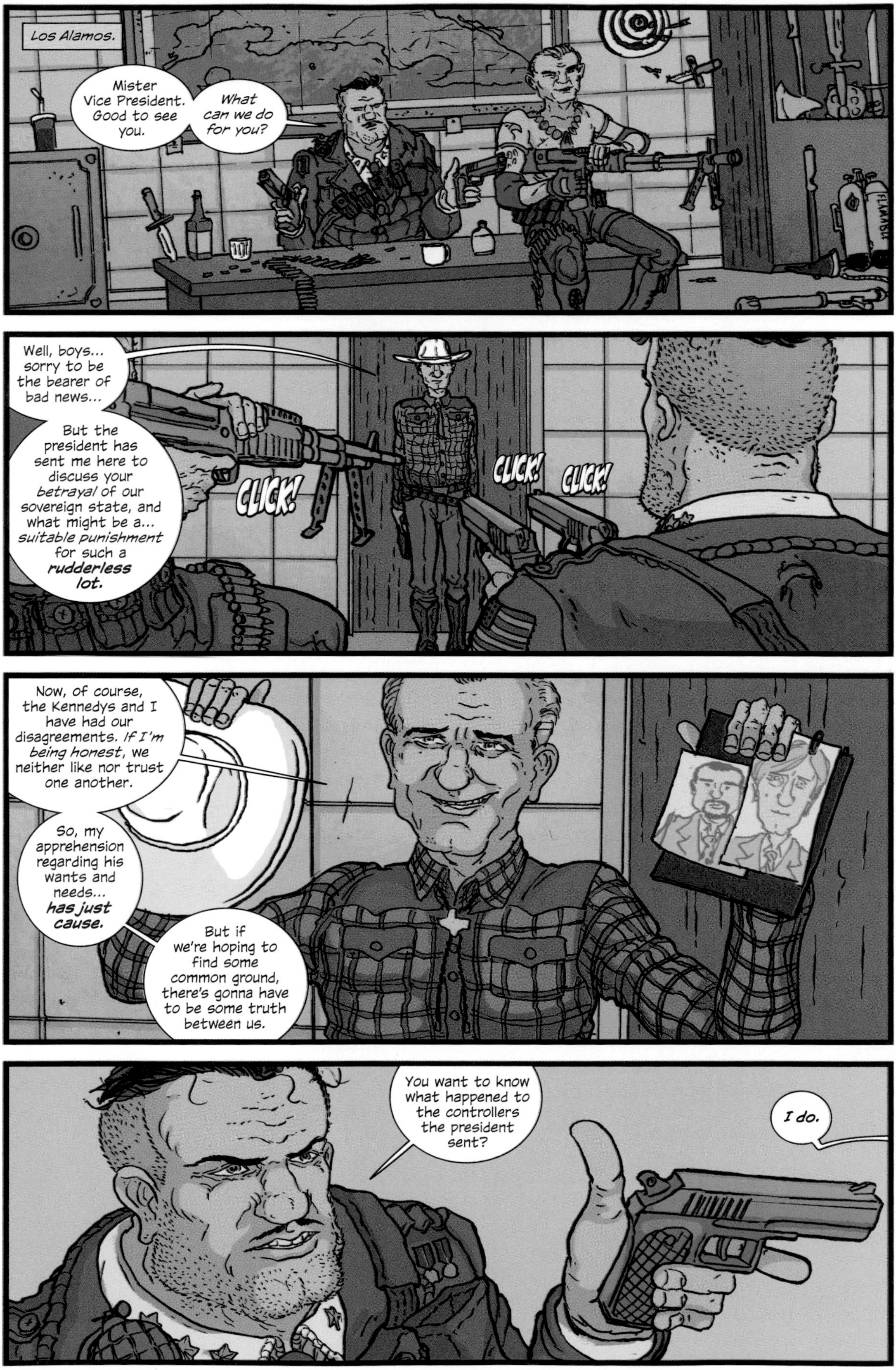
Los Alamos.
Mister Vice President. Good to see you.
What can we do for you?
Well, boys... sorry to be the bearer of bad news...
But the president has sent me here to discuss your betrayal of our sovereign state, and what might be a... suitable punishment for such a rudderless lot.
CLICK!
CLICK!
CLICK!
Now, of course, the Kennedys and I have had our disagreements. If I'm being honest, we neither like nor trust one another.
So, my apprehension regarding his wants and needs... has just cause.
But if we're hoping to find some common ground, there's gonna have to be some truth between us.
You want to know what happened to the controllers the president sent?
I do.

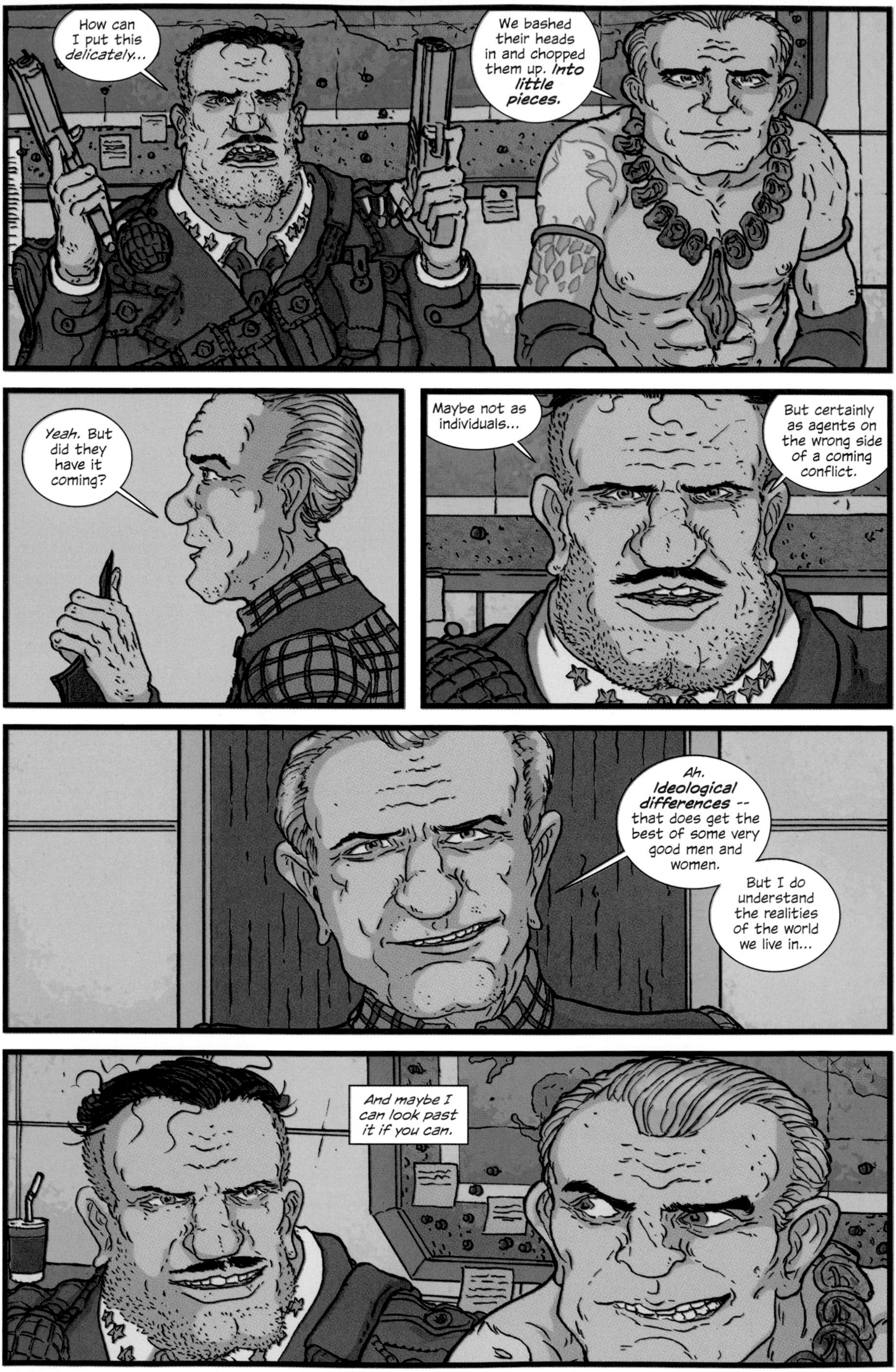

How can I put this *delicately*...
We bashed their heads in and chopped them up. ***Into little pieces.***
Yeah. But did they have it coming?
Maybe not as individuals...
But certainly as agents on the wrong side of a coming conflict.
Ah. ***Ideological differences*** -- that does get the best of some very good men and women.
But I do understand the realities of the world we live in...
And maybe I can look past it if you can.

Control.
It's a subtle art... one not easily understood by most base humans.
Sure, our new flesh -- *the combined primate-xenological super being* -- affords us the luxuries of both observation and manipulation...
But the real craft is not in the deconstruction of a mind, as we did with Minister Ustinov...
Art, you see... is ***controlling a population.***
Art... is the ***cultivation*** of a ***human crop.***
And for that, you need useful, charismatic tools to infect the people with propaganda.
Weaponized ideas that subjugate an entire nation without firing a single bullet.

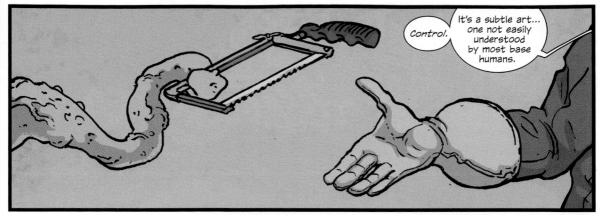

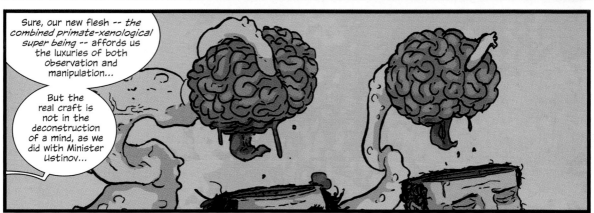

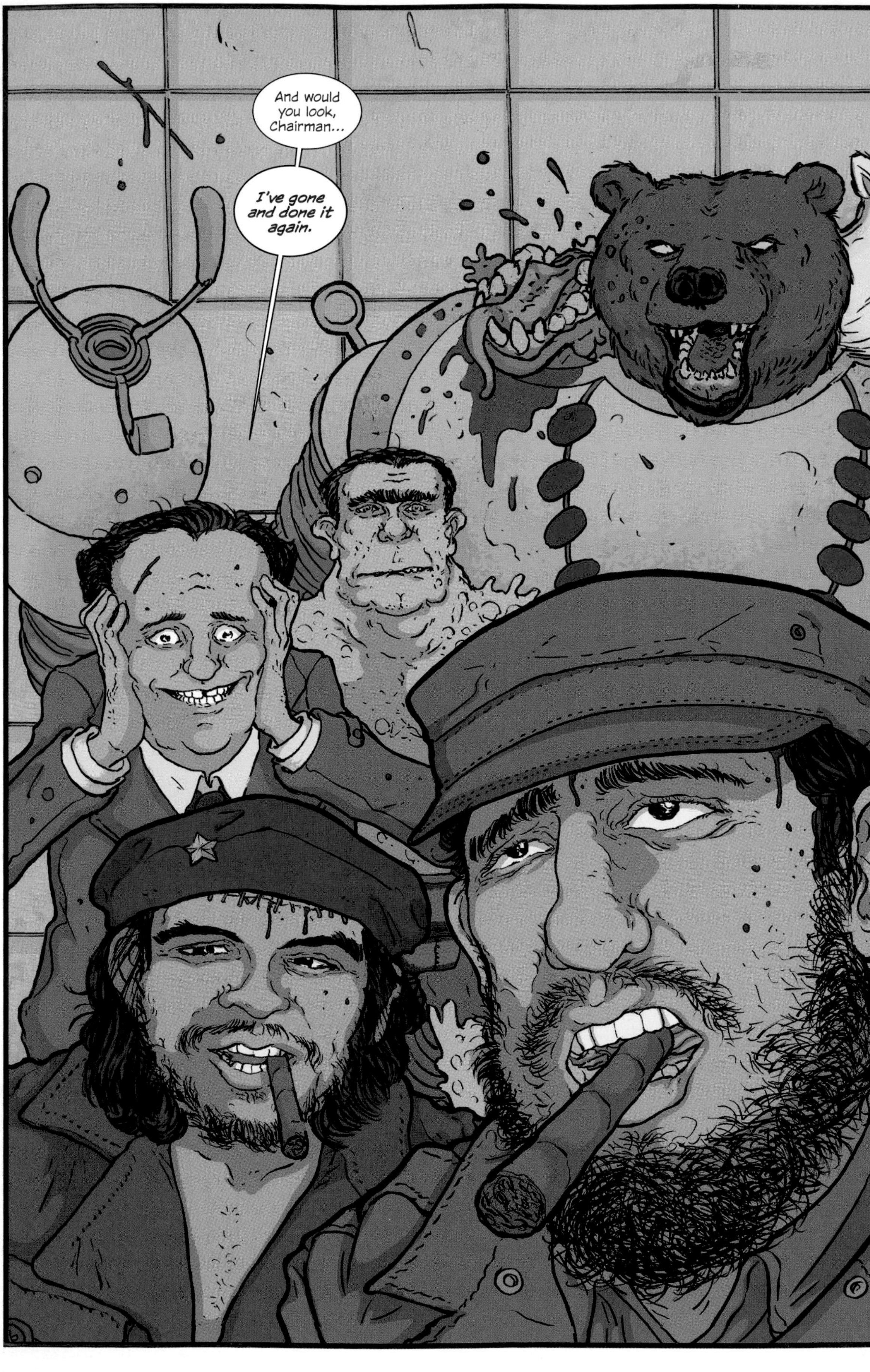
And would you look, Chairman...
I've gone and done it again.

"HISTORY CREATES REVOLUTIONARIES OUT OF THIN AIR. IT SUMMONS THEM FROM NOTHING."

CLAVIS AUREA
THE RECORDED FEYNMAN | **VOL. 4**

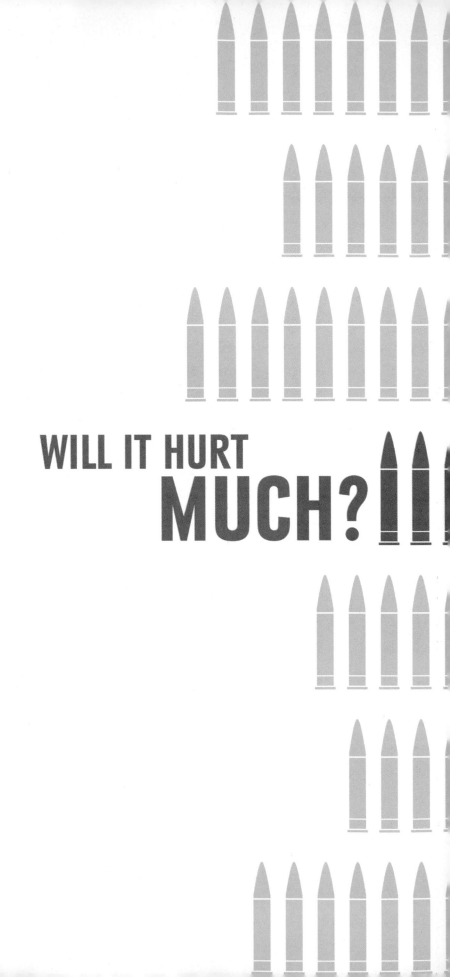

WILL IT HURT MUCH?

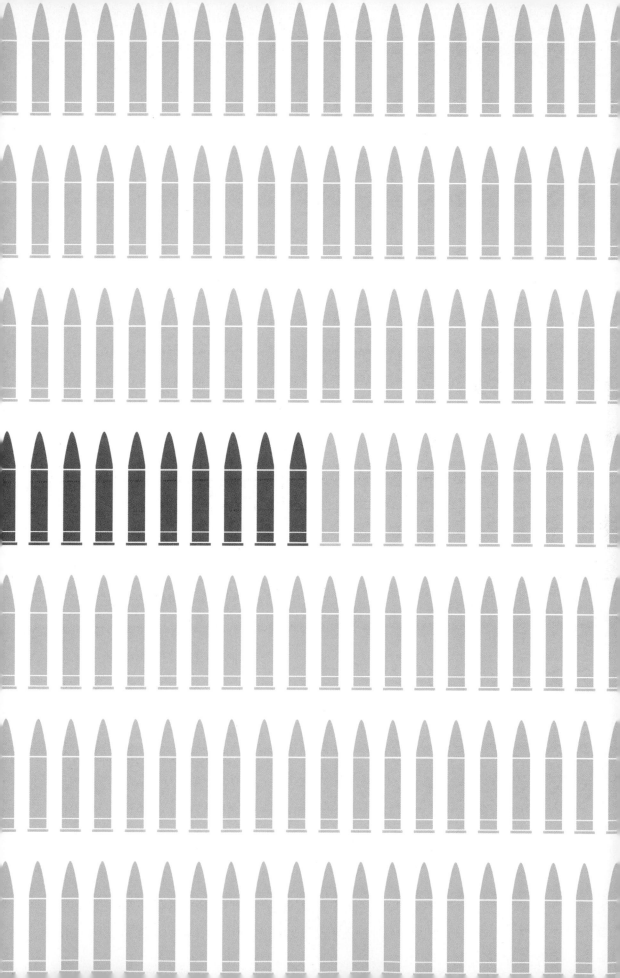

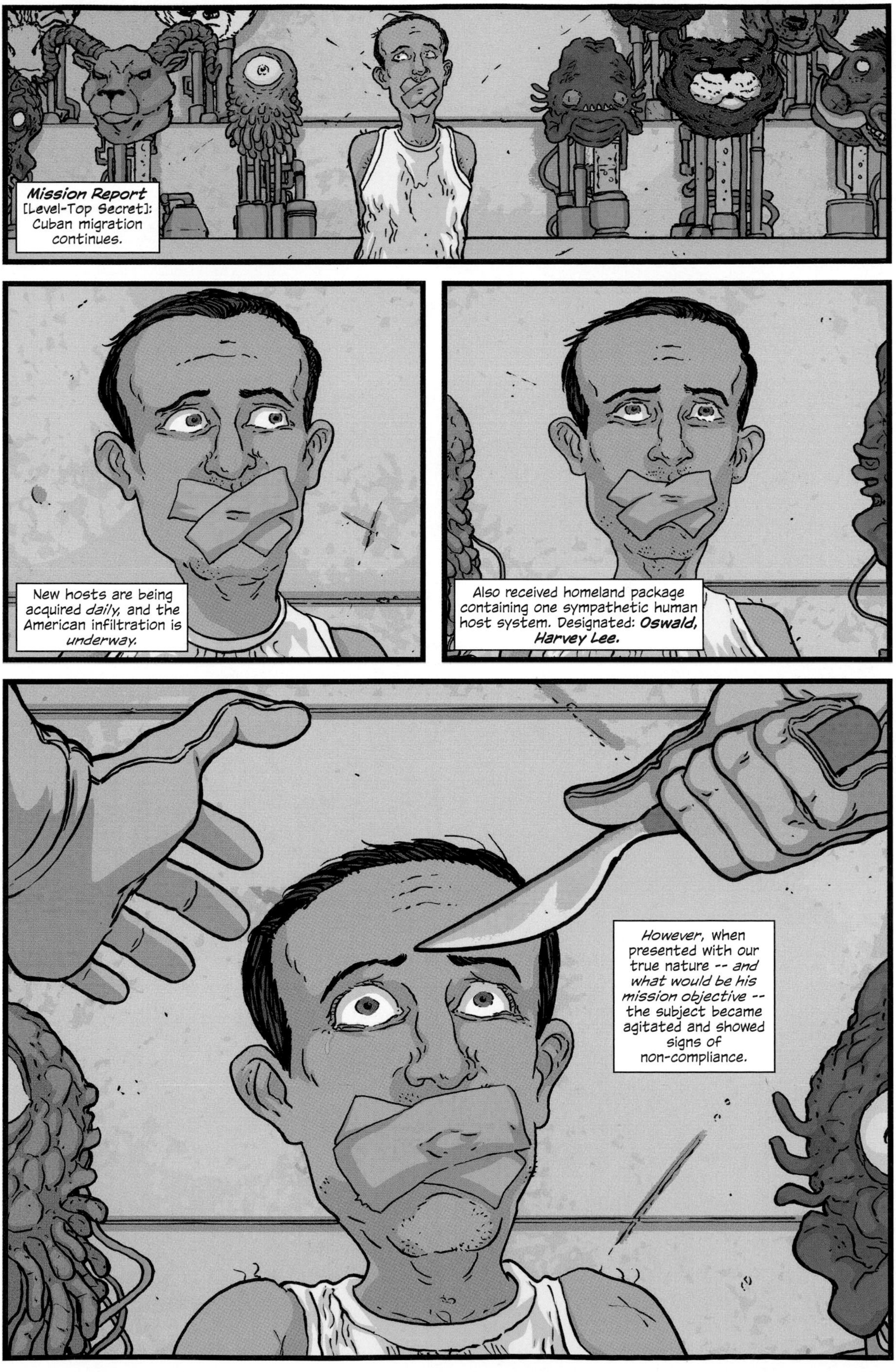
Mission Report
[Level-Top Secret]: Cuban migration continues.
New hosts are being acquired *daily*, and the American infiltration is *underway*.
Also received homeland package containing one sympathetic human host system. Designated: ***Oswald, Harvey Lee.***
However, when presented with our true nature -- *and what would be his mission objective* -- the subject became agitated and showed signs of non-compliance.

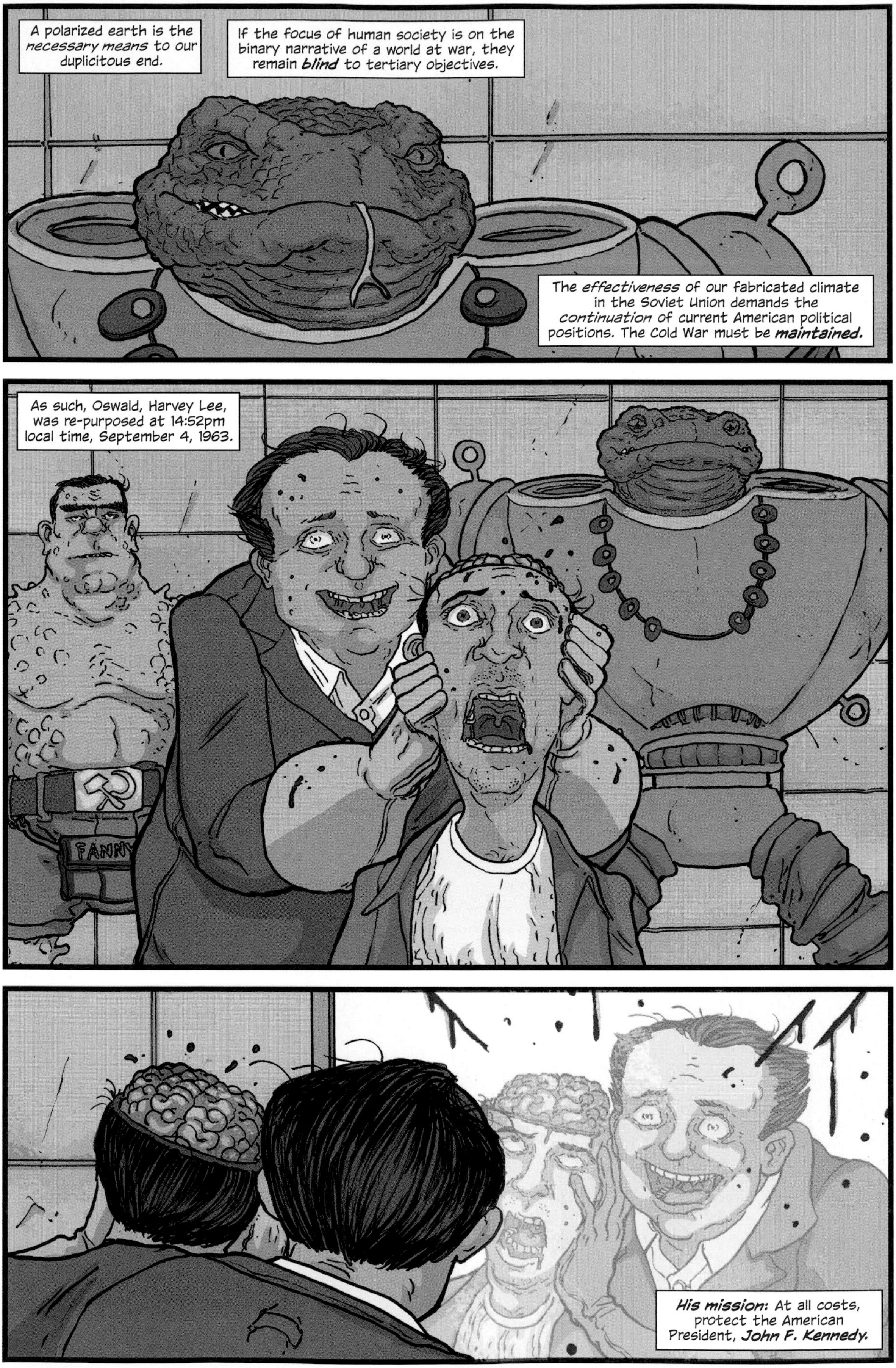
A polarized earth is the *necessary means* to our duplicitous end.
If the focus of human society is on the binary narrative of a world at war, they remain ***blind*** to tertiary objectives.
The *effectiveness* of our fabricated climate in the Soviet Union demands the *continuation* of current American political positions. The Cold War must be ***maintained.***
As such, Oswald, Harvey Lee, was re-purposed at 14:52pm local time, September 4, 1963.
FANNY
His mission: At all costs, protect the American President, ***John F. Kennedy.***

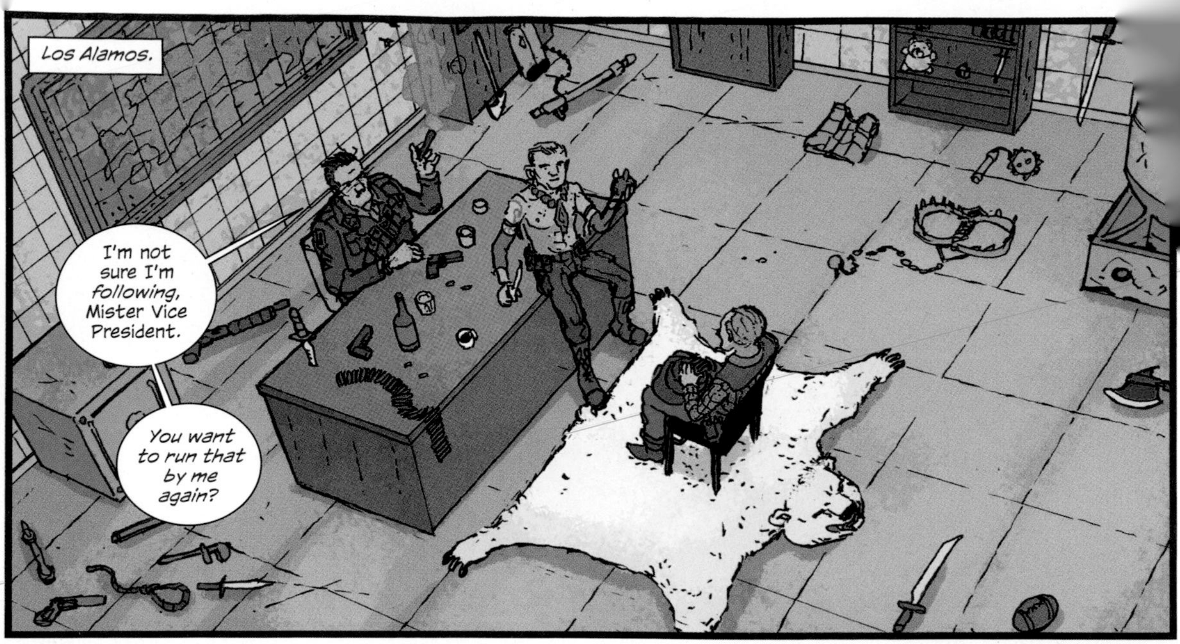
Los Alamos.
I'm not sure I'm *following*, Mister Vice President.
You want to run that by me again?

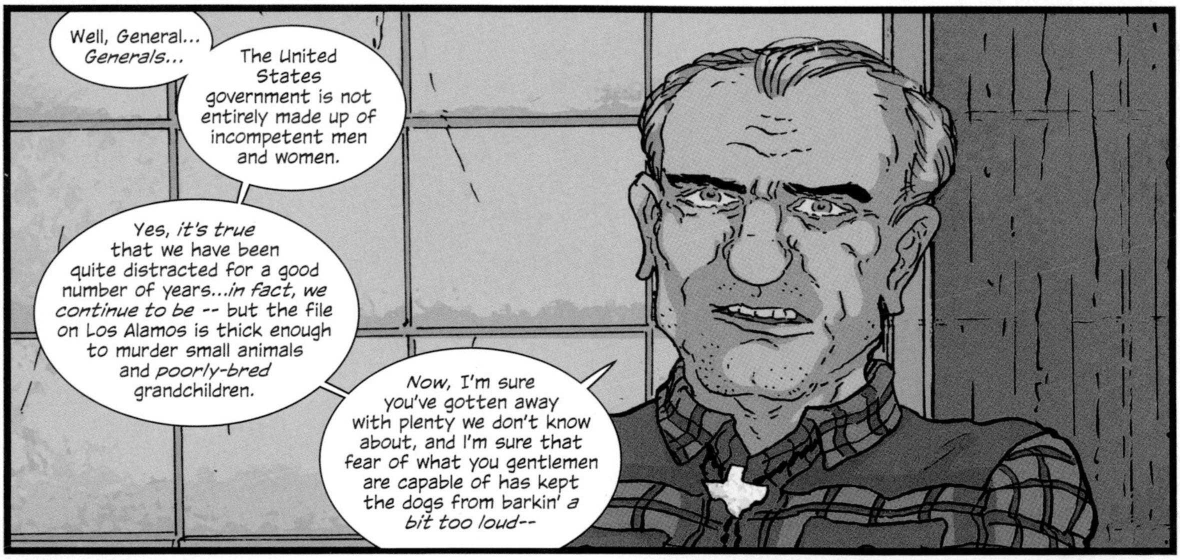
Well, General... *Generals...*
The United States government is not entirely made up of incompetent men and women.
Yes, *it's true* that we have been quite distracted for a good number of years...*in fact, we continue to be* -- but the file on Los Alamos is thick enough to murder small animals and *poorly-bred* grandchildren.
Now, I'm sure you've gotten away with plenty we don't know about, and I'm sure that fear of what you gentlemen are capable of has kept the dogs from barkin' *a bit too loud--*

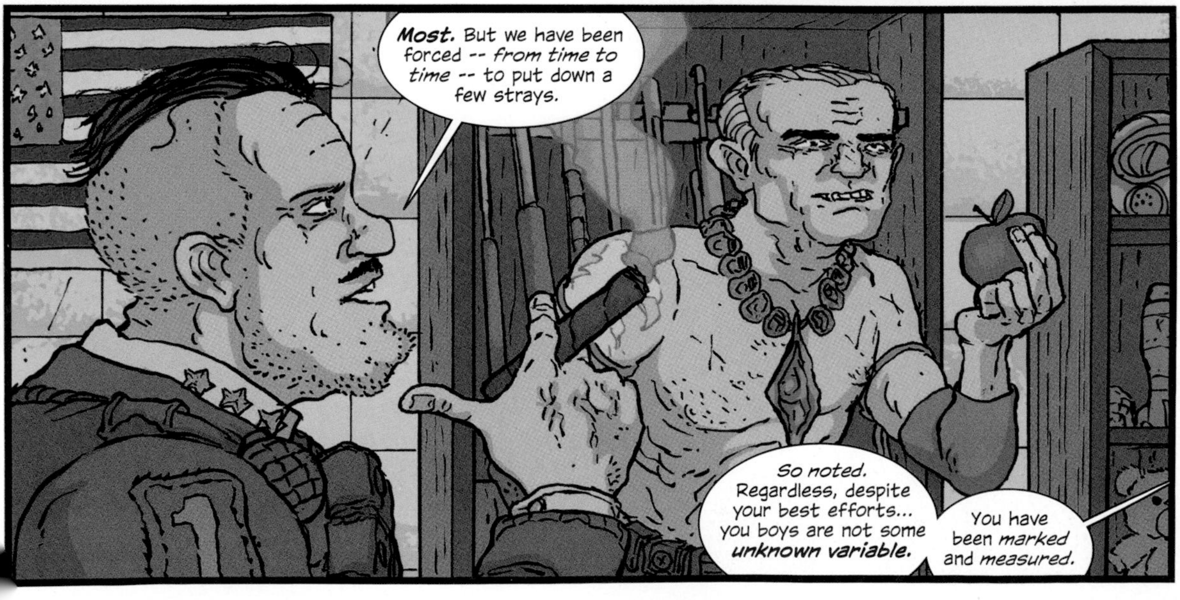
Most. But we have been forced -- *from time to time* -- to put down a few strays.
So noted. Regardless, despite your best efforts... you boys are not some ***unknown variable.***
You have been *marked* and *measured.*

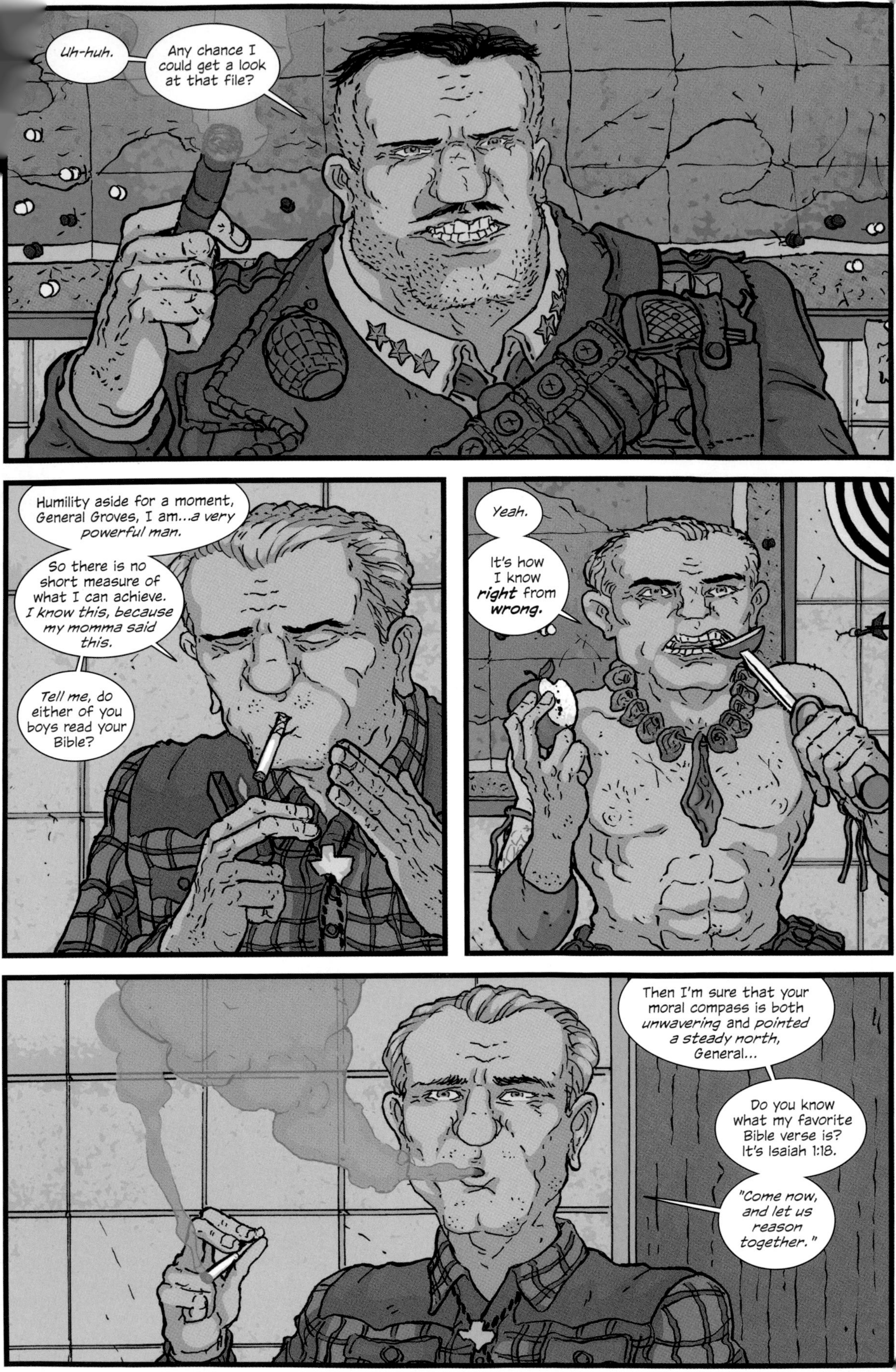
Uh-huh.
Any chance I could get a look at that file?
Humility aside for a moment, General Groves, I am...*a very powerful man.*
So there is no short measure of what I can achieve. *I know this, because my momma said this.*
Tell me, do either of you boys read your Bible?
Yeah.
It's how I know **right** from **wrong.**
Then I'm sure that your moral compass is both *unwavering* and *pointed a steady north,* General...
Do you know what my favorite Bible verse is? It's Isaiah 1:18.
"Come now, and let us reason together."

I am here because I see great *purpose* and *reason* in what you are doing.
I am also here because I believe that ***together*** -- *if such a thing were made possible* -- we could do great things for our country...
PTOOO!
And, dare I say, the world...*as it is in need of rescue.*
Do you agree?
PTOOO!
I do.
What about you, Westy?
A consolidated power structure is easily fortified and defensible from multiple positions. ***It's sound strategy.***

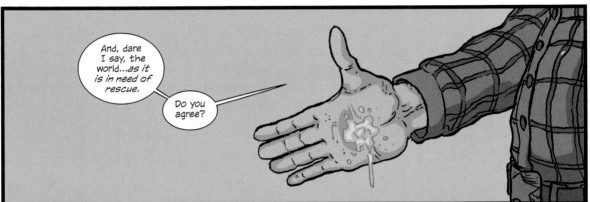

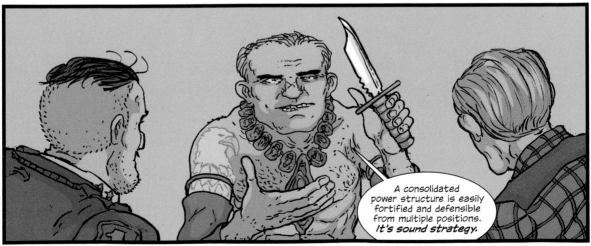

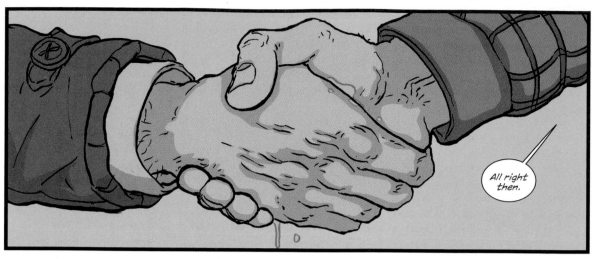

All right then.

So...I assume there's a quid pro quo in play here. *That's fairly obvious...*

But what's this talk of rescue? *What do we not know?*

I'm aware you lost Star City -- but how much do you know about what's really going on at the Kremlin?

And after that, I'd like to fill you in regarding an operative named Oswald.

"WE HAVE NOT BEEN TOLD THE TRUTH ABOUT OSWALD."

- HALE BOGGS
THE WARREN COMMISSION

CLAVIS AUREA
THE RECORDED FEYNMAN | **VOL. 4**

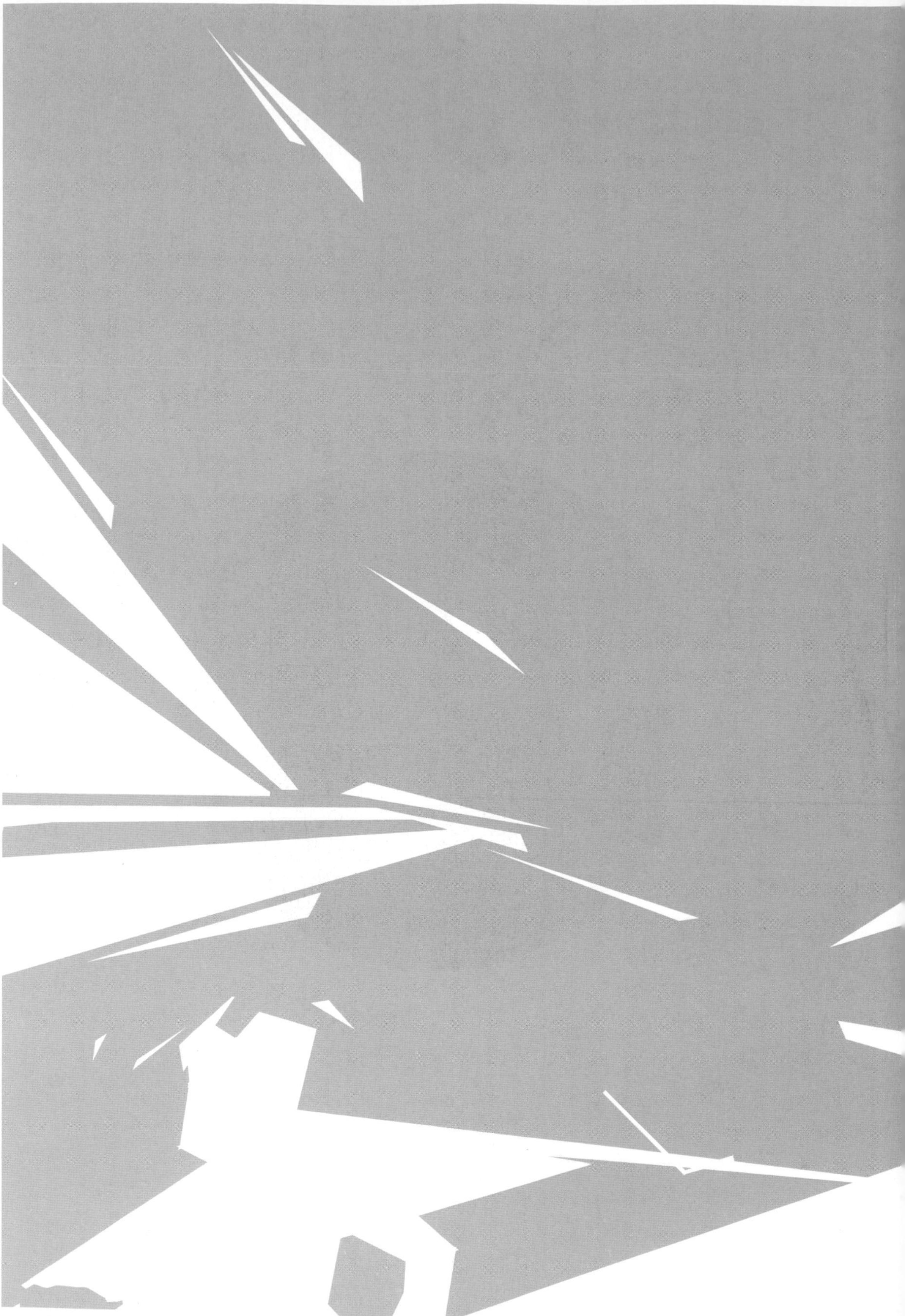

24

TEXAS ROULETTE

"HE WAS QUITE A MYSTERIOUS FELLOW, AND HE DID HAVE A CONNECTION . . . THE EXTENT OF THE INFLUENCE OF THOSE CONNECTIONS ON HIM I THINK HISTORY WILL DEAL WITH MORE THAN WE'RE ABLE TO NOW."

- PRESIDENT LYNDON BAINES JOHNSON

CLAVIS AUREA
THE RECORDED FEYNMAN | **VOL. 4**

November 22, 1963

Dallas, TX

I'm not sure why we need this guy.

Alive, I mean.

In my experience, it's always best to discard a useless -- and poorly purposed -- tool.

I think you know that, normally, "kill 'em all" is a pretty rock solid philosophy for me...but this time you're wrong, Leslie.

Sure...the primary objective here is simple regime change...

But we also have other goals:

Like the peaceful transition of leadership, and the continued illusion of an ongoin' Cold War.

I mean, we don't want the people to devolve into a mob, but conflict is good...

It means *money* -- and money means *operational longevity.*

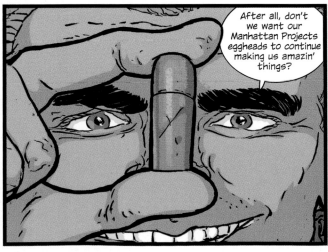

After all, don't we want our Manhattan Projects eggheads to continue makin' us amazin' things?

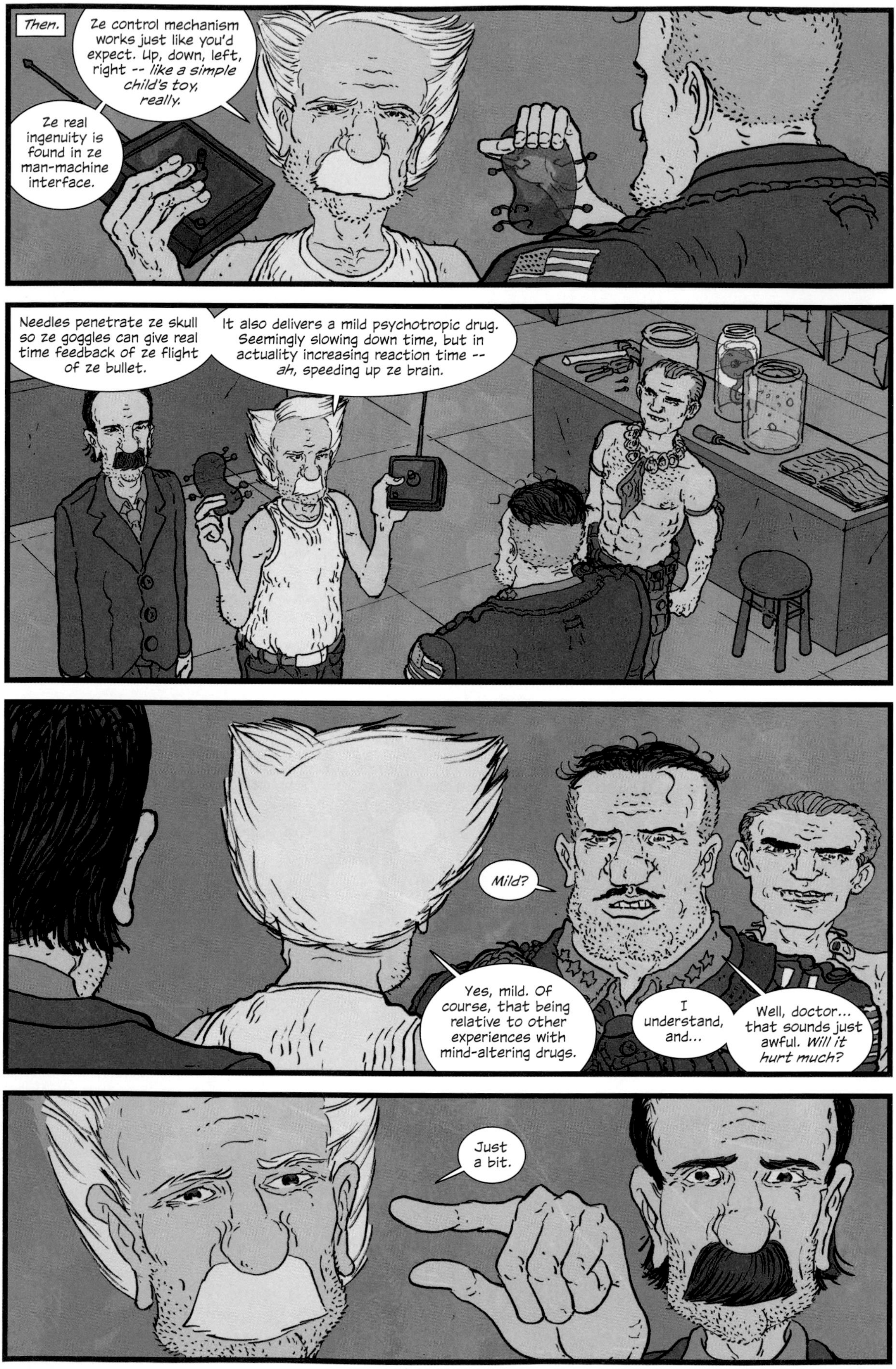
Then.
Ze control mechanism works just like you'd expect. Up, down, left, right -- *like a simple child's toy, really.*
Ze real ingenuity is found in ze man-machine interface.
Needles penetrate ze skull so ze goggles can give real time feedback of ze flight of ze bullet.
It also delivers a mild psychotropic drug. Seemingly slowing down time, but in actuality increasing reaction time -- *ah*, speeding up ze brain.
Mild?
Yes, mild. Of course, that being relative to other experiences with mind-altering drugs.
I understand, and...
Well, doctor... that sounds just awful. *Will it hurt much?*
Just a bit.

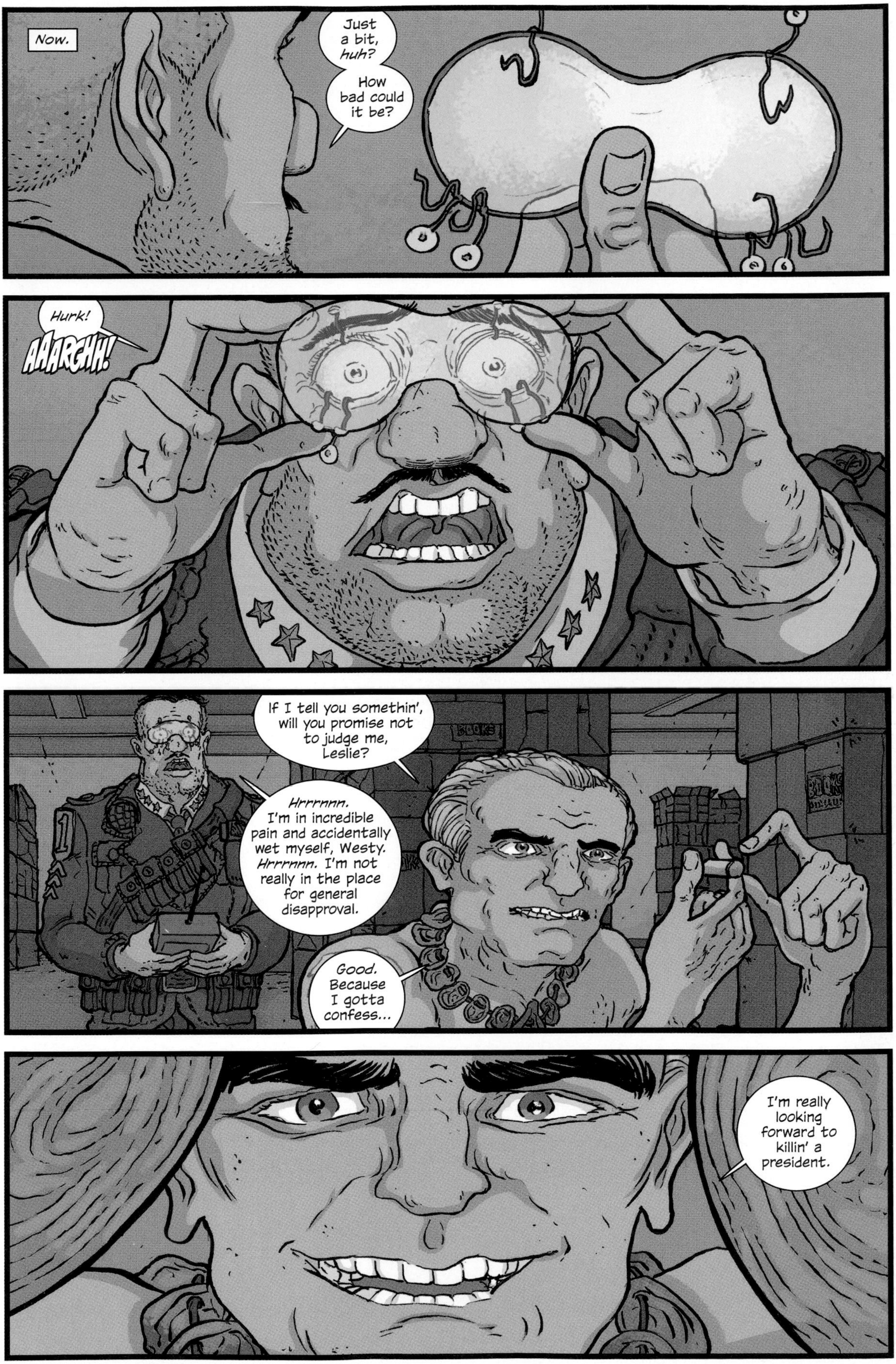
Now.
Just a bit, *huh?*
How bad could it be?
Hurk!
AAARGHH!
If I tell you somethin', will you promise not to judge me, Leslie?
Hrrrnnn. I'm in incredible pain and accidentally wet myself, Westy. *Hrrrnnn.* I'm not really in the place for general disapproval.
Good. Because I gotta confess...
I'm really looking forward to killin' a president.

Although I suppose that even though it's my finger pullin' the trigger...

That it's me who sets the killin' object on its way...

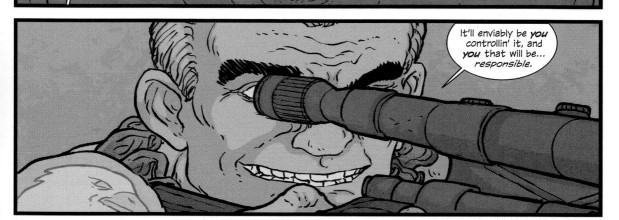

It'll enviably be *you* controllin' it, and *you* that will be... *responsible.*

CLICK!

BANG!

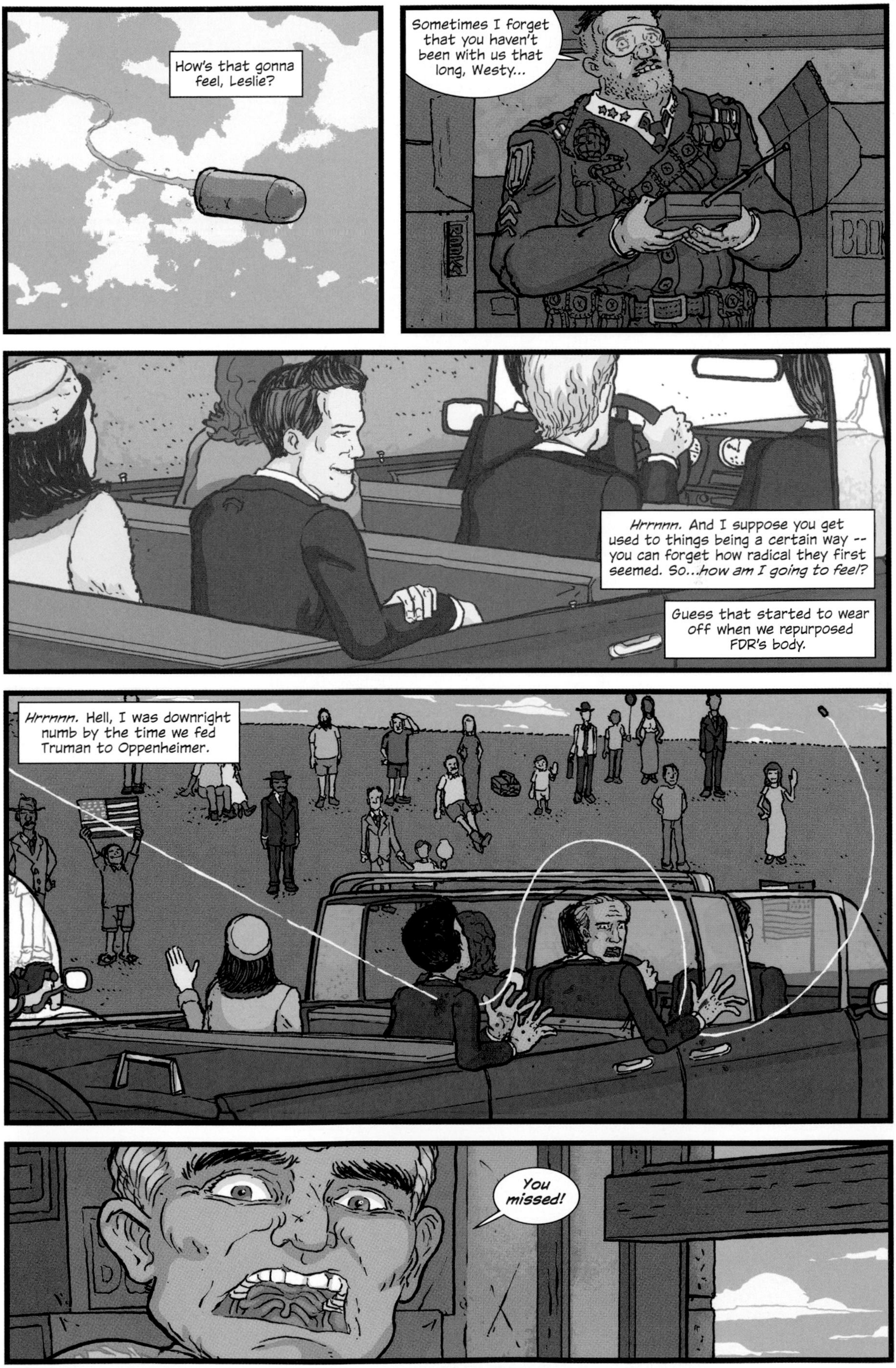
How's that gonna feel, Leslie?
Sometimes I forget that you haven't been with us that long, Westy...
BOOM
Hrrnnn. And I suppose you get used to things being a certain way -- you can forget how radical they first seemed. So...*how am I going to feel?*
Guess that started to wear off when we repurposed FDR's body.
Hrrnnn. Hell, I was downright numb by the time we fed Truman to Oppenheimer.
You missed!

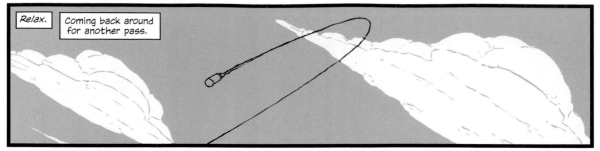

Relax.

Coming back around for another pass.

Anyway...here's the thing you need to remember about these fellas in the big white house...

They're all the same -- replaceable.

Sure, many of our god-fearing citizens like to pretend that they're not -- and I gotta admit, sometimes I find it hard to respect people so goddamn gullible -- but that's exactly what these...statesmen are.

High-end cogs.

Watch. You'll see...

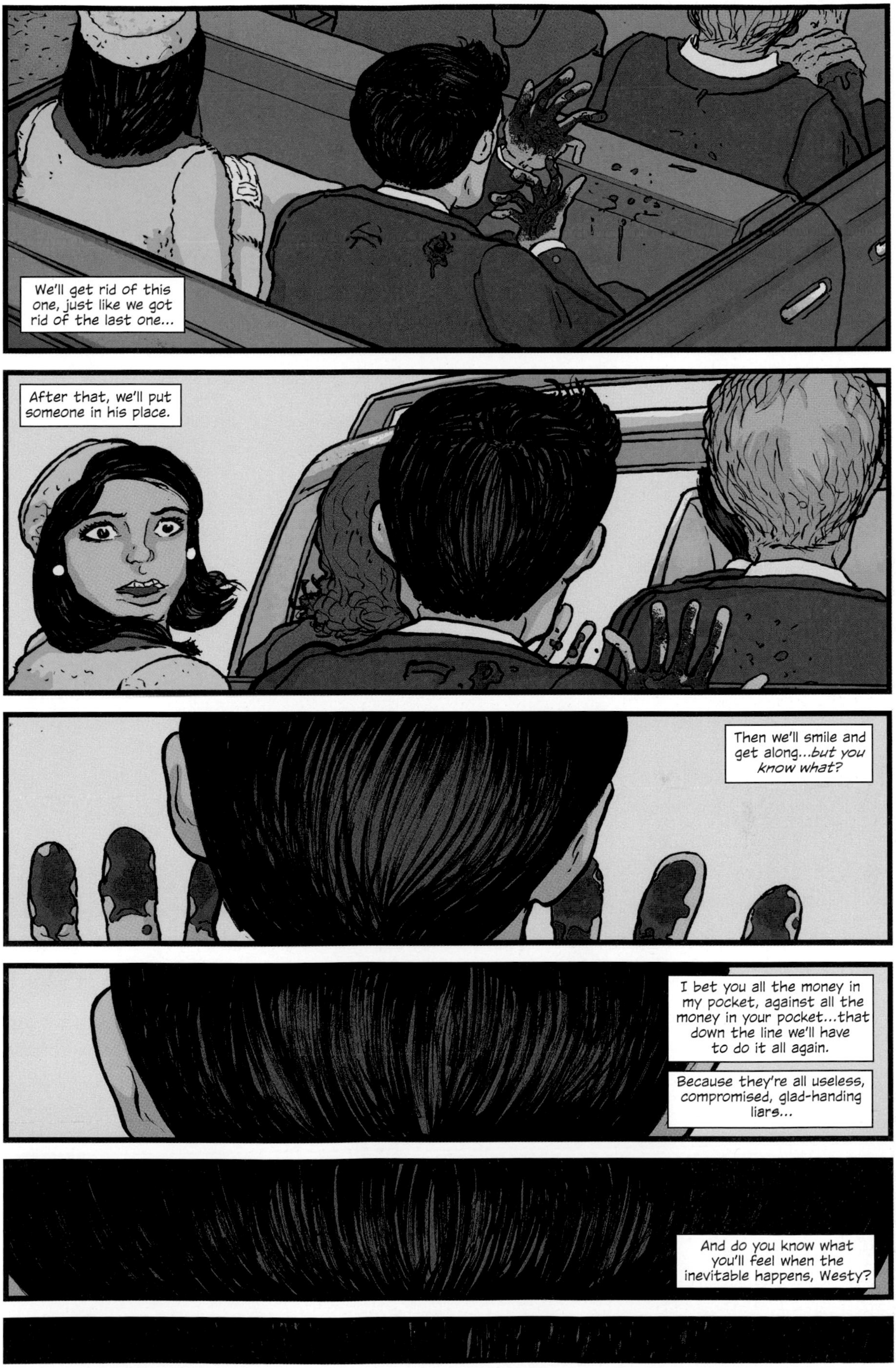
We'll get rid of this one, just like we got rid of the last one...
After that, we'll put someone in his place.
Then we'll smile and get along...*but you know what?*
I bet you all the money in my pocket, against all the money in your pocket...that down the line we'll have to do it all again.
Because they're all useless, compromised, glad-handing liars...
And do you know what you'll feel when the inevitable happens, Westy?

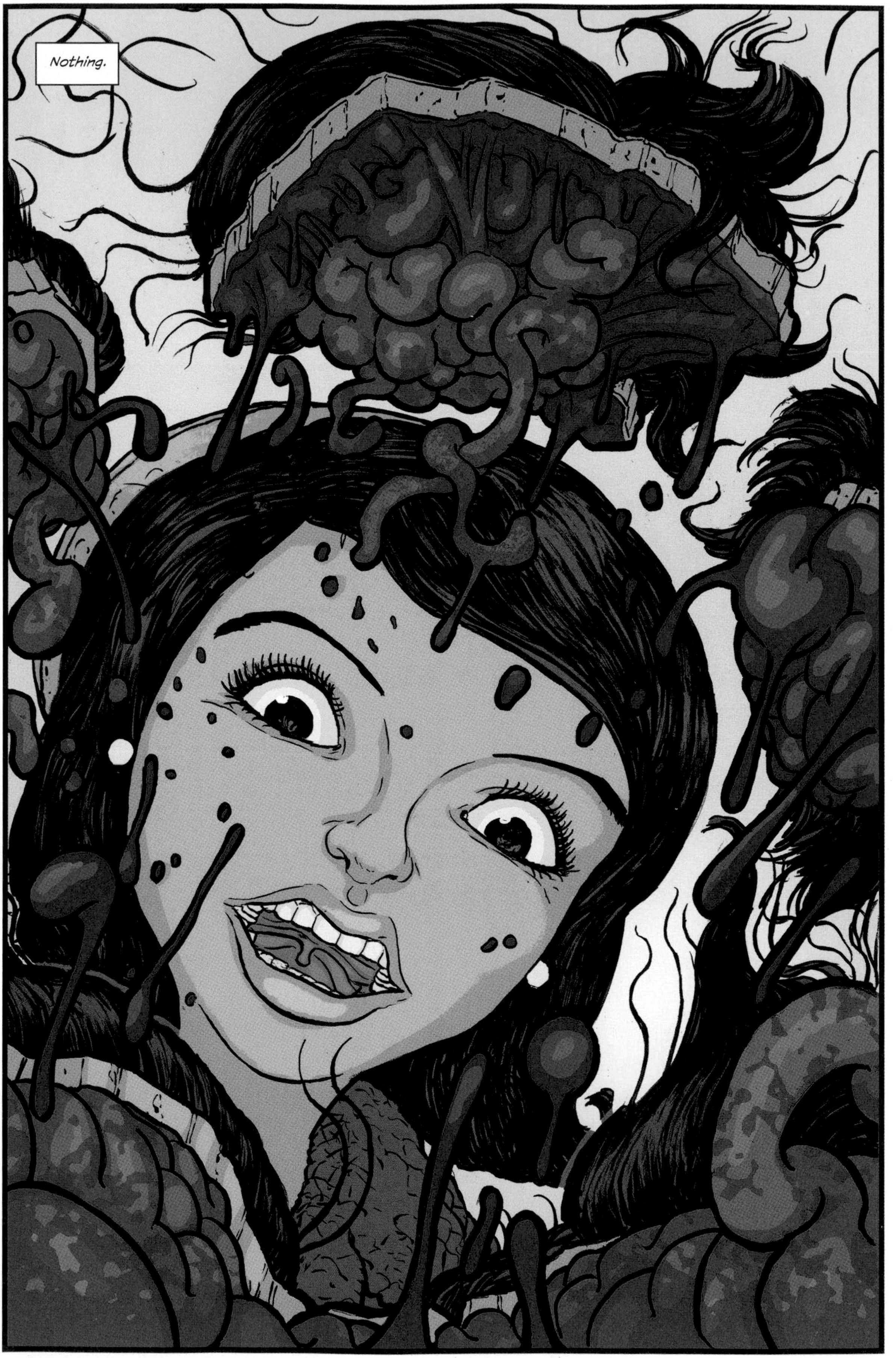
Nothing.

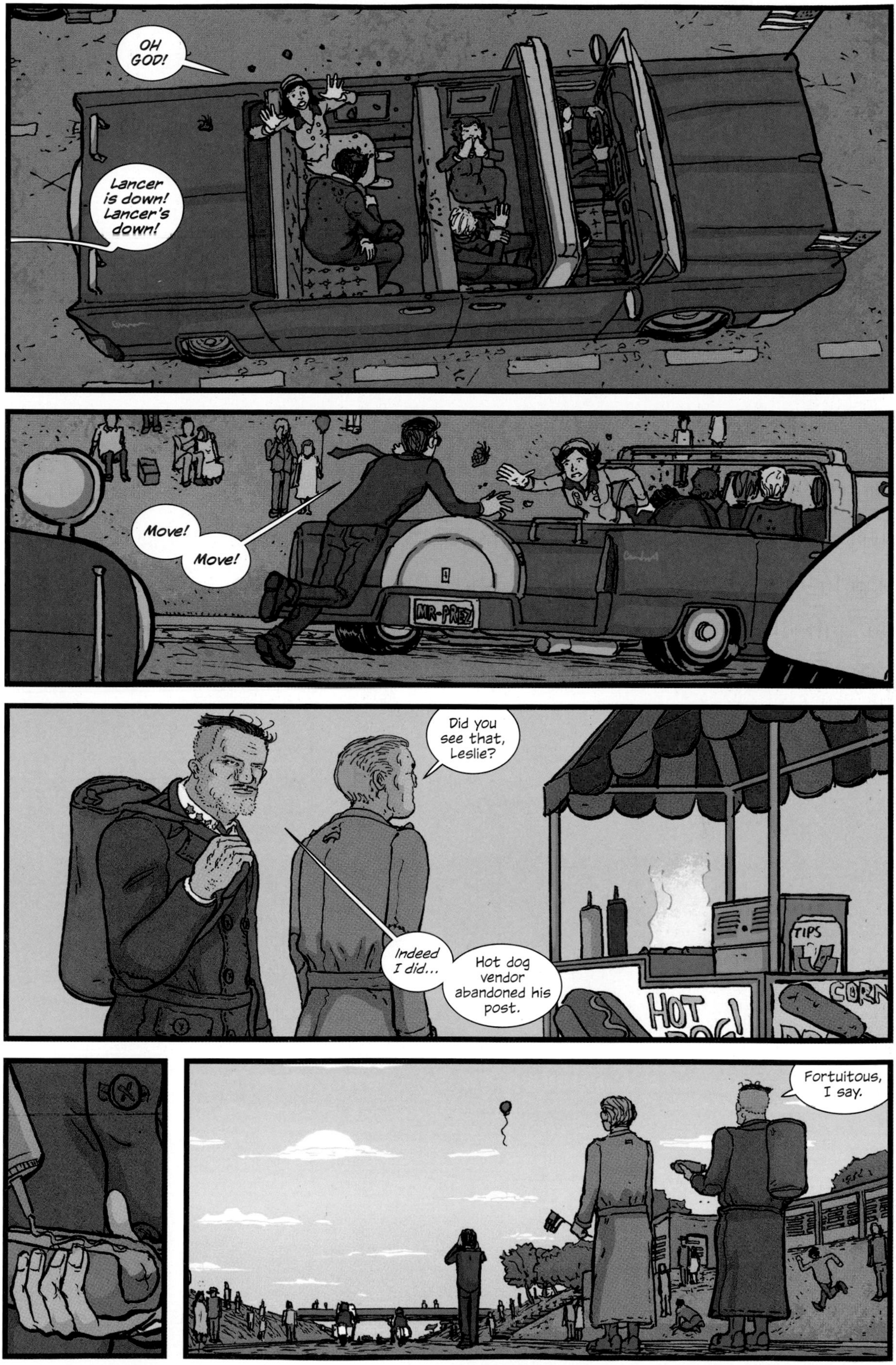
OH GOD!
Lancer is down! Lancer's down!
Move!
Move!
MR-PREZ
Did you see that, Leslie?
Indeed I did...
Hot dog vendor abandoned his post.
TIPS
HOT DOG!
CORN
Fortuitous, I say.

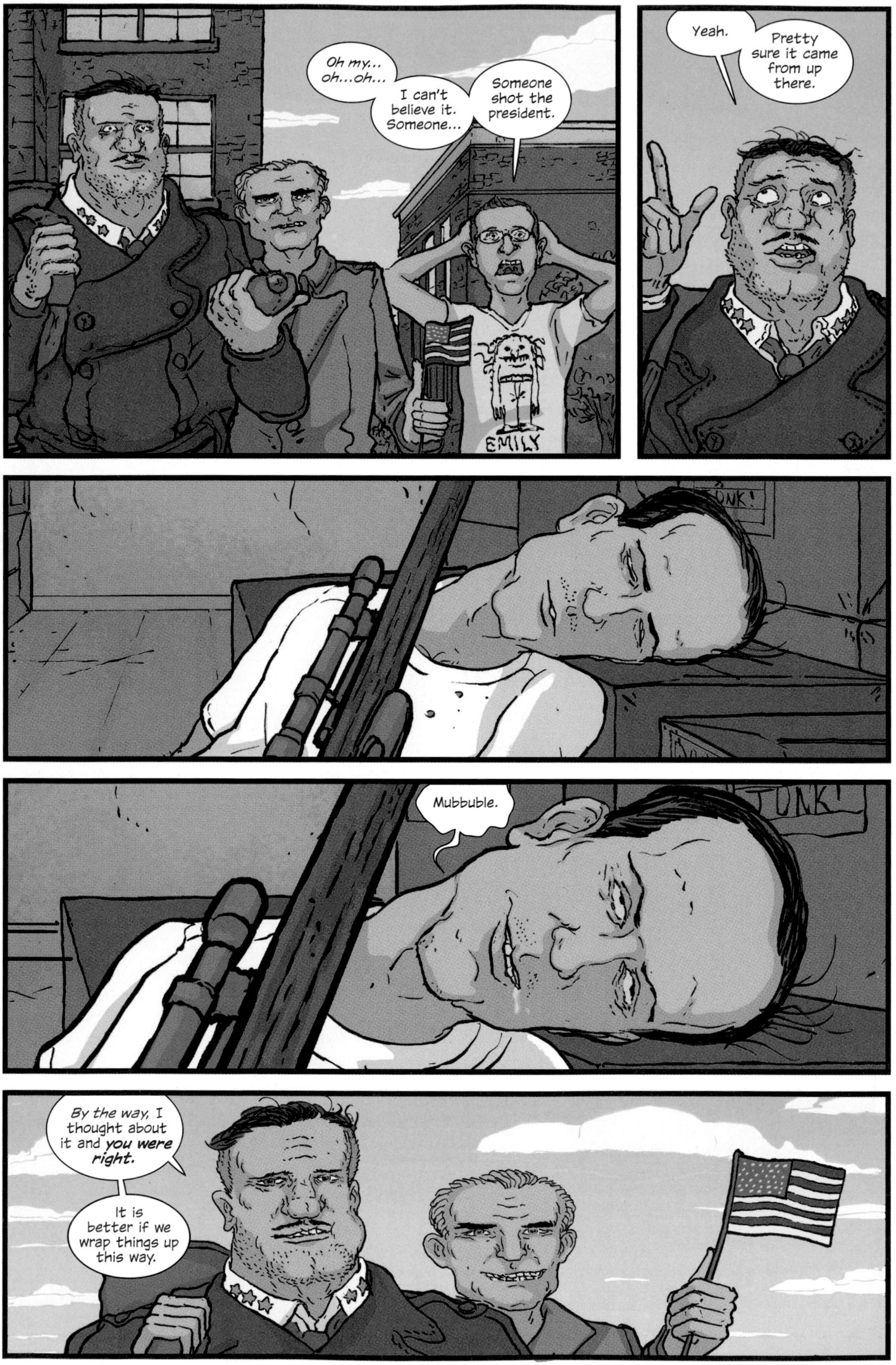

Oh my... oh...oh...
I can't believe it. Someone...
Someone shot the president.
EMILY
Yeah.
Pretty sure it came from up there.
JUNK!
Mubbuble.
JUNK!
By the way, I thought about it and *you were right.*
It is better if we wrap things up this way.

Space.

I don't want to upset you, Yuri...

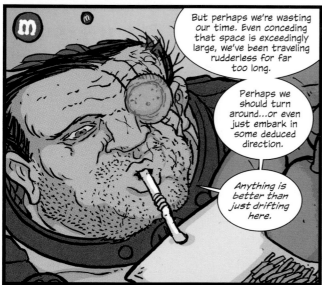

But perhaps we're wasting our time. Even conceding that space is exceedingly large, we've been traveling rudderless for far too long.

Perhaps we should turn around...or even just embark in some deduced direction.

Anything is better than just drifting here.

Just because we haven't found anything yet doesn't mean we should give up, Doctor.

This area is where the signal Laika sent originated from.

We just have to wait a little longer...

We have to keep looking until we...find...

SKKRRZZZ!

Do you hear that?

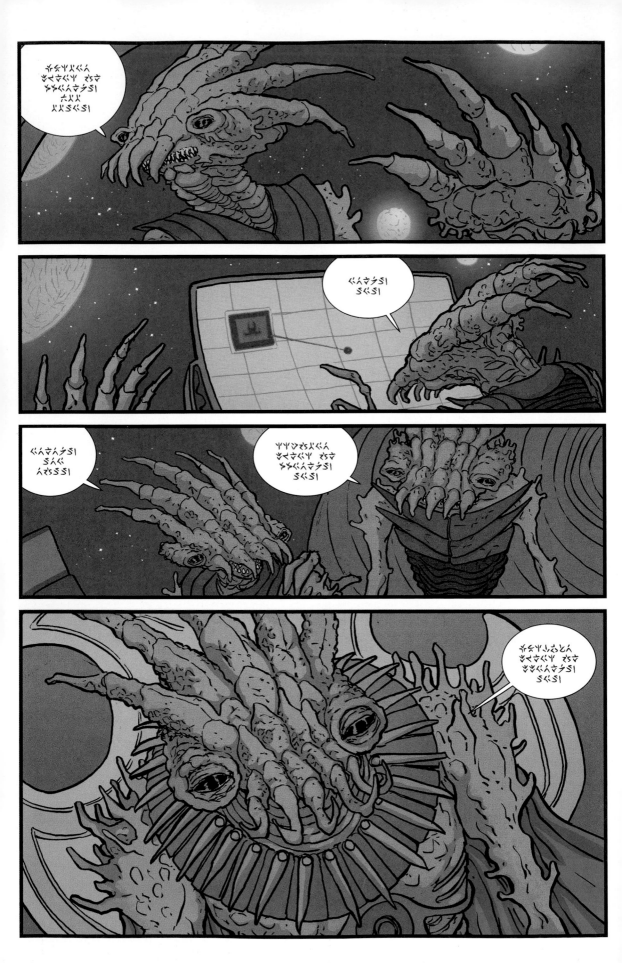

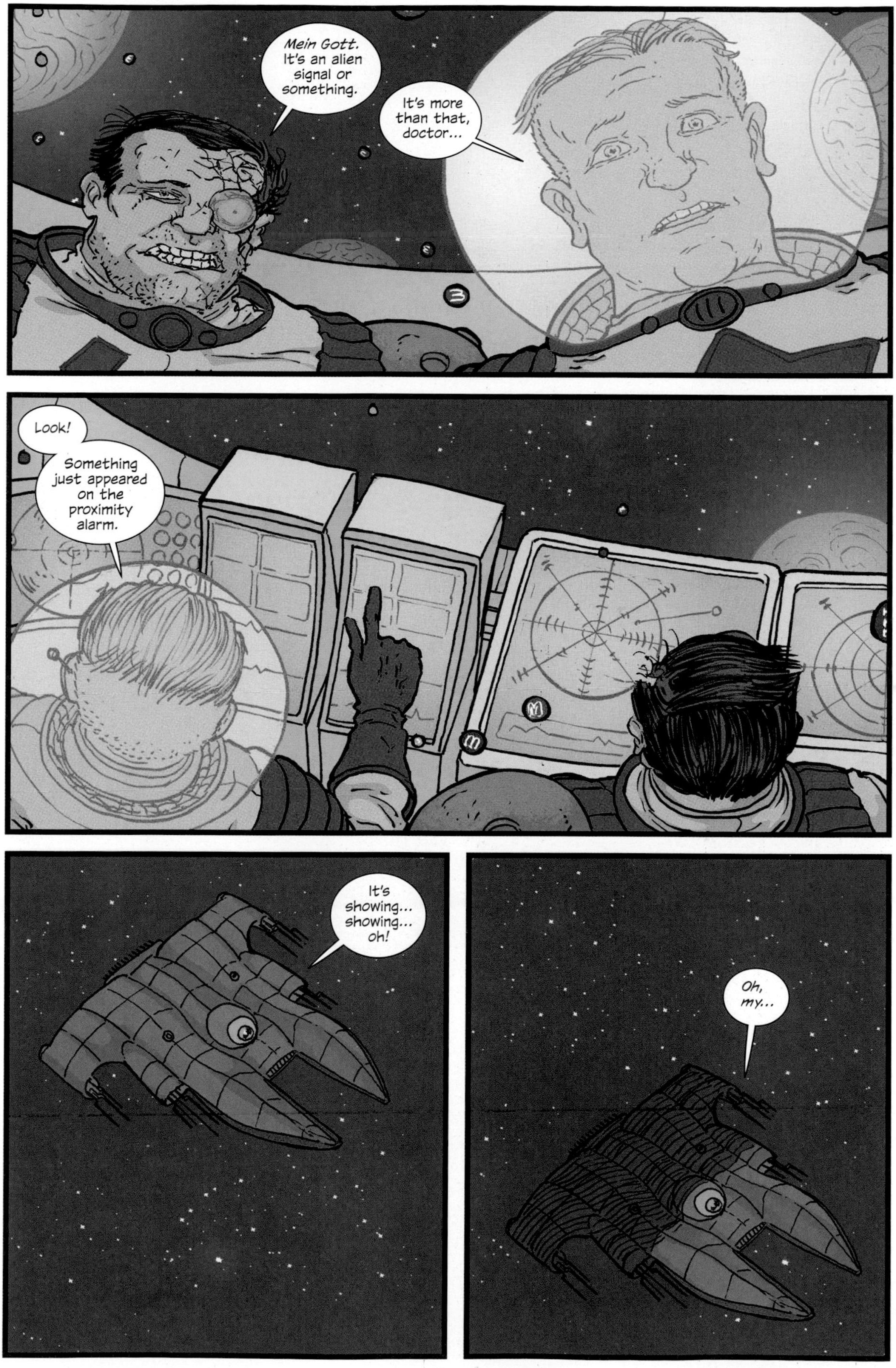

Mein Gott. It's an alien signal or something.
It's more than that, doctor...
Look!
Something just appeared on the proximity alarm.
It's showing... showing... oh!
Oh, my...

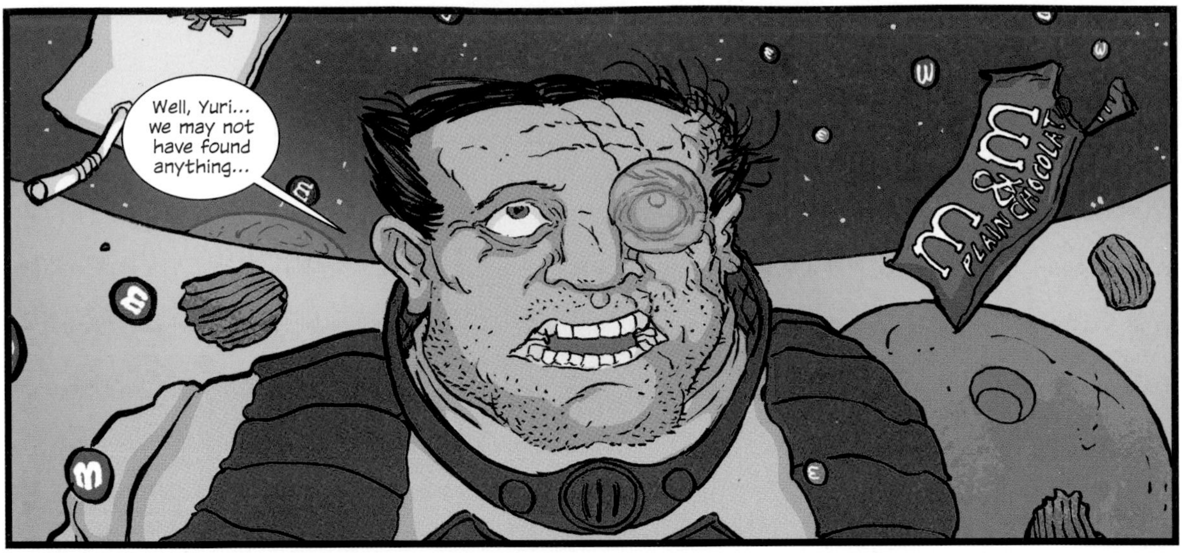
Well, Yuri... we may not have found anything...
m&m PLAIN CHOCOLATE

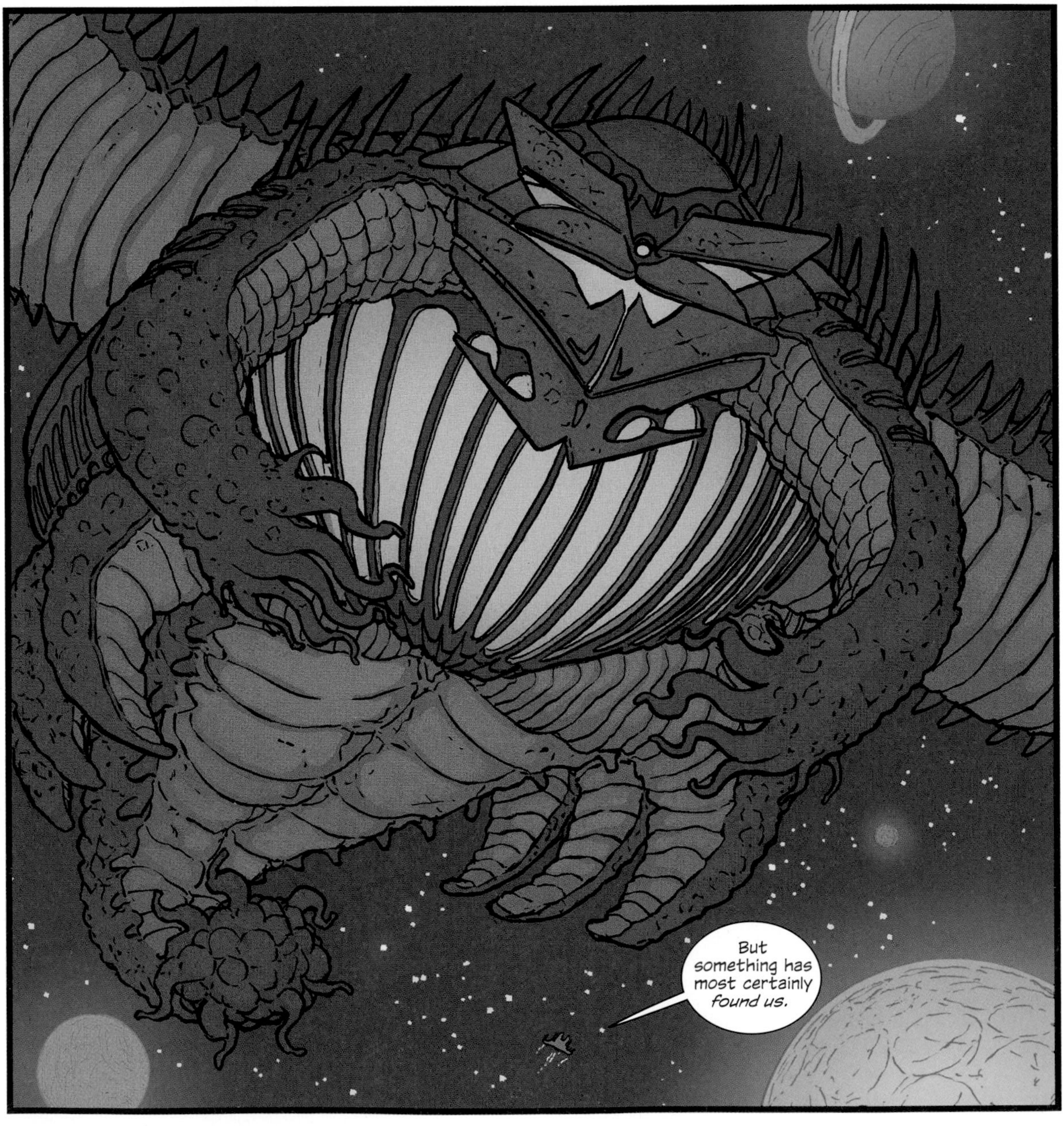
But something has most certainly *found us.*

"I DIDN'T SHOOT ANYBODY, NO SIR . . . I'M JUST A PATSY. WITH A XENOLOGICALLY MODIFIED BRAIN."

- LEE HARVEY OSWALD

CLAVIS AUREA
THE RECORDED FEYNMAN | **VOL. 4**

LET THE EXPERIMENTS
CONTINUE

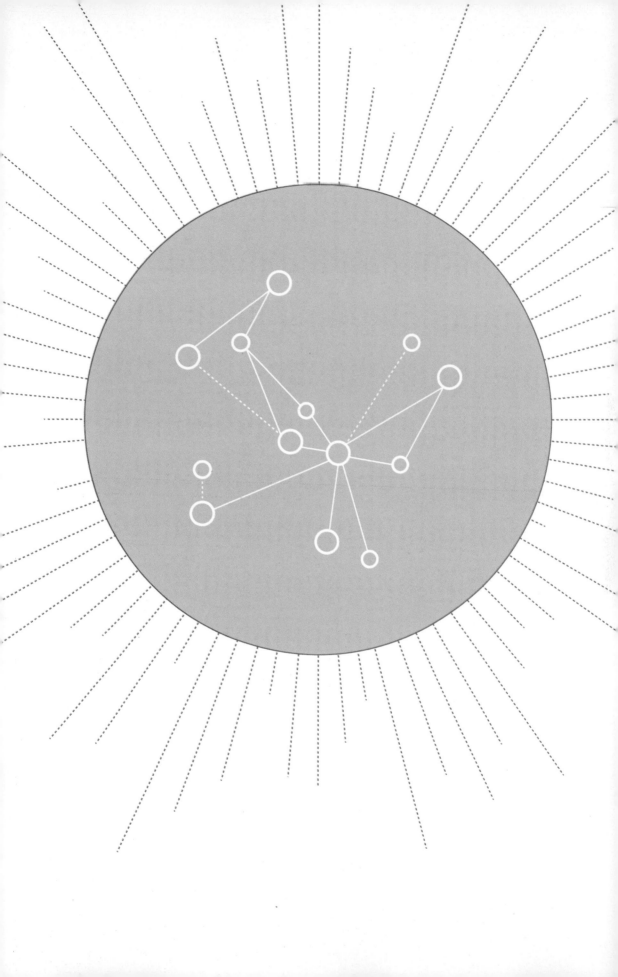

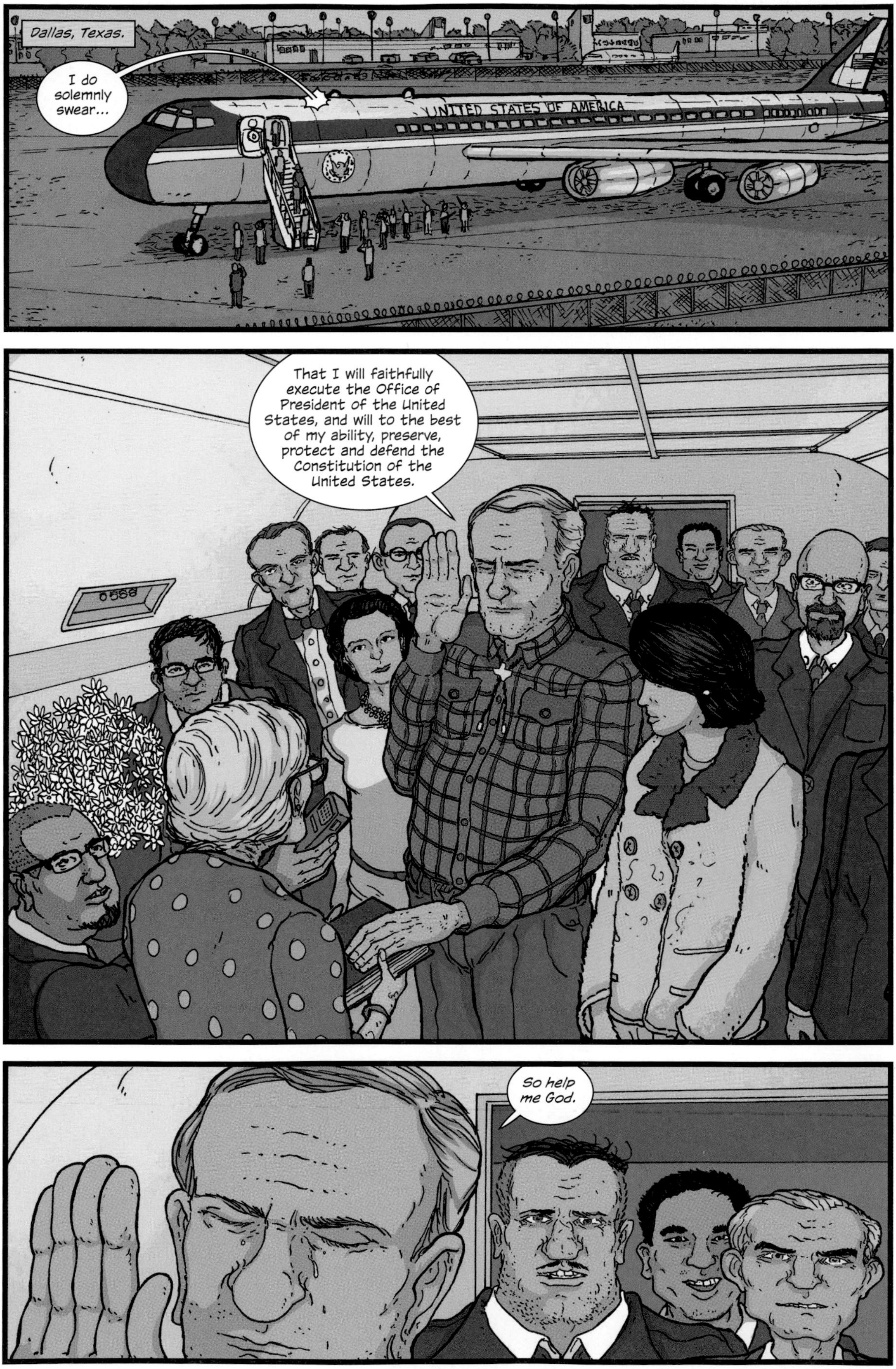
Dallas, Texas.
I do solemnly swear...
UNITED STATES OF AMERICA
That I will faithfully execute the Office of President of the United States, and will to the best of my ability, preserve, protect and defend the Constitution of the United States.
So help me God.

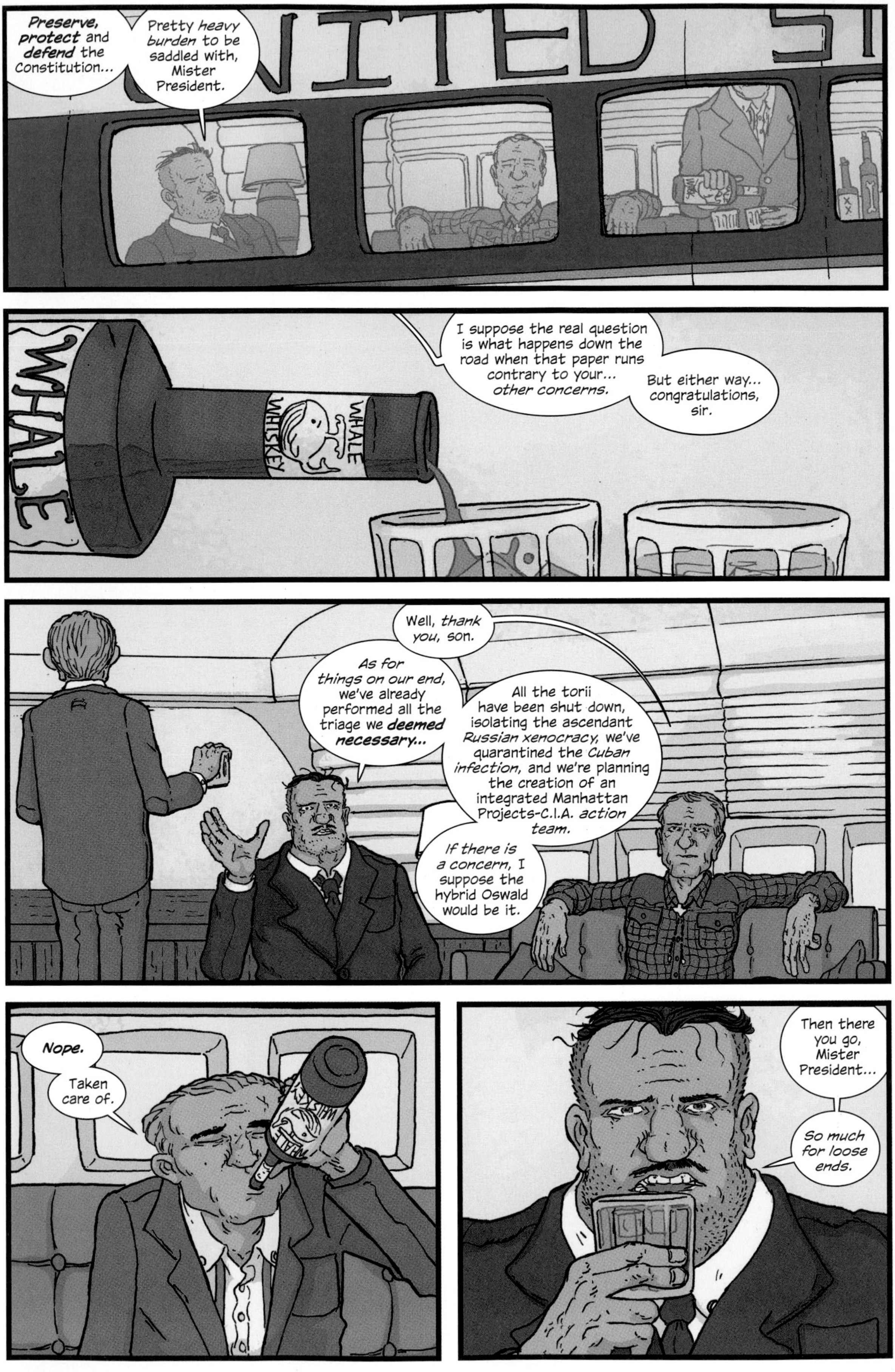
Preserve, protect and defend the Constitution...
Pretty heavy burden to be saddled with, Mister President.
WHALE
WHALE WHISKEY
I suppose the real question is what happens down the road when that paper runs contrary to your... other concerns.
But either way... congratulations, sir.
Well, thank you, son.
As for things on our end, we've already performed all the triage we deemed necessary...
All the torii have been shut down, isolating the ascendant Russian xenocracy, we've quarantined the Cuban infection, and we're planning the creation of an integrated Manhattan Projects-C.I.A. action team.
If there is a concern, I suppose the hybrid Oswald would be it.
Nope.
Taken care of.
Then there you go, Mister President...
So much for loose ends.

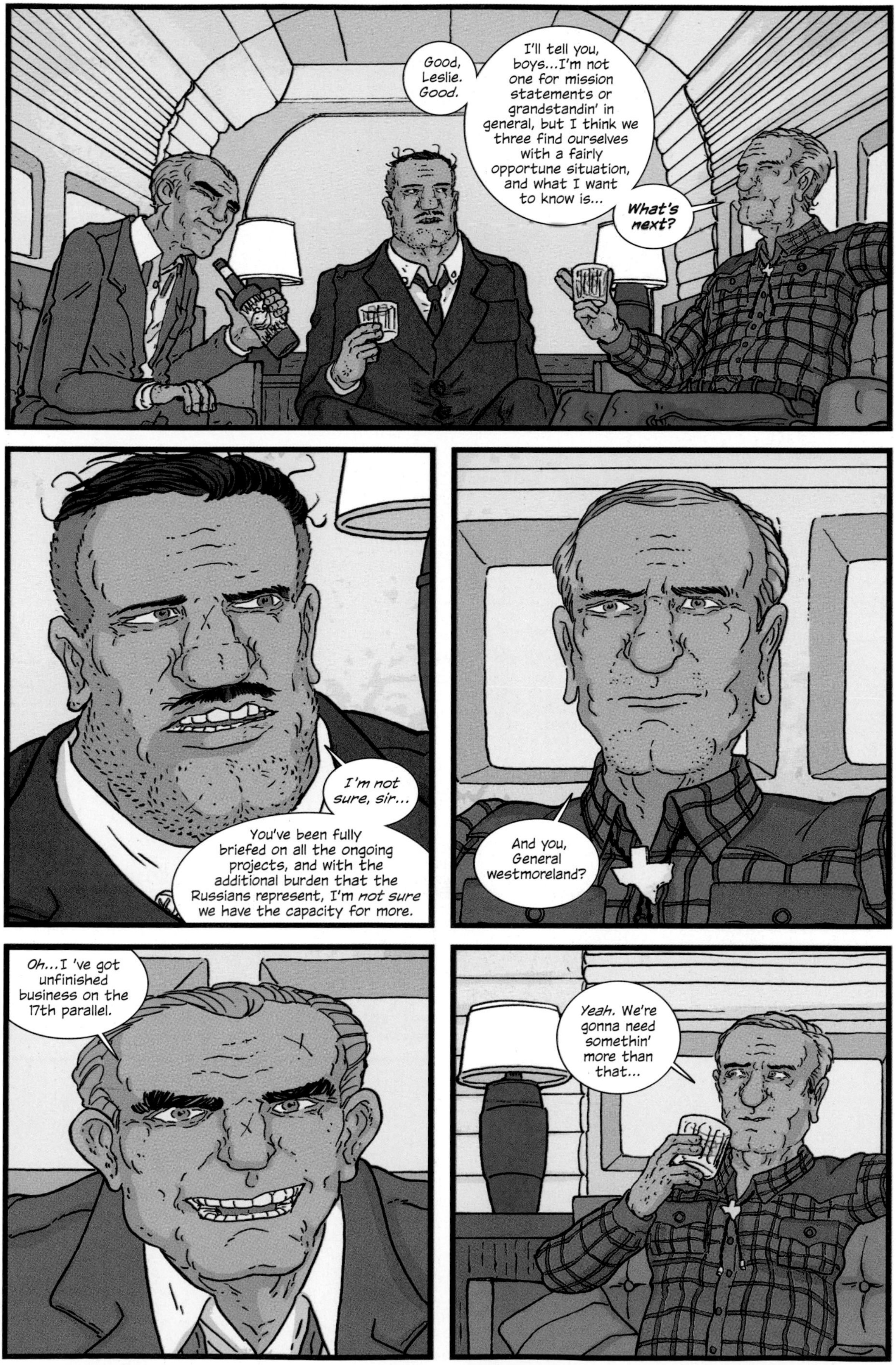
Good, Leslie. Good.
I'll tell you, boys...I'm not one for mission statements or grandstandin' in general, but I think we three find ourselves with a fairly opportune situation, and what I want to know is...
What's next?
I'm not sure, sir...
You've been fully briefed on all the ongoing projects, and with the additional burden that the Russians represent, I'm not sure we have the capacity for more.
And you, General westmoreland?
Oh...I 've got unfinished business on the 17th parallel.
Yeah. We're gonna need somethin' more than that...

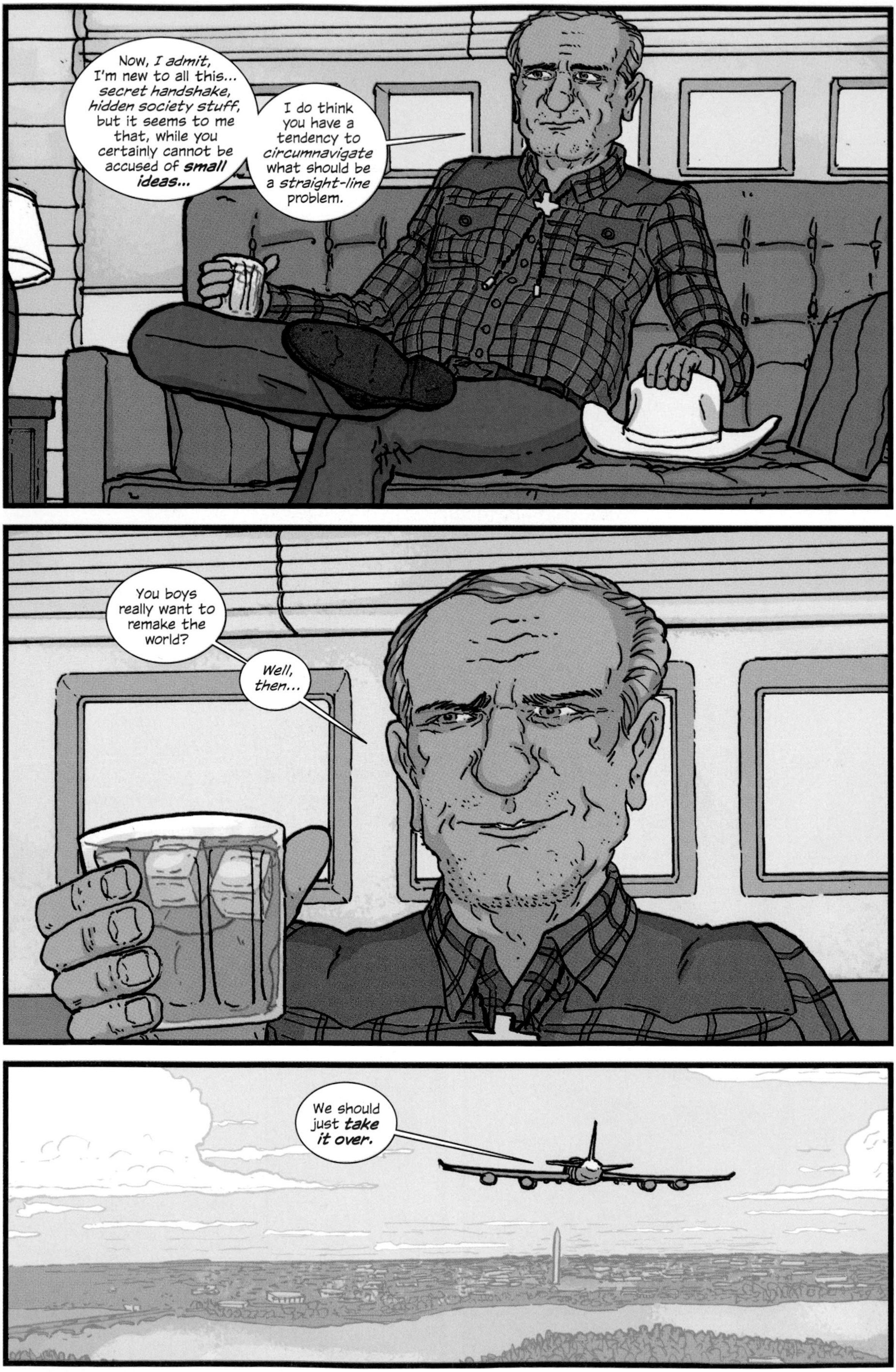
Now, *I admit*, I'm new to all this... *secret handshake, hidden society stuff*, but it seems to me that, while you certainly cannot be accused of ***small ideas...***
I do think you have a tendency to *circumnavigate* what should be a *straight-line* problem.
You boys really want to remake the world?
Well, then...
We should just ***take it over.***

"I CAN'T BELIEVE HOW FAR WE'VE COME."

CLAVIS AUREA
THE RECORDED FEYNMAN | VOL. 4

25

DEPARTURE POINT

"I CAN'T BELIEVE HOW FAR WE HAVE LEFT."

CLAVIS AUREA
THE RECORDED FEYNMAN | **VOL. 4**

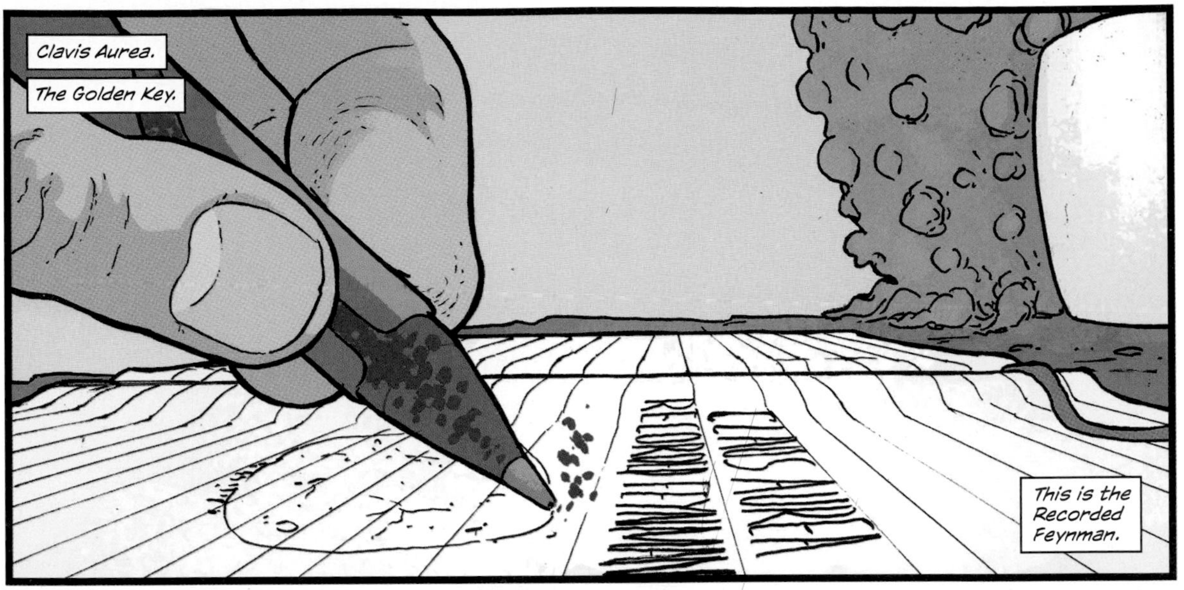
Clavis Aurea.
The Golden Key.
This is the Recorded Feynman.

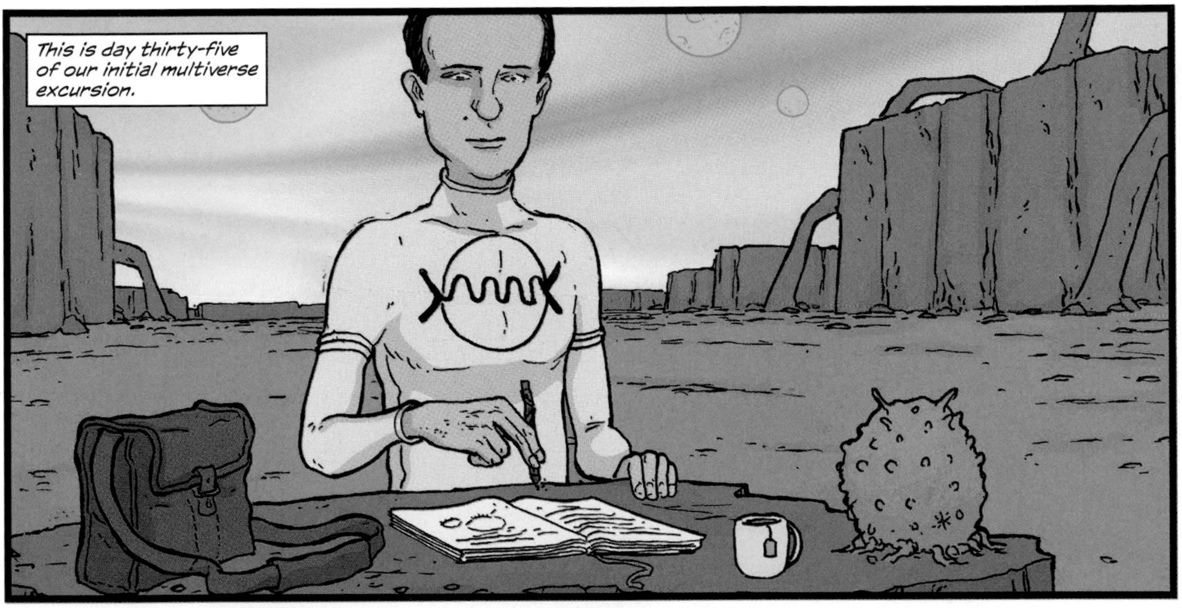
This is day thirty-five of our initial multiverse excursion.

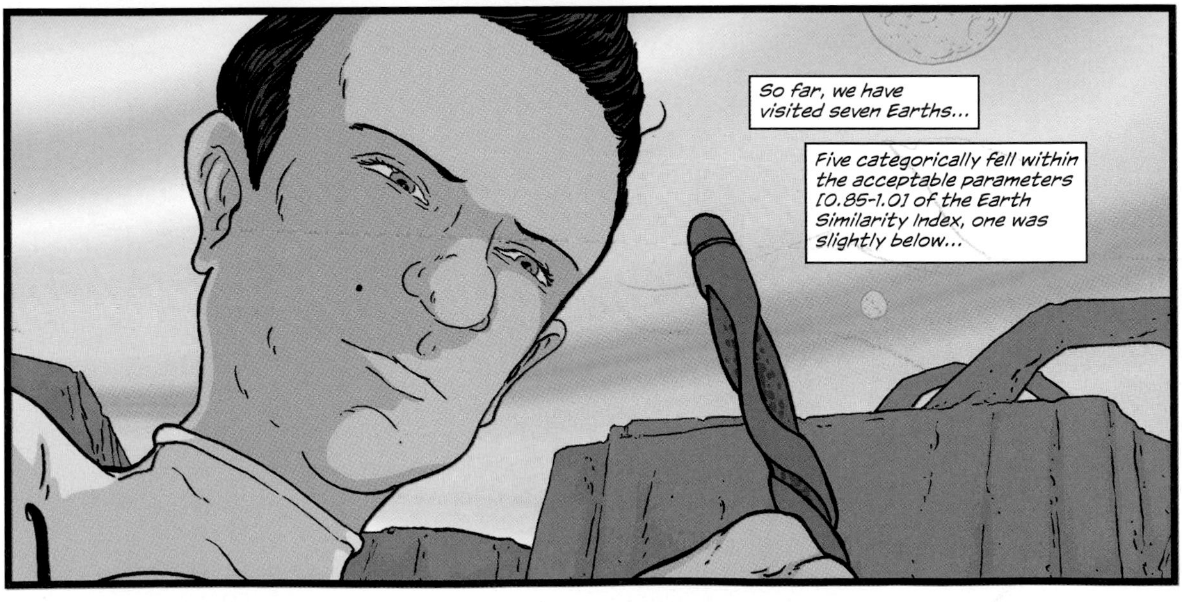
So far, we have visited seven Earths...
Five categorically fell within the acceptable parameters [0.85-1.0] of the Earth Similarity Index, one was slightly below...

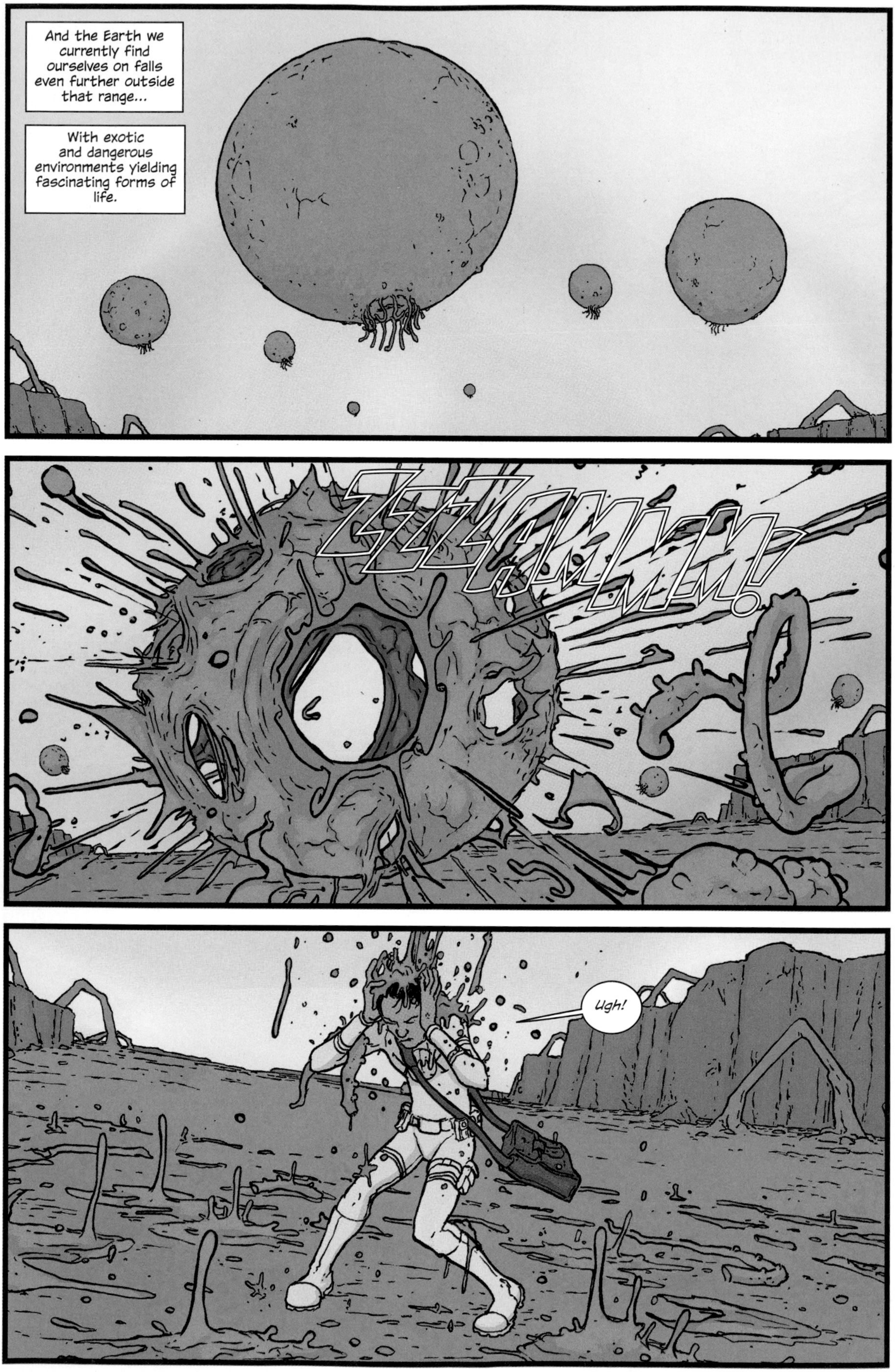
And the Earth we currently find ourselves on falls even further outside that range...
With exotic and dangerous environments yielding fascinating forms of life.
ZZZLAMMMM!
Ugh!

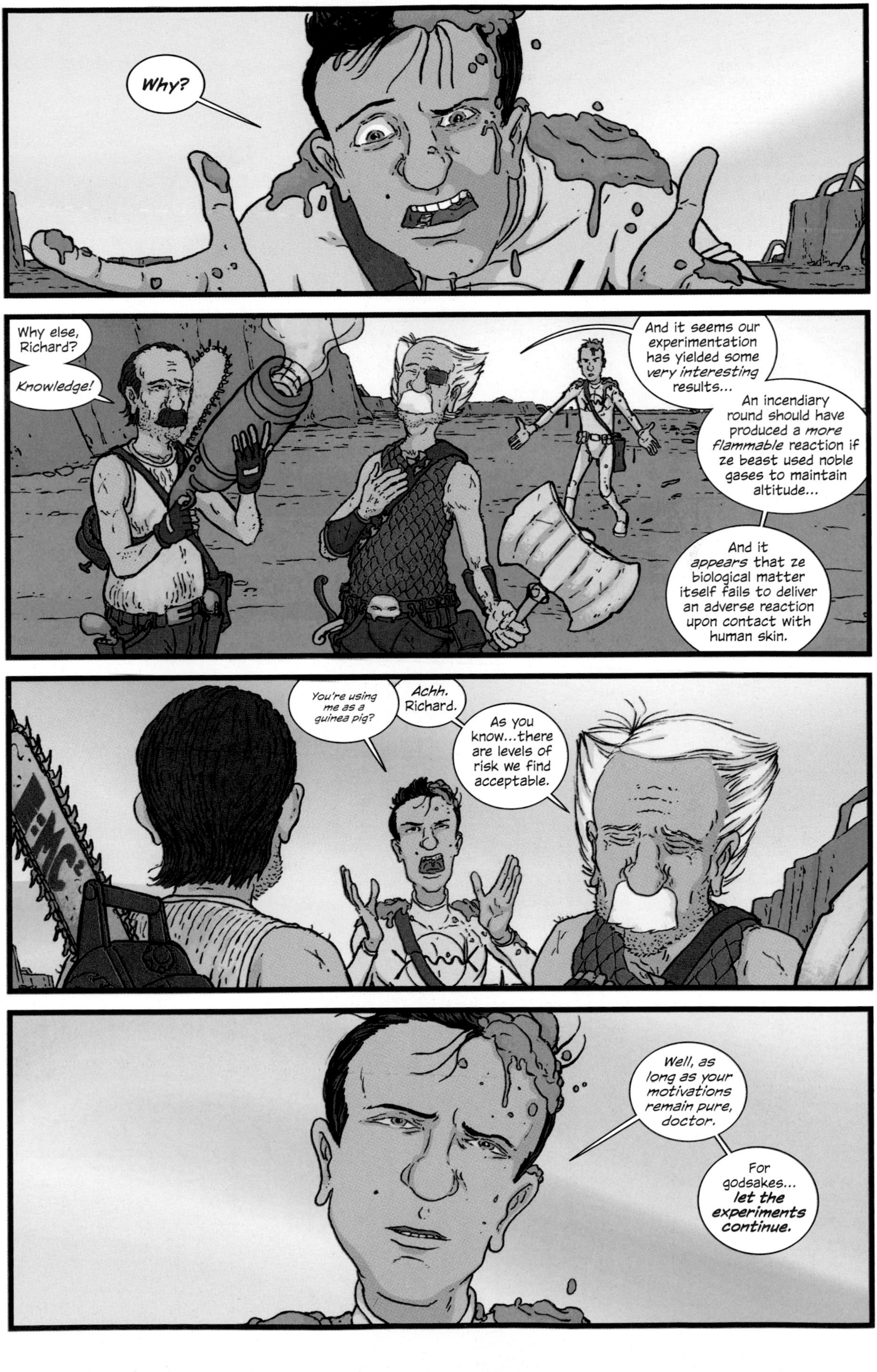
Why?
Why else, Richard?
Knowledge!
And it seems our experimentation has yielded some very interesting results...
An incendiary round should have produced a more flammable reaction if ze beast used noble gases to maintain altitude...
And it appears that ze biological matter itself fails to deliver an adverse reaction upon contact with human skin.
You're using me as a guinea pig?
Achh. Richard.
As you know...there are levels of risk we find acceptable.
Well, as long as your motivations remain pure, doctor.
For godsakes... let the experiments continue.

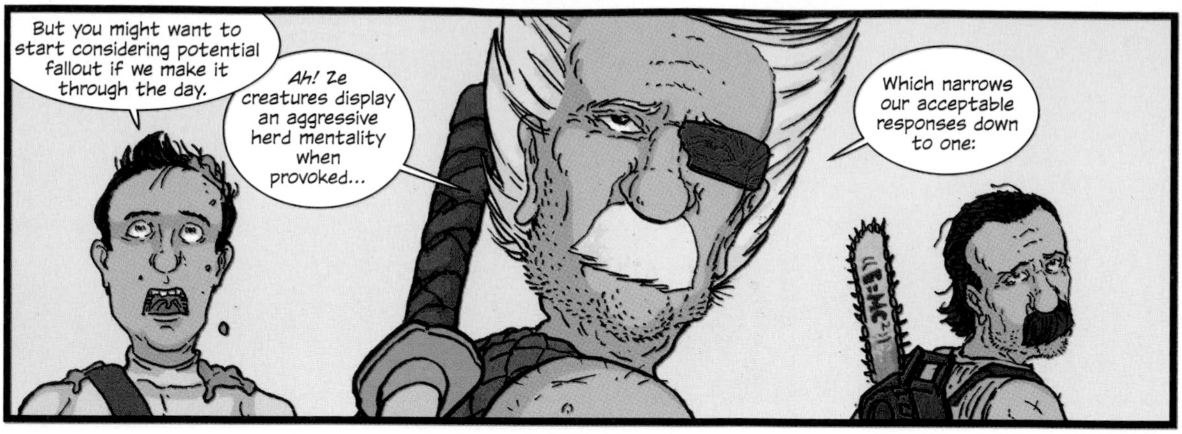
But you might want to start considering potential fallout if we make it through the day.
Ah! Ze creatures display an aggressive herd mentality when provoked...
Which narrows our acceptable responses down to one:

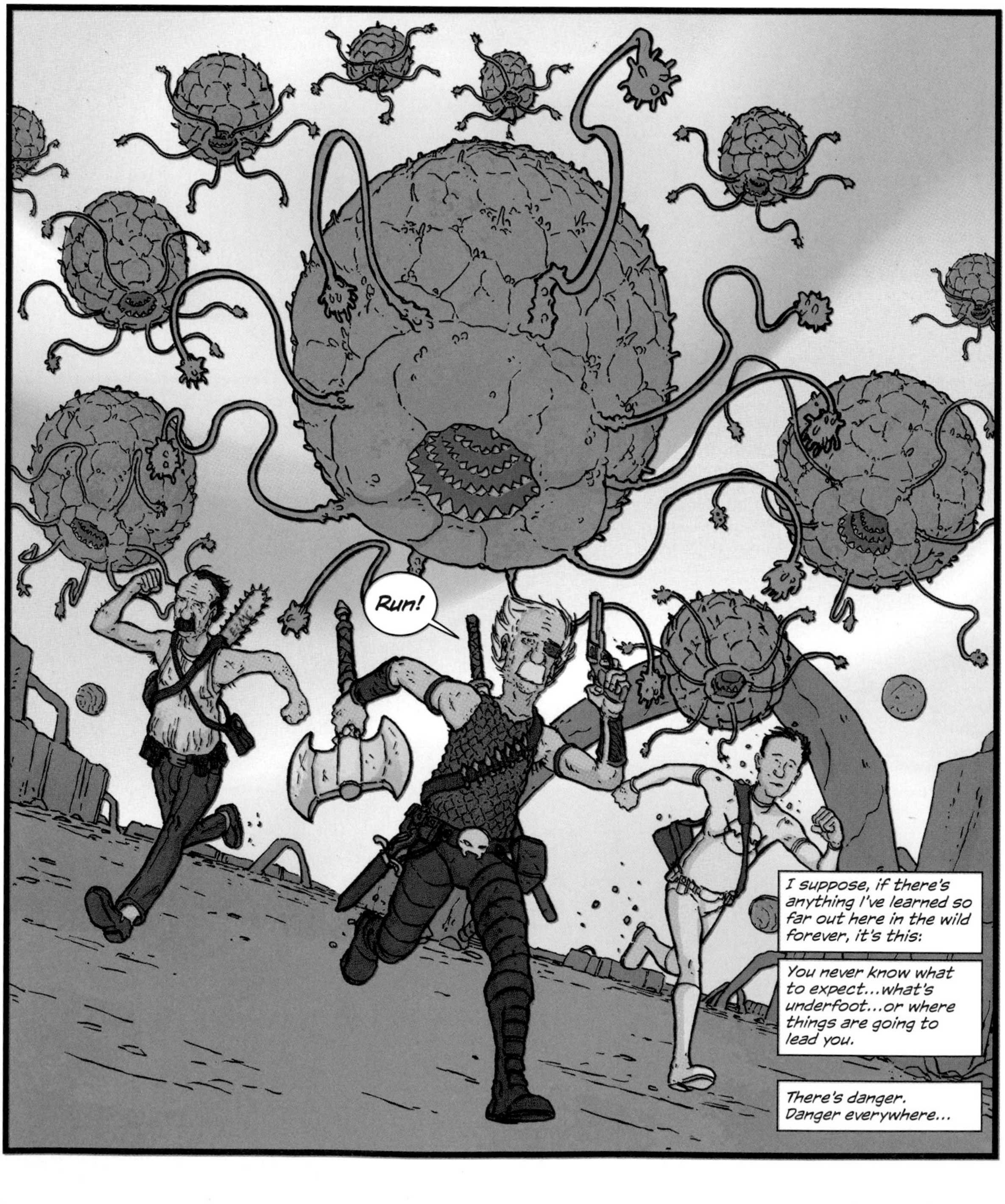
Run!
I suppose, if there's anything I've learned so far out here in the wild forever, it's this:
You never know what to expect...what's underfoot...or where things are going to lead you.
There's danger. Danger everywhere...

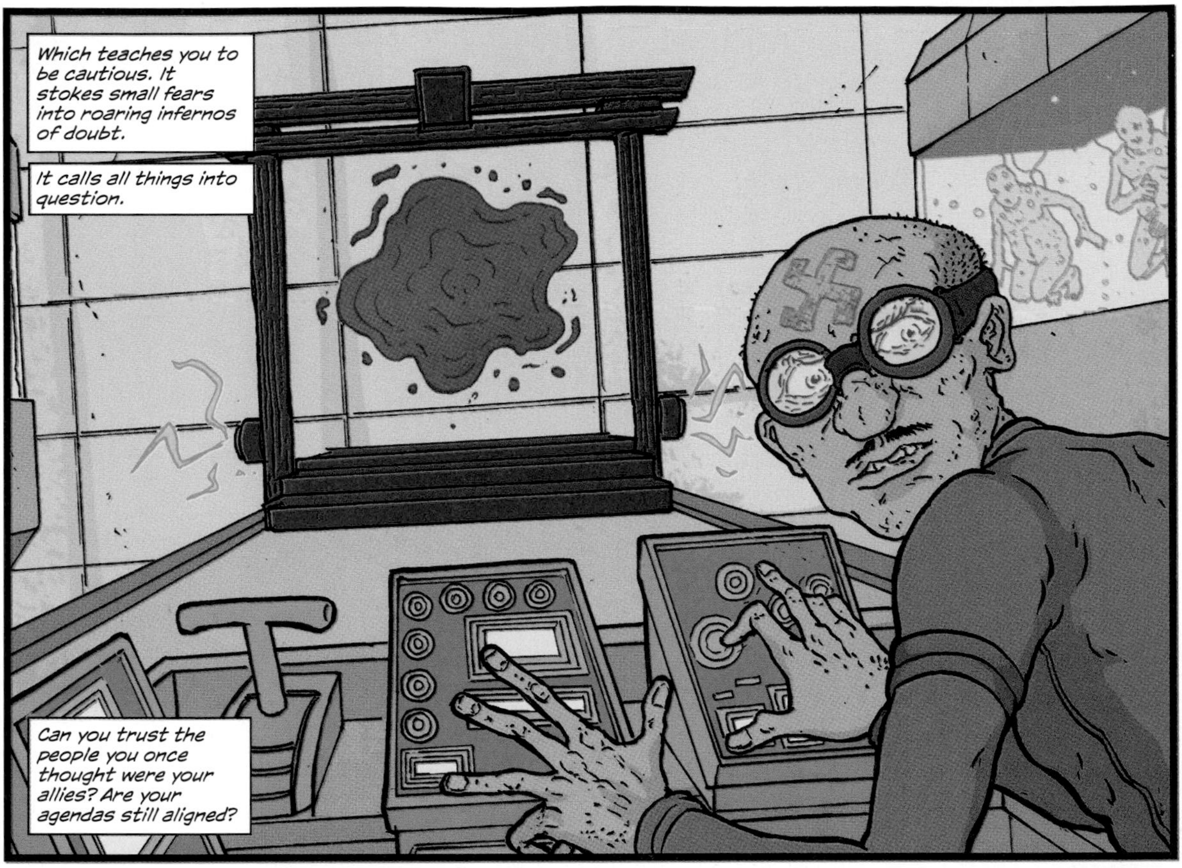
Which teaches you to be cautious. It stokes small fears into roaring infernos of doubt.
It calls all things into question.
Can you trust the people you once thought were your allies? Are your agendas still aligned?

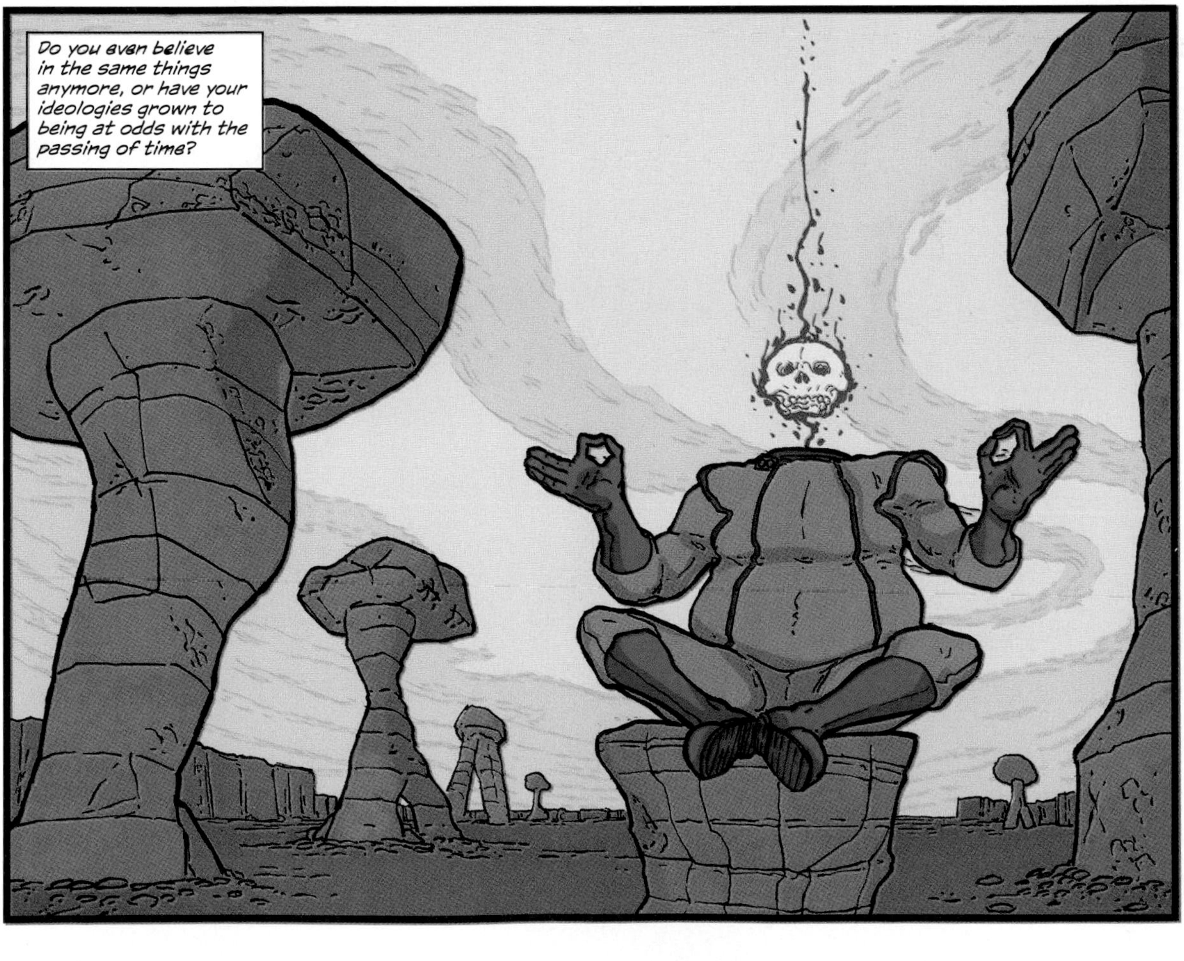
Do you even believe in the same things anymore, or have your ideologies grown to being at odds with the passing of time?

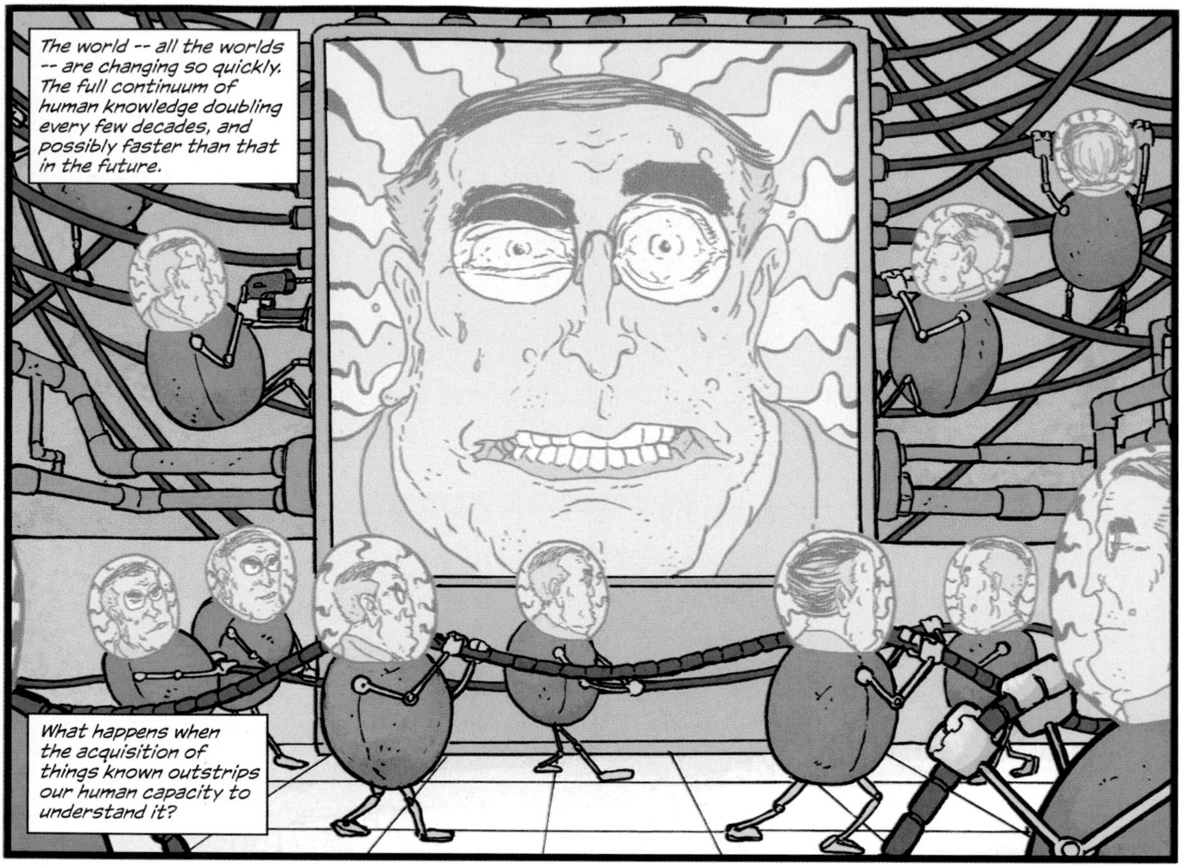
The world -- all the worlds -- are changing so quickly. The full continuum of human knowledge doubling every few decades, and possibly faster than that in the future.
What happens when the acquisition of things known outstrips our human capacity to understand it?

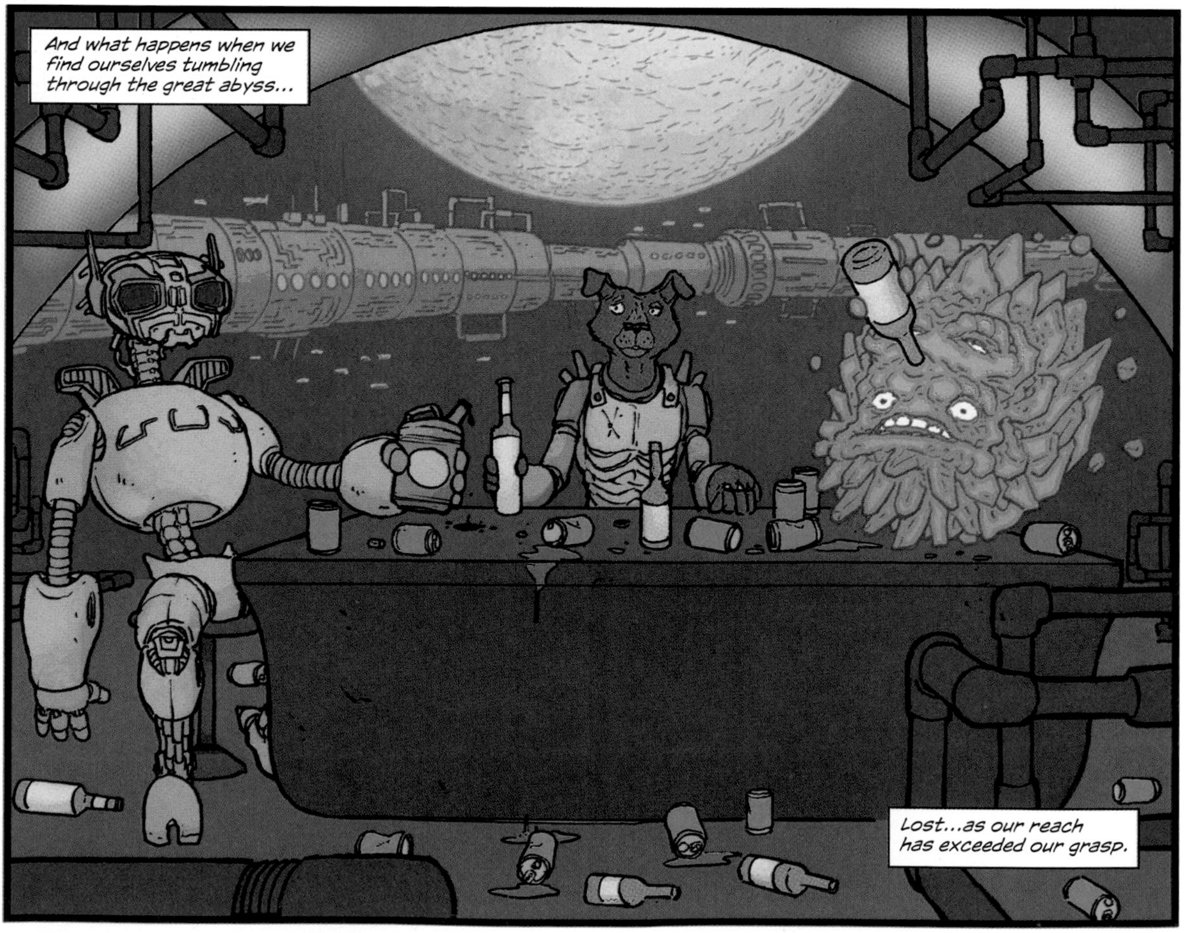
And what happens when we find ourselves tumbling through the great abyss...
Lost...as our reach has exceeded our grasp.

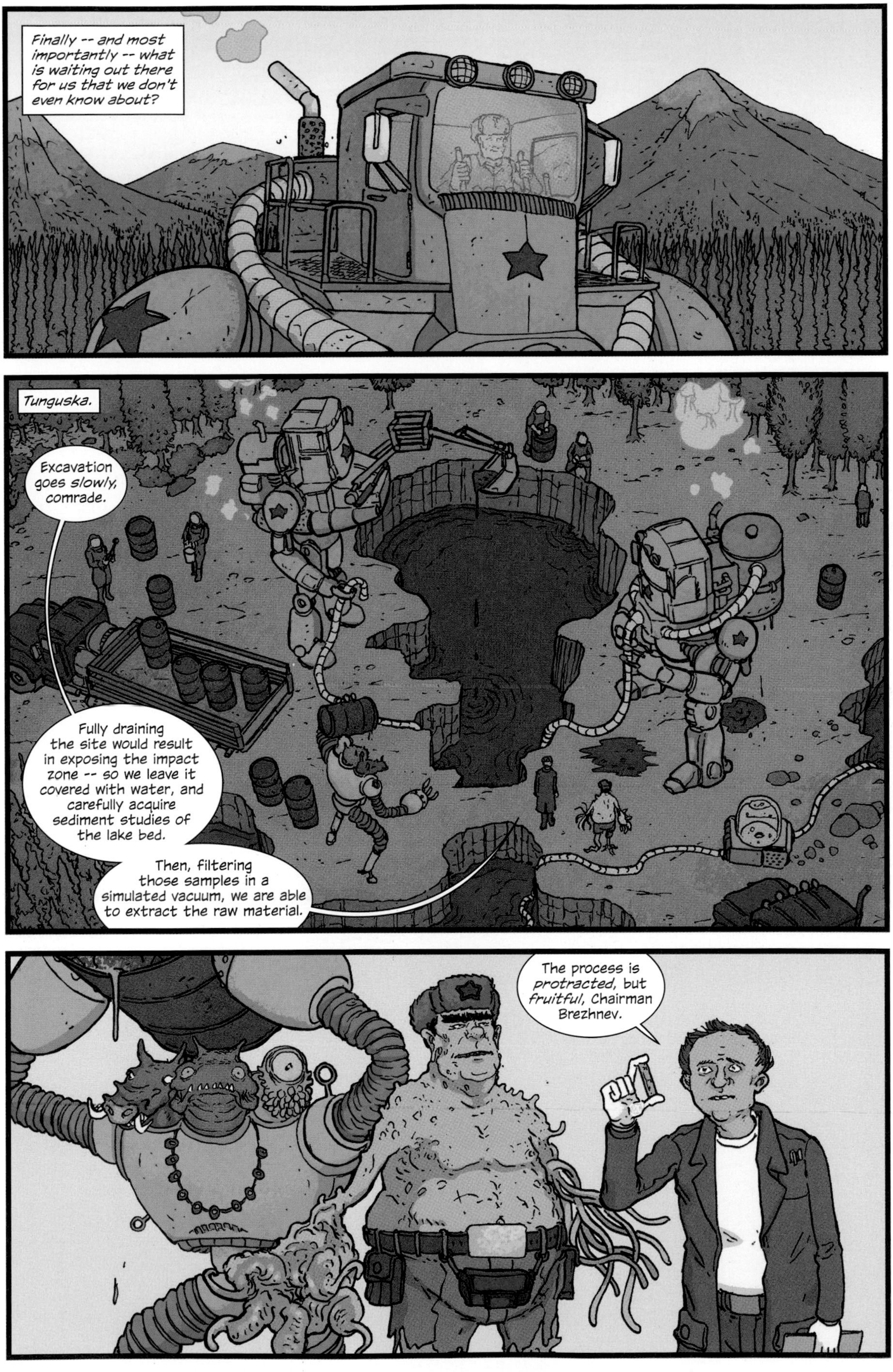
Finally -- and most importantly -- what is waiting out there for us that we don't even know about?
Tunguska.
Excavation goes slowly, comrade.
Fully draining the site would result in exposing the impact zone -- so we leave it covered with water, and carefully acquire sediment studies of the lake bed.
Then, filtering those samples in a simulated vacuum, we are able to extract the raw material.
The process is protracted, but fruitful, Chairman Brezhnev.

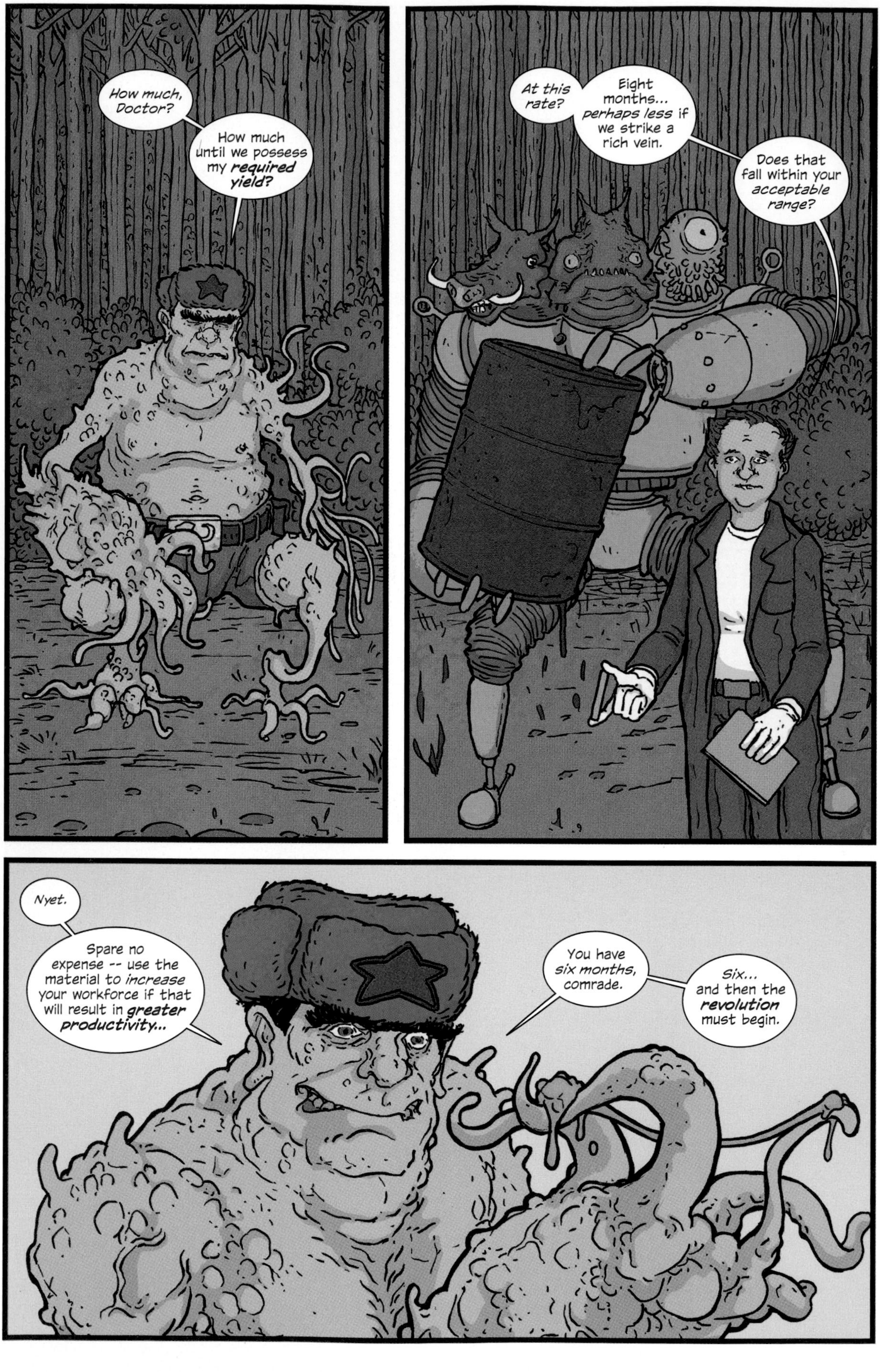
How much, Doctor?
How much until we possess my *required yield?*
At this rate?
Eight months... *perhaps less* if we strike a rich vein.
Does that fall within your *acceptable range?*
Nyet.
Spare no expense -- use the material to *increase* your workforce if that will result in ***greater productivity...***
You have *six months,* comrade.
Six... and then the ***revolution*** must begin.

Space.

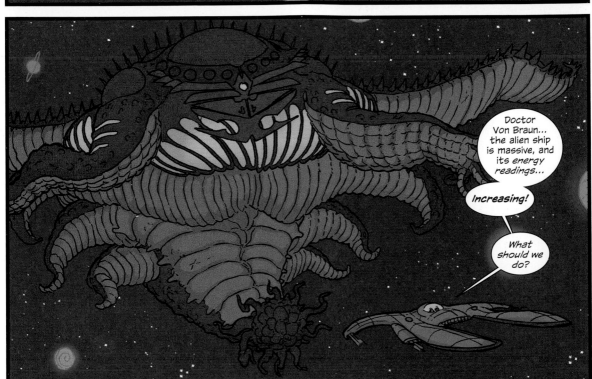

Doctor Von Braun... the alien ship is massive, and its *energy* readings...

Increasing!

What should we do?

What do you think, Yuri?

Accelerate. Evade. Mein Gott... get us the hell *out of here!*

Got it!

But, doctor...

What if sweet Laika is on board that ship?

Maybe we should just --

SKASH!!

Ooooff!

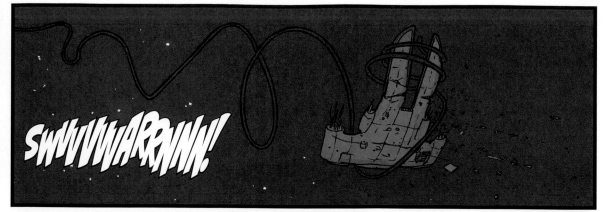

SWVVWARNNN!

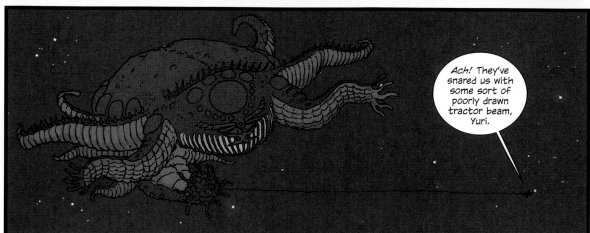

Ach! They've snared us with some sort of poorly drawn tractor beam, Yuri.

Hurry! You have to get to the ejector before that behemoth gobbles us whole.

You? Don't you mean us, doctor?

Nein. You escape and continue your quest...I will stay here and, if there is time, attempt to scuttle the ship.

Doctor... I didn't know that you cared.

SLAAMMM!

I don't.

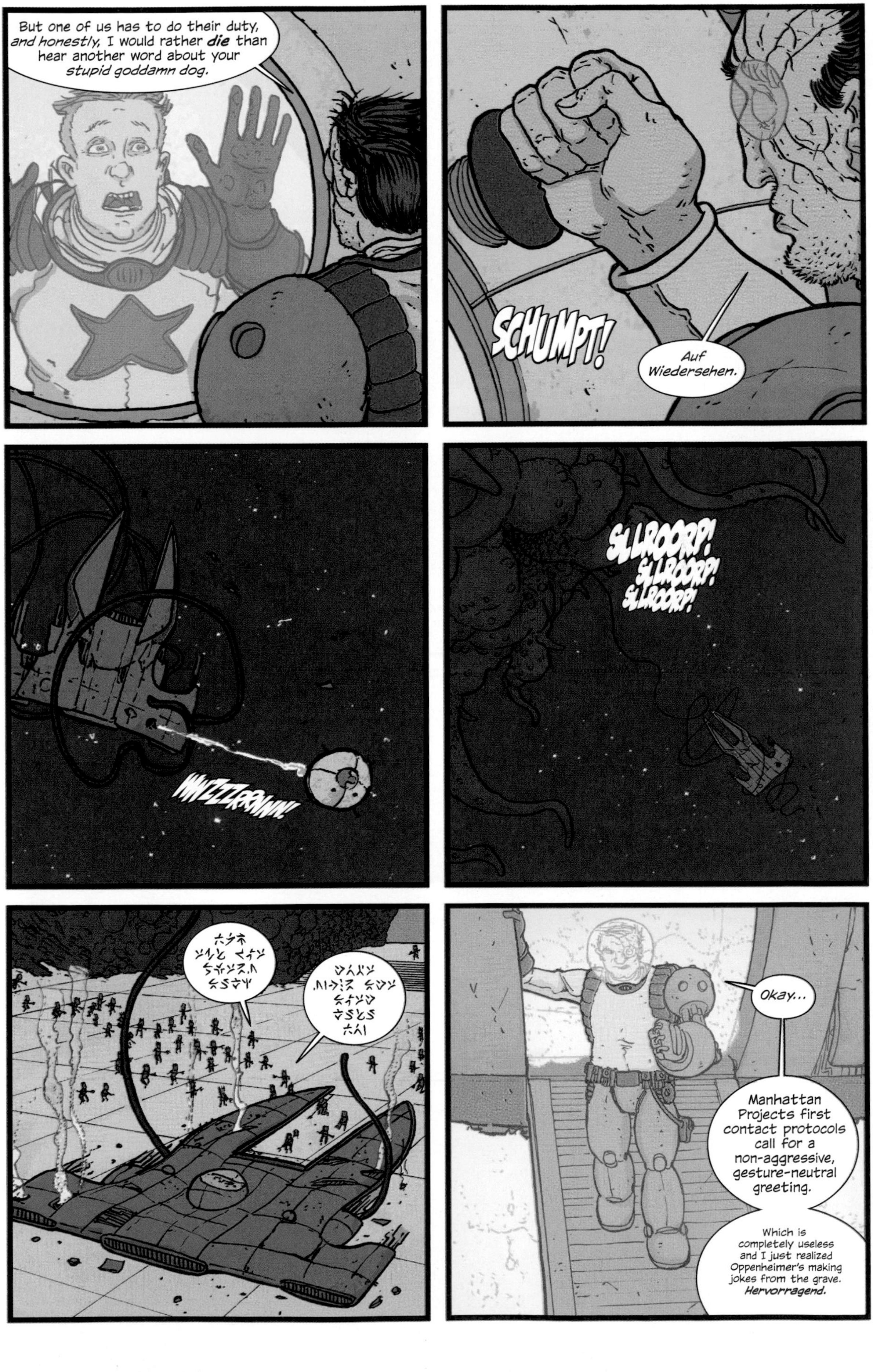
But one of us has to do their duty, *and honestly,* I would rather ***die*** than hear another word about your *stupid goddamn dog.*
SCHUMPT!
Auf Wiedersehen.
WWZZZRRNNN!
SLLROORP! SLLROORP! SLLROORP!
Okay...
Manhattan Projects first contact protocols call for a non-aggressive, gesture-neutral greeting.
Which is completely useless and I just realized Oppenheimer's making jokes from the grave. ***Hervorragend.***

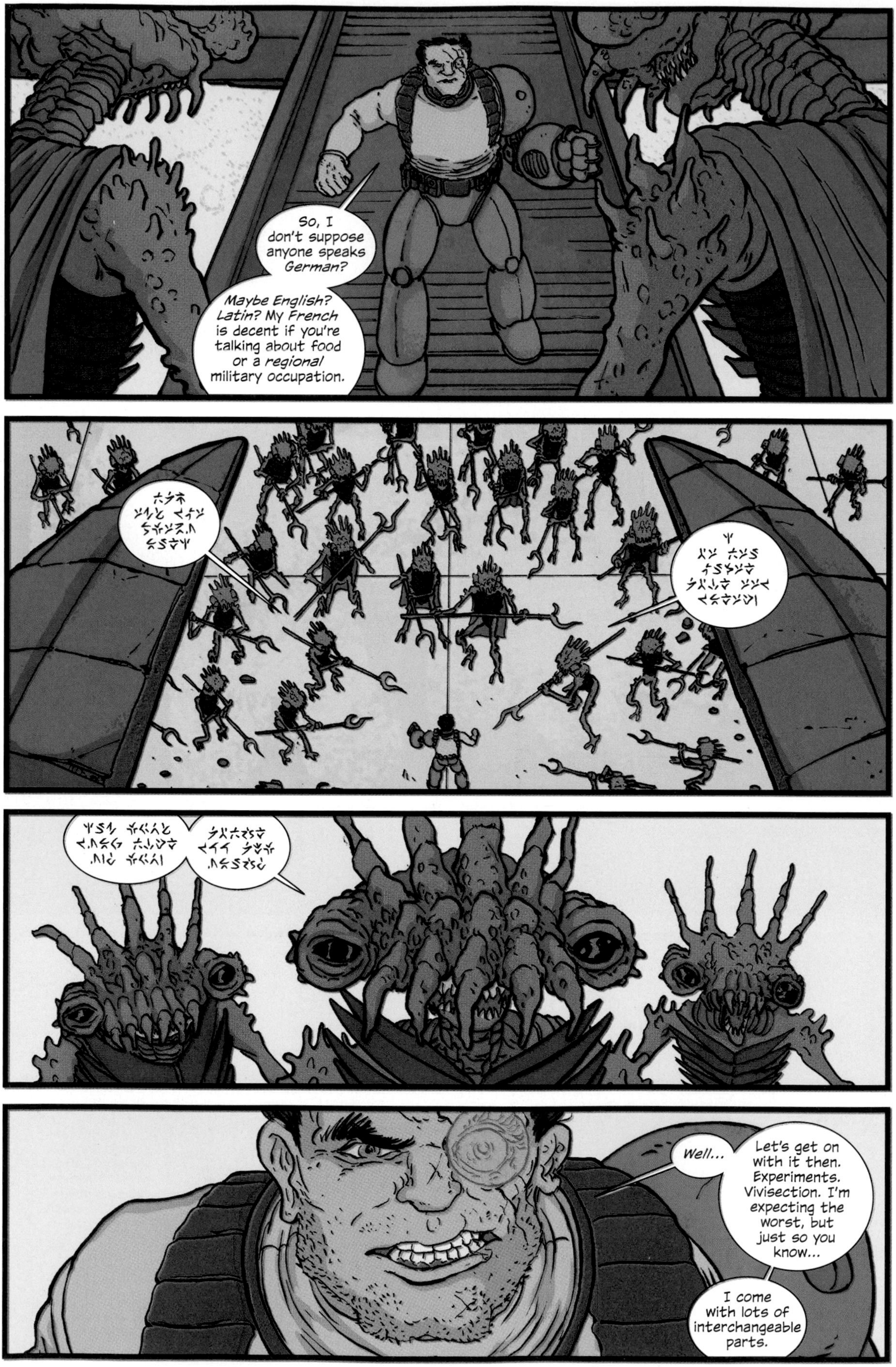
So, I don't suppose anyone speaks *German*?
Maybe English? Latin? My *French* is decent if you're talking about food or a *regional* military occupation.
Well...
Let's get on with it then. Experiments. Vivisection. I'm expecting the worst, but just so you know...
I come with lots of interchangeable parts.

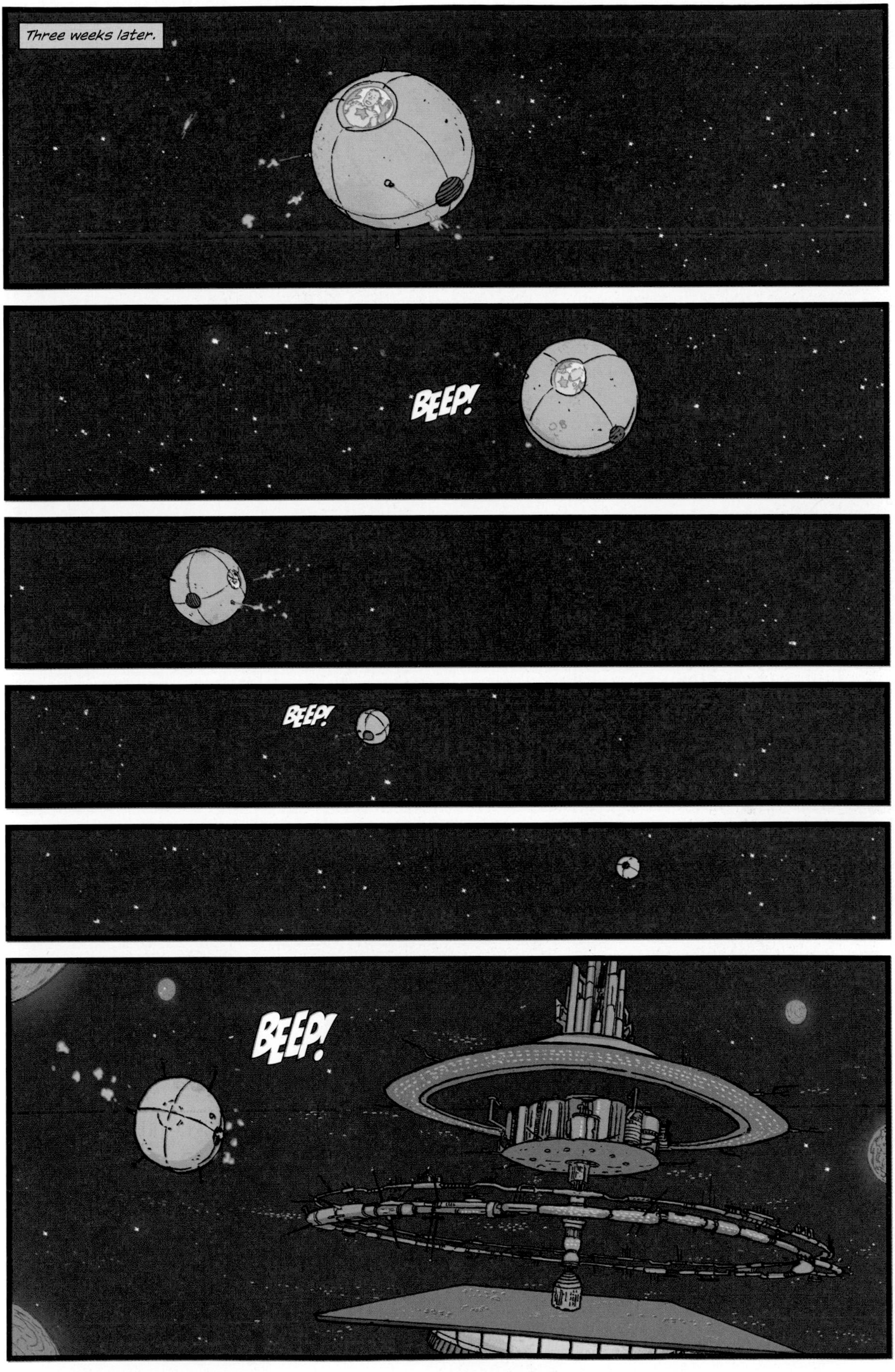
Three weeks later.
BEEP!
BEEP!
BEEP!

Five weeks later.

BEEP!

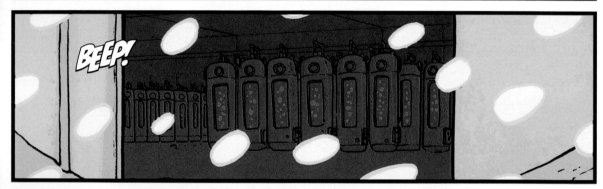

BEEP!

BEEP!

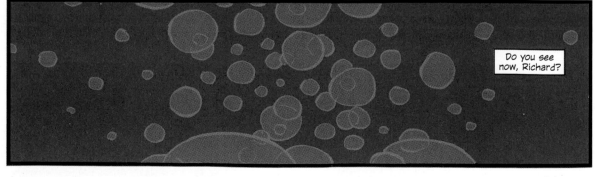

Do you see now, Richard?

Experimentation is its own reward.

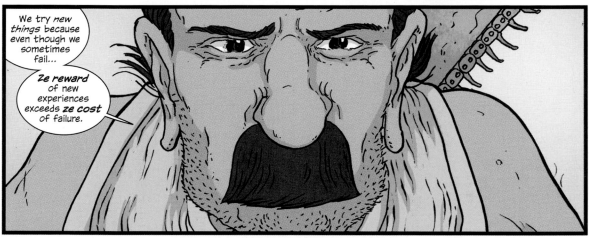

We try *new things* because even though we sometimes fail...

Ze reward of new experiences exceeds *ze cost* of failure.

So you got a bit of alien ordure on you...

I was covered in it, doctor.

We all have our own process. If immersion is yours, so be it...

My point is, you have to stop *being afraid of dangerous things.* Some people spend their entire lives locked in a room because they think it's safe.

But you know better, Richard...

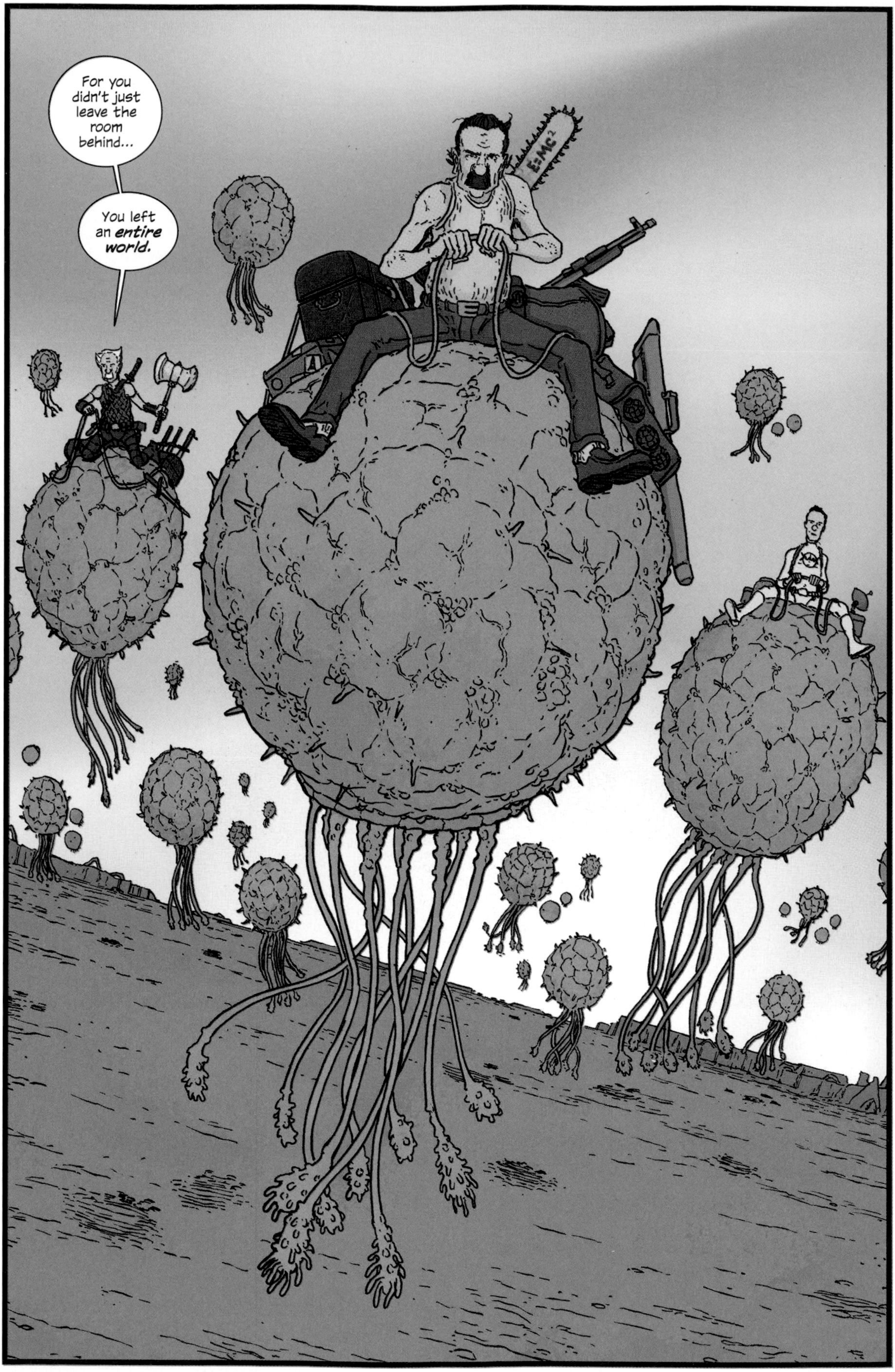
For you didn't just leave the room behind...
You left an *entire world.*
E=MC²

"BUT NOW WE GO...FORWARD."

CLAVIS AUREA
THE RECORDED FEYNMAN | **VOL. 4**

THE CAST

ALBERT EINSTEIN

Super genius.
German. Physicist.
Barbarian.

ALBRECHT EINSTEIN

Highly intelligent.
German. Physicist.
Drinks.

RICHARD FEYNMAN

Super genius.
American. Physicist.
Wormholer.

WILLIAM WESTMORELAND

Not a genius.
American. General.
Butcher.

HARRY DAGHLIAN

Super genius.
American. Physicist.
Messiah.

WERNHER VON BRAUN

Super genius.
German. Rocket scientist.
Robot arm.

LESLIE GROVES

Not a genius.
American. General.
Smokes. Bombs.

FDR: A.I.

Computational super genius.
American. President.
Dead.

LBJ

Not a genius.
American. President.
Texan.

THE CAST

YURI GAGARIN

Not a genius.
Russian. Cosmonaut.
Hero.

LAIKA

Explorer.
Russian. Former Dog.
Walks.

HELMUTT GRÖTTRUP

Super genius.
German. Rocket scientist.
Slave.

DMITRIY USTINOV

Not a genius.
Russian. Minister.
Disassembled.

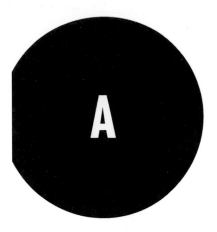

Jonathan Hickman is the visionary talent behind such works as the Eisner-nominated **NIGHTLY NEWS**, **EAST OF WEST** and **PAX ROMANA**. He also plies his trade at MARVEL working on books like **FANTASTIC FOUR** and **THE AVENGERS**.

His twin brother, Marc, builds custom machines for Confederate Motorcycles.

Jonathan lives in South Carolina near a lowcountry nature reserve.

You can visit his website:***www.pronea.com***, or email him at:***jonathan@pronea.com***.

·

Nick Pitarra is a native Texan and all around nice guy. As a senior in high school he was kicked out of honors English, and subsequently fell in love with comic illustration while doodling with a friend in his new class.

Sometimes it pays not to do your homework.